KT-074-891

KING JAMES THE SECOND

Nat. Port. Gallery]

JAMES II
From the portrait by Kneller

KING JAMES THE SECOND

By

F. M. G. HIGHAM

Author of 'Charles I'

HAMISH HAMILTON
90 GREAT RUSSELL STREET LONDON

First Published 1934

PRINTED IN GUERNSEY, C.I., BRITISH ISLES,
BY THE STAR AND GAZETTE COMPANY LTD.

CONTENTS

LIST OF ILLUSTRATIONS

PART I

EXILE

CHAPTER I

PRINCE OF THE BLOOD ROYAL

'Newes we have none but the birth of the Duke of Yorke, the 14th of this instant. . . . The King and Queene are well and jolly.' – *Newsletter*, 31 Oct., 1633.

KING CHARLES the second has come into his own again, riding triumphantly into the hearts of posterity as he rode down the cheering streets of London on his birthday in 1660. The other side of the question, which the Whigs of the eighteenth century kept well from view in their teaching of Stuart history, has been painted with skill and artistry and has stirred the potential Jacobite that lurks in most of us. Few talk with enthusiasm of the 'glorious' Revolution in an age when moderation is an unfashionable virtue, and the ideal of liberty beneath the law has, for many, been replaced by the panacea of dictatorship either of the mob or of the individual. Yet one figure stands aloof, unloved as he has always been, condemned by a people who have never understood him, James II, the King whom Whigs and Tories combined to drive from England. In common decency, he should be given a fair trial. And if, when this has been done, the events of 1688 still appear as the manifestation of a great wave of national feeling against the mistakes of a deluded king, it will need more than a twist of fashion to lessen the glory of a Revolution that was a triumphant declaration of a people's faith.

. . . .

The story begins at eleven at night on the fourteenth of October, 1633, when a 'goodly lusty child' was born to Queen Henrietta of England. A month later he was christened with all the pomp of procession and ceremony, that rejoiced his father's heart. The crowds besieged the chapel of St. James's and, as the strains of the anthem died away, the doors were thrown open and the heralds proclaimed the name of the newly-christened child.

> 'Almighty God of his infinite grace and goodness preserve and blesse with long life in health, honor and all happiness the most high, mighty and excellent Prince James Duke of York, second sonne to the most high, most mighty and most excellent Prince Charles, by the grace of God King of England, Scotland, France and Ireland, Defender of the Faith.'

The cheers of the loyal citizens of London drowned the beat of the drums, and rose to a crescendo on the distant sound of cannon from the shipping in the Thames.

It was November, 1633, the most prosperous year of Charles I reign. Prince James had been held at the font by Lord Treasurer Portland, whose careful if uninspired labours had saved the King from penury, while William Laud, the new Archbishop of Canterbury, who officiated at the baptism, had not yet lashed into open resentment the tempers of the malcontents. Foreign commitments, it is true, were impossible and Elizabeth of Bohemia, the King's sister, had realised that she could expect nothing from her brother beyond a genuine if limited affection. But she instanced her goodwill by sponsoring *in absentia* the new prince, to whom her son was godfather. The other godparent was Frederick Henry, Prince of Orange, a name honoured by all who loved the Protestant cause. The Londoners approved the choice as a gesture of friendliness to the reformed Faith in Europe, where Dutch and Swede and German princeling still waited for Richelieu's men and money to make headway against Hapsburg Emperor and Hapsburg Spain.

For James was born into a world in which religion was

still the dominant force in politics and social life. It mattered vitally what one believed and what one's neighbour believed, not merely for one's salvation in the next world but for one's safety in this. The ladies at court and the young men at the University struggled to apprehend theology as to-day they endeavour to understand economics, while the writer of tracts and the purveyor of false news worked havoc with men's fears by rumours of intended massacre, potent with a generation whose grandfathers remembered the fires of Smithfield and to whom Gunpowder Plot was a horror that had well-nigh succeeded.

At his very birth, religious discord troubled James. The wet-nurse, selected by the Queen, was a Roman Catholic, and the strained relations which resulted between Her Majesty and the Lords of the Council only ceased when the nurse's anxiety had begun to affect her charge's health. Charles allowed his wife her own way, thus needlessly adding to the suspicions of his people. But as the years passed, the fears seemed groundless, for, under the kindly and capable governance of the Countess of Dorset, James grew up in a staunch Protestant atmosphere rendered the more compelling by the example of his father's true religious fervour.

The nursery at St. James's was a happy refuge for the King and Queen, as their public life at Whitehall grew more exacting. Charles, the Prince of Wales, who was three years older than his brother, was an ugly but attractive youth, a thorough Latin in his lazy insolence, a Frenchwoman's son and the grandson of a Medici. Yet some shrewd Scot ancestor had bequeathed him a sense of humour and proportion, which combined with an unusual sweetness of nature to win the affections of all about him. James, fairer in complexion, with better looks and gentler manners, had the English defects of stubbornness and stolidity. Between the two in age was Mary the Princess Royal, a tall child, reserved and self-opinionated, but passionately devoted to her parents and her brothers.

The three spent most of their early years together. London was no healthy spot, when the heat of summer or a spring drought gave rise to a wave of pestilence, the plague that scourged the narrow streets or the smallpox that would not be shut out from the court of kings. So the royal nursery was often to be found in the country. At Hampton Court, the children ran wild in the Home Park and climbed the trees, unchecked. At Richmond, they absorbed unawares the beauty of the English countryside. At Greenwich, they watched the ships. And James, who at five had been made Lord-Admiral of England, looked forward with a child's impatience to the time when he would be old enough to order his father's navy.

Strengthened by fresh air and healthy exercise and fortunate in the happy family life that encircled him, James had reached his eighth year, when security, the birthright of every child, was snatched from him. His father's absence in the north to subdue the Scottish rebels may have seemed of little import to him, except as the cause of his mother's unusual irritability. But by the spring of 1641 even a child could tell things were awry. Parliament, that body of querulous lawyers and stupid gentlemen of which he was hearing for the first time, swooped upon his father's greatest servants, imprisoned Archbishop Laud and charged the Earl of Strafford with treason. To James, a parliament seemed more like an insatiable monster than a collection of human beings, and his first impression was never uprooted; to the end of his life he never had, nor could be expected to have, any gleam of sympathy or understanding for the ideas of government for which all parliaments stood.

At this stage his distracted father arranged for the marriage of Mary, the Princess Royal, to Prince William of Orange. It was a popular alliance by which Charles hoped to conciliate the moderate section of his opponents. To James and his brother, it was a welcome occasion of subdued rejoicing. William of Orange arrived in London in April, 1641. The princes ran out to meet the young Dutchman on the water-stairs of the Palace of Whitehall, when he arrived by boat from Gravesend. They told him that their sister was in bed with a cold, and took him for a walk in the Privy Garden. But William insisted on seeing his future bride, as she sat up in bed with a pale and swollen face, as miserable as a nine-year-old could be. William was fifteen, and very solemn. But the two soon made friends, and on Low Sunday the wedding was solemnised. Prince Charles and the Duke led their sister into the Chapel of Whitehall. The family dined together in state and went for a walk in Hyde Park afterwards. There was a feeling of unreality about the festivities, but the children only half-understood the tragedy that was imminent. A few days later it was brought home to them by the flight of the gayest and most assured of the courtiers who hovered round the Queen, their mother. For a moment she talked wildly of flight herself, when she heard that Henry Jermyn had gone, the ne'er-do-well who had planned with his army friends to save the situation by a military rising in the King's favour. Before the week was out, the attainder of Strafford was an accomplished fact and James had lived through the horror of the days when the people yelled outside the Palace and were not appeased till the King had agreed to sacrifice his friend. It was a week of experience far too intense for a child of eight to undergo.

A year of uncertainty ensued; there was an atmosphere of apprehension and discomfort, more galling to a child's spirit than spectacular alarms. At last, one unhappy January day, the King's spirit broke, and the sudden decision was reached to leave London. The King and Queen with their elder children left hastily for Hampton Court. Their arrival was unexpected. The shutters were closed, the rooms icily cold, and the beds unaired. It was a miserable day. At the end of it the two boys were thrust into the same four-poster bed as their parents, to find comfort in their mother's nearness from the uncomprehended fears of the future. There was no more ordinary home-life. A month late, in February 1642, the Princess Royal, who had been left in England after her marriage on account of her youth, went out with her mother to Holland. Henrietta's aim was to raise money for the unavoidable struggle and she did not return to England for over a year. Charles, on tenterhooks lest his opponents should seize the person of the Prince of Wales, hurried back to Windsor, where he had left his son, and set out with him to York. James was sent back to St. James's to join his younger sister and brother, Princess Elizabeth and Henry, Duke of Gloucester. But the King was now equally fearful for the Duke of York's welfare, and anxious lest he should be used as a figurehead by the rebels. At Easter, the Earl of Hertford smuggled James out of London, against the orders of Parliament. His safe arrival at York was the sign for an outburst of mild festivities, and on Easter Monday he was invested with the Order of the Garter, and felt himself free of the nursery, ready to participate in great events.

The immediate future held an adventure for him. When Charles determined to summon Hull to surrender, he adopted a characteristic and disingenuous manœuvre. James and his cousin, the Elector Palatine, were sent to visit the town, ostensibly for the Duke of York's pleasure and recreation. Should they be well received, it was the King's intention to follow them next day and take possession. Sir John Hotham, the Governor of Hull, gave them the respect due to folk of high degree, and the lads might well mistake courtesy for friendship. But, unhappy though the conflict of loyalties made him, Hotham was a Parliament man at heart. James tells the story himself in one of the few surviving fragments of his autobiographical jottings.

'Sir L. Dyves came the next day before dinner and told

> the Governor, that the King would dine with him. They were on a platform, by the water-side. The Governor turned pale. He desired the Duke and company to retire to their lodgings. The gates were shut and the garrison put to arms.'

The King came, but no persuasions had any effect. Hotham would not let him in. At Charles's request, however, the Duke and his companions were allowed to leave the town one by one. According to James, only the officers' threats forced the garrison to arm unwillingly against their King. He believed that his father could have taken Hull, had he acted more precipitately.

> 'Some vigorous bold men, that went with the Duke of York should have been trusted with the design, with an order on the rest to obey the Duke. For it was in their power, several times after Hotham ordered the gates to be shut, to have secured him, or knocked him on the head. Either would have done the work.'

So James in his adult years recorded the angry sense of frustration, which embittered him on this, his first experience of failure, still believing with the uncomplicated outlook of youth that a knock on the head would solve political problems.

Disappointed at Hull, the Royalists plunged all the more eagerly into the maelstrom of events, which at length put an end to the lethargy of the months at York. The raising of the standard in August, and the quick march into Shropshire was followed in October by the first battle of the Civil War. At Edge Hill, a week after his ninth birthday James had his first sight of bloodshed. It was in the confident hope of triumph, that the King marched into battle, a son on either side. But when his men faltered and the fortunes of war wavered, he found himself father as well as King. His first thought was to remove his sons to safety. He himself wished to renew his troops' courage by putting himself at their head, so he called upon the Duke of Richmond to take the young princes out of battle. But Richmond excused himself. Dorset, the sturdy husband of the governess of happier days, was given the charge. But he, more blunt than the other, replied that 'he would not be thought a coward for any king's son in Christendom'. Another was put in command, and with a small escort of pensioners, the princes left the field. There was momentary danger as a body of enemy horse appeared, but the Royalists took refuge behind a close-set hedge, in a small barn which was in use as a dressing-station for the King's wounded. The enemy force passed on, unconscious of the illustrious prisoners they might have taken. As dusk fell, the tired lads reached the summit of the low hill, whence they could view in safety the dishevelled battlefield. When it was dark, the King joined them. Victory had eluded his arms; the struggle must go on. The tragedy of the future cast its shadow across their lives, but their spirits were saved from breaking and their minds from apprehending by the blessed necessity of fulfilling the tasks of the moment. Royalist headquarters were fixed at Oxford and thither James was sent, for obviously he was too young for a prolonged campaign. But none the less he had seen war: its terror, its hideousness and its thrill. It was to be the dominant passion of his youth.

From the age of nine to eighteen, with the exception of the glorious episode of his flight from England, the Duke of York was condemned to an enforced idleness as harmful as the previous excess of experience. It is possible that his mental rigidity and lack of imagination as an adult may be attributed to his inability to find a natural outlet for his energy and emotions in adolescence. Oxford in wartime was a hot-bed of intrigue and jealousy. The best men went out to fight, and did not return. The Queen came back in the summer of 1643 but after the birth of her last child at Exeter, she fled broken in health and spirit to her beloved France, her own country as England had never been. Next year the Prince of Wales was sent into the West with some well-chosen counscllors, and in due course escaped to the Continent. But the Duke of York was still at Oxford. In April 1645 it was suggested that he should go into Ireland, to be a rallying-point for the royal cause. The Queen in France was consulted, and after some weeks' delay declared that she saw nothing in the plan she could approve! The Duke chafed at the decision, resenting for the first time his mother's dominant will. But he was by nature an obedient child, and intensely loyal to those in authority over him. He fretted, but remained.

Naseby was fought and lost. In the spring of 1646 Charles, after weeks of hesitation, turned with pathetic futility to his countrymen the Scots. In his last Odyssey from Oxford, he would have liked to take James with him. But he was too uncertain of the future, and regretfully he left his son with his cousins, Richmond and Prince Rupert. Oxford was besieged. James was in charge of Sir George Radcliffe, a sincere and able man, the old friend and servant of the Earl of Strafford. The Queen sent him word to smuggle the Duke of York, either to France or Ireland. But Radcliffe was a man of honour – and he did not love Henrietta. He replied that he must receive an order from the King. Oxford surrendered, and the victors waited upon the Duke. They were rough soldierly men, and only one of their number, General Cromwell, was sufficiently touched by the forlorn figure of abandoned royalty, to kneel and kiss his hand. Radcliffe was ordered to take the Duke to London, there to hand him over to the charge of the Earl of Northumberland. They arrived in August, 1646, to be given a state welcome, by a parliament and people uncertain of the road upon which victory had set them. The King's younger son might be a good figurehead for a limited monarchy. His old servants were dismissed and even his pet dwarf was taken from him, but Northumberland proved a kindly and respectful guardian, and the companionship of his younger sister and brother, who had been in London throughout the war, made him in some ways less lonely than he had been at Oxford. They occupied their own quarters at St. James's with occasional visits to Northumberland's country mansion, Sion House, where James looked out on the river and fretted for the freedom he had lost. The confinement, however formal, chafed his spirits, and he was ill with a succession of childish ailments throughout the spring of 1647. The news that Parliament had discovered plans for his escape, engineered by the King's friends without, added to his misery. In June a happy episode broke the tedium of their lives and they were allowed to spend two days with their father at Caversham, on his way to Hampton Court as the Army's prisoner. Before they parted, the King in a few whispered words had urged the Duke to endeavour his escape. Soon afterwards, Charles succeeded in sending him a cipher to use in writing to him when and how he could. During the summer, plots were in abeyance, as the King's fate wavered in the balance and Parliament and Army strove for mastery. In August, while Charles was at Hampton Court his children saw him frequently, but in November his rash flight, that finished in renewed captivity at Carisbrooke, put an end to all chance of his rehabiliation. Then James concentrated upon the plans for his own escape, with a foresight and determination remarkable in a boy of fourteen.

His accomplices at St. James's were a barber, placed in his service by the Parliament but won over to his designs, and a Mrs. Kilvert, who waited upon the Princess Elizabeth. Running one day up the stairs from the Palace garden to his own apartments, the Duke pushed open the door and felt that somebody was concealed behind it. A hand slipped a letter into his. It contained money from the King for his requirements. But again the fates were unpropitious. A cipher-letter in the Duke's handwriting was intercepted by the authorities; the barber was imprisoned, and James could not this time, as in the previous winter, deny knowledge of the plot. Fortunately Mrs. Kilvert was not suspected, and to her the Duke had entrusted the cipher as soon as he heard that he was discovered. In March he was examined by a committee of both Houses but they could extract nothing from him. He declared that the cipher was burnt, and no threat of the Tower would induce him to betray his accomplices. The committee could report nothing further to the Commons, many of whom urged that the Tower was indeed the safest place for the Duke. The committee, however, had been moved by his fearless behaviour; they counselled leniency and he was left at St. James's, the anxious Northumberland protesting that he would not be answerable for his charge. The most that the Duke would promise was to receive no letters whatsoever, without his guardian's knowledge. 'But nothing they could do or say to him was capable of hindering him from endeavouring his escape.'[1]

The third attempt was lucky. There was a Colonel Joseph Bampfield, whose share in the previous efforts had not been disclosed. James determined to work through him only, and not to run the risk of many conspirators, nor be involved in other plans. None the less, he must have been tempted, when one day on his way to the tennis-court a letter was offered to him with the whisper, 'It is from the Queen.' But he replied, 'I must keep my promise and for that reason cannot receive it.' Henrietta was furious when she heard of his refusal, and James had much ado to placate her. The action was typical of him, and of a natural honesty that never diminished; while no less illuminating was the determined self-sufficiency, with which he worked out his plans regardless of friend and enemy alike.

[1] Clark : *Life of James II*, p. 33, *seq.*

On April 20th, 1648, he escaped. About a fortnight before that date, he had delighted his brother and sister by suggesting a game of hide-and-seek, after they had finished their seven o'clock supper. The other young people in the house were asked to join in, and a joyous hour followed, in and out of the garden, up the stairs and down the passages. Nor was the Duke's condescension for one evening only. To the joy of his juniors, the games of hide-and-seek went on. The kindly Northumberland was glad to see the children happy, and felt that perhaps he had been worrying unnecessarily about James, who seemed to be enjoying himself as much as the rest. Naturally he knew the best places in which to hide, and he played with such zest that sometimes it took the children an hour to find him. As the novelty wore off the younger ones grew weary of so one-sided a game, and often they gave up looking, knowing that he would come out of his hiding-place when he was tired. And so, on April 20th, nobody worried when the children came in without the Duke.

That evening he had run off as usual to hide, followed by Elizabeth's little dog, who liked to join in the game. As soon as he was out of sight he picked up the dog, ran to his sister's bedroom and locked him safely in. Then he slipped quickly down the back-stairs into a small garden, whence a door opened into St. James's Park. Bampfield was awaiting him outside with a footman carrying cloak and periwig. At Spring-gardens, they took coach to Salisbury House. Here James alighted boldly, as if to pay a visit, and the coachman drove on into the city. The fugitives slipped down Ivy Lane to the river, and rowed to London Bridge. Thence, they reached a doctor's house close by the bridge where, as previously arranged, James was disguised as a girl. Bampfield had hired a barge to take them down to the Hope beyond Gravesend, where a ship awaited them. The barge belonged to a certain John Owen, who knew nothing of his passengers. And here danger first threatened them, for Owen began to suspect the runaways when he saw a young woman in the party. The Duke's own indiscretion confirmed the bargeman's suspicion, for spying into the cabin, Owen saw the 'young woman' hitching up her garter with her leg upon the table 'in so unwomanish a manner' that his doubts became certainties.

Fortunately, James did the only wise thing. He told the bargee everything and asked his help. He would have been a hard-hearted fellow, who could have resisted the youth's eager appeals, and the Duke's luck held. Owen consented to take them down to the ship. All lights on board were extinguished and the barge drifted down with the tide past the blockhouses at Gravesend to the Dutch ship in the Hope, ready to sail at daybreak for Holland and freedom.

The ship anchored next morning before Flushing, and the last thrill of the adventure was again due to Owen, who for his own safety had sailed with them. Sighting a distant ship, he declared it to be a Parliamentary frigate and urged them to set sail at once for Middleburgh. The tide did not serve, but, less affrighted of sand-banks than Parliament, Owen declared he could pilot the ship through the passage. They were twice on the verge of shipwreck, but their pilot persevered and only admitted that the pursuer was a harmless merchantman when the ship was safely anchored across the bar. Bampfield posted at once to The Hague to tell the Princess Royal the good news and to bring back some clothes for the Duke. Mary set out to meet her brother, and brought him in triumph to her home at Honslärdyke. He had accomplished his first great adventure, the only one in his life that was to be entirely successful.

At St. James's, it had seemed that, once abroad, all his troubles would be over. But the new set of circumstances were in some ways more difficult than any he had yet experienced, requiring from him qualities of implicit obedience which he did possess, and of patience and adaptability which he could never achieve. At this stage in his life, his chief need was an elder friend to guide him. His brother, the Prince of Wales, might have supplied the lack, but not only was Charles himself unsettled and unhappy, not yet having learnt the insouciance which helped him in later crises, but he was jealous of his brother, whose romantic escape from England combined with his better looks and more docile ways to make him a favourite among the little band of exiles. The two brothers were of too dissimilar a nature for there to be much real sympathy between them before the passage of years had dimmed the vital difference of personality, and shared experiences and common memories had bound the two more closely.

Rupert was also in Holland, the cousin from Germany whose exploits in the recent wars might well stir a boy to enthusiastic affection. But the Queen had never liked him; he had offended King Charles in the last months at Oxford, and he suffered under a sense of injury which showed itself in a growing moroseness. There are few things more exhausting to nerves and temper than continuous shortage of money: one of them is continuous shortage of occupation. The exiles suffered from both, and in consequence the various small groups, surrounding the Queen, the Prince and the Duke, indulged unchecked in intrigue and mischief-making. James, when he came from England, turned for advice as was natural to Colonel Bampfield, whose loyalty and skill he had experienced. But Bampfield had Presbyterian sympathies, he was not therefore *persona grata* with the Prince of Wales, who knew that a section of the Presbyterians would like to oust the army leaders from their control of English affairs and set up a limited monarchy, using the Duke of York for their purpose. To counteract Bampfield's interest, the Queen made the mistake of setting about James a large number of gentlemen, for whom he could provide neither sustenance nor work. In place of his titular governor,

Lord Byron, who was still in England, she sent down a kinsman of her friend Jermyn, Sir John Berkeley, a vigorous and remarkably successful adventurer. James at first resented his intrusion, though Berkeley, always cool-headed and untrammelled by scruple, stood his ground till he made headway in the Duke's affections. Bampfield hated him, and the unquiet atmosphere of James's household was accentuated by the arrival of eight ships of the English Navy, which had revolted from Parliament and wished to submit themselves to one or other of the princes. This was Bampfield's opportunity. The Duke, as Lord-Admiral, would naturally take command, an expedition would sail for England, and Bampfield declared that he could vouch for support in that country not merely from Royalists, but from a large section of disillusioned and war-weary Presbyterians. James went proudly on board, in ecstasy at the prospect of going to sea in real earnest and rescuing his father from the power of his enemies. But word was sent to the Prince of Wales. He came down hurriedly to the coast, dismissed Bampfield as 'a man of a turbulent intriguing head', and dispatched James back to The Hague like a disobedient schoolboy.

A few months later the Prince of Wales joined the Duke, as dejected as his brother, for the naval expedition which had set out under his command had failed as completely as the other ill co-ordinated Royalist efforts of 1648. Charles explained to James that Bampfield had meant to set him up in opposition to his father, and the Duke, dismayed, promised absolute obedience. He was not however to be allowed to command the fleet. It was sent to the West Indies on a three years' voyage, under the joint leadership of Rupert and his brother Maurice. James's disappointment and his sense of Rupert's rivalry affected their relationships to the end of their lives. But he need not have grudged his cousin his command. Rupert returned alone. In a storm at sea, the ship, which bore his brother, had vanished, never to be seen or heard of again. The loss soured the spirit of a brave and honest man, already embittered by the ingratitude of the world.

In the New Year, Charles and James were destitute at The Hague, reduced to further misery by a recent attack of smallpox. Nor could Mary give them the comfort she would have wished. Her husband was their loyal friend, but his position as stadt-holder was precarious. For his sake alone, the brothers must seek a fresh refuge. The Duke left for France, and arrived in Paris in February, 1649. His mother and her youngest child, Princess Henrietta, were living in penury at the Louvre. It was of little help to her that she was the French King's aunt, for that Christmas, young Louis XIV had been driven from his capital by the rebellious citizens, distrustful of his mother and her Italian favourite Mazarin. The French royal family at St. Germain were for the moment only one whit less wretched than their English cousins. The Duke of York reached the Louvre while the Queen was at dinner, knelt down and asked his mother's blessing. But the joy of their meeting was clouded by suspense. Everybody awaited news from England, and dreaded its arrival. Then the terrible rumour arose that would not be denied. King Charles had been condemned and executed. Nobody dare tell the Queen. The days passed and she became anxious that no word had reached her. She attributed the delay to the unsettled state of affairs in Paris, and at length she smuggled a messenger through to the French court, with whom the rebels did not permit her communication. Louis would be able to tell her. While they awaited the messenger's return, the Queen and the Duke and their immediate attendants sat in uneasy conversation, the latter trying in vain to start a subject, which would have 'the effect of diverting the mind of the Queen.' Why was the messenger so long, she asked, and the devoted Jermyn murmured that the delay must mean bad tidings. 'You know, then, full well,' cried the Queen with sudden suspicion. Then at last Jermyn told her. 'She stood motionless as a statue,' wrote one who was present, 'without words and without tears.' At last when they had begun to fear that too great control would mean mental derangement, the comforting words of another woman brought the tears of healing.

James, who was the least introspective of people, used to note down his experiences but never his feelings. What he thought on this tragic occasion is unrecorded, but to the end of his life he showed by his words and deeds how deeply his father's fate impressed him as a dread answer to all who were lenient to rebellion.

Until the catastrophe of Worcester put a stop to all hope of change in the present posture of affairs, the years were spent in unquiet efforts to achieve the impossible and regain the crown. In September, 1649, the Duke went with Charles to Jersey. Henrietta did not wish him to go: it was foolhardy to expose both the brothers to danger. But Charles could not brook any interference with his authority and James was taken 'more to annoy his mother . . . than because prudence required it'. He proved surprisingly able, and gave sound advice on matters of seamanship. He was happy to be active and full of hope. But the expedition proved valueless, and Charles, restless and uncertain what course to pursue, was away again at the beginning of the year to negotiate with the Scots, leaving James in Jersey till September, 1650.

In the autumn he returned to his mother's tutelage in Paris and found it a sorry exchange for the petting of the Jersey loyalists. Henrietta had little skill in managing her sons. She had never been immune from the feminine sin of possessiveness, and now that her husband's death and the authority, which hedged her eldest son as King, had lessened the range of her activities, she found the power she always craved in a close control of the affairs of her younger children. James resented her insistence in treating him as a child, and her attempts to organise his household. She still regarded Lord Jermyn as her best friend, and he did in part compensate for his lack of character by his loyalty in distress. His buccaneering kinsman Berkeley, who enhanced the role of successful man-of-the-world with a spice of rashness and jollity, attracted James, but was still regarded by him as Jermyn's nominee and his mother's agent and was kept at arm's length in consequence. The Duke's new secretary, Henry Bennet, was the friend of the other section of the exiled court, which was led by Hyde, the honest and learned lawyer whom Henrietta disliked but who had a disconcerting way of proving himself right. Bennet was regarded as Hyde's friend, but he was an unprepossessing creature, able in a deprecatory fashion, incapable of any sort of idealism and all the more likely to succeed in a cynical world. But he was no mentor for active and eager youth. In the absence of a congenial companion it was not surprising that James, a young man of seventeen with a superabundance of energy and no legitimate means of expressing himself, fell a ready victim to the designs of two men of a very different type from the average Cavalier. Sir Edward Herbert, the Attorney-General, was a dour lawyer who had begun his career alongside of Eliot and Pym, as an active member of an obstreperous House of Commons. But he had been won over by the court in the first days of the Long Parliament when the King's concessions broke the unanimity of the opposition. He stood now for the policy, earlier advocated by Bampfield and stringently opposed by Hyde, of endeavouring to regain the throne by making use of the Presbyterian malcontents. Charles, in spite of his former reluctance, was at this juncture won over to a like policy, thus entering upon the alliance with the Scots and the disastrous adventure, which began with Dunbar and ended with Worcester.

Meanwhile Herbert combined with Sir George Radcliffe, who had rejoined the Duke's household with something of his old authority, to persuade James to flee to Holland. Once free of his mother's apron-strings, they urged that he might do something to assist his brother in the plans he was concerting; they were necessarily vague as to details, and a less ingenuous youth might have gathered that their real aim was to have control of the person who would be heir to the throne, if Charles died in the forthcoming attempt. But the Duke, candid himself by nature, loved the adventure inherent in any sort of 'design', without being subtle enough ever to appreciate its causes or consequences. In this case, he gladly agreed to the plan. His mother, the Queen, forbade him, but, as always, opposition only made him the more determined to go on. Berkeley stayed behind, not as yet feeling strong enough to challenge the others' influence; Bennet, characteristically, went to crab the scheme with his constant criticism. On October 4th, 1650, they set out for Brussels, intending to proceed to The Hague. Things went ill from the start. Mary of Orange was pregnant and less equal to managing her difficult relations than usual, and, having received an irate letter from her mother, told James unhappily that he had better stay where he was till he had made his peace with the Queen. He lingered at Brussels, where the news reached him of his sister Elizabeth's death in England. She had been sent under surveillance to Carisbrooke, the very place where her father had been imprisoned. The perpetual reminder of his tragedy wore down her health, already overstrained by her last meeting with him on the eve of his execution, too great a sorrow for a delicate and sensitive child. Only the Duke of Gloucester was left in England. Cromwell, they said, was about to apprentice him to a shoemaker.

At Brussels, bad news continued to pour in. The accounts of defeat at Dunbar were followed by a rumour that Charles was dangerously ill in Scotland. Herbert and Radcliffe, anxious to maintain their hold over James, concerted a scheme for marrying him to the natural daughter of the Duke of Lorraine, an independent princeling, who, with valour and diplomatic skill, fought and coquetted in turn with France and Spain. He treated his visitors with courtesy, though he disliked Radcliffe's propensity for conversing in Latin. But he had no intention of going beyond words, and even James began to realise that the designs of the wiseacres, to whom he had trusted, were as much the fruit of impotent idleness as the less harmful escapades of the addle-pates in Paris. He was feeling homesick. The fortunes of the Stuarts were at their nadir, and it was no time to be flouting his mother and displeasing Charles. In November, news had come of another death. The Prince of Orange had been struck down by smallpox, a few weeks before the expected birth of his first child. His death was a severe blow to the cause of the Stuarts; to his wife, the Princess Royal, it was a bitter personal loss. For she had loved him well, and her joy in the child-to-be was engulfed in despair at the tragic devastation that evil chance had wrought in her life. The bejewelled bed in which she was to be confined lay unoccupied, and she abandoned herself to her sorrow. But the new life within her would not be denied, and her child was born and lived, and gradually, in caring for him and defending his rights against the jealous burghers of Amsterdam, she found again a purpose in existence. Only, as the child grew out of babyhood did his wizened little face, his over-anxious ways and his inability to enjoy the pastimes and carefree extravagances of youth bear witness to a twist in his nature, a perpetual reminder that he, conceived in joy, had been brought forth in desolation. They christened him William, and from Brussels, the Duke of York, his uncle, wrote in eager congratulation to ask whom he was like. He came in January to see the baby for himself, the child who was one day to break his heart, and to rule in his stead as William III of England.

James passed the spring in aimless inactivity in Flanders, too proud to admit the fiasco of his bid for independence but not sorry when in June, 1651, a categorical letter from his brother bade him return to Paris and submit himself in all things to the Queen. Radcliffe was dismissed, though he made his peace with Henrietta later. Herbert ingratiated himself with the Queen by playing upon her hostility to Hyde. James turned in natural reaction to Berkeley, and welcomed to his household the latter's two nephews, Harry Jermyn, an ugly and fascinating oddity, and Charles Berkeley, a brave man who had no principles beyond loyalty to his friends and disregard of his own interests, in honest adherence to which tenets he excelled far better men.

Perhaps at Charles's instigation, Henrietta received James with an affectionate disregard of his escapade. It was a critical moment, and temporarily all divergences of policy and interest were swept aside among the exiles at the Louvre. Charles, recovered from his indisposition, had gathered a new army and marched into England, forbearing with difficulty the Presbyterian Divines whom an ironic fate had made his strange allies. Hopes ran high, and the suspense was almost unbearable. Then like a thunder-clap came news of Worcester. It was the end! But had the King escaped? Nobody knew. October ushered in a host of rumours, each in turn proved false. Hope began to fade: the worst had happened. Then came the incredible truth. He had escaped; he was in France. James rode out to meet him, and on November 7th, 1651, Charles entered Paris in a caricature of a costume, with a single lackey in attendance. He talked readily enough about his adventures, from the moment when he escaped from the battlefield with a 'gentleman' who was a highwayman by trade and knew the hidden bypaths well. Charles laughed and jested, and flirted with Orleans's daughter, La Grande Mademoiselle, but he was changed. Gone were the fair though excessive illusions of youth; he had experienced hypocrisy, bloodshed, despair and, recoiling from tragedy, henceforward he sought security from life in a shrewd irony and good-natured detachment, which did not ill become a King without a throne. But for James, incapable of loosing the rein, in all ways more intense than his brother, no pleasures of court or countryside could stifle the urge to be up and doing. Now that all plots to regain the crown were in abeyance he was free, and he determined to follow the French flag as a soldier of fortune. Henrietta made violent objections; less vehemently but with more authority Charles echoed her disapproval. But the Duke persisted. The matter was brought up in Council. James, like all who are ill at ease with the world, never forgot a favour nor an injury. He did not forget that, on this occasion Hyde by his subtle euphemisms enabled Charles to give his consent. For Hyde argued that while it would ill become the King to advise his brother to a dangerous undertaking, if the Duke out of his own princely courage wished to visit the French army, it were ungracious to restrain him. A large part of the prejudice with which the Duke had hitherto regarded Hyde trembled into nothingness, as with the last words of his ponderous discourse he came down on James's side in the dispute. His support was decisive and the royal permission was given without further demur. Unfortunately the Duke had no money, and no horses! Charles solved the latter difficulty by lending him some coach-horses, and James borrowed three hundred 'pistoles' from a Gascon to buy the necessary equipment. The French army was in the field near Chartres, and with two companions, Sir John Berkeley and Colonel Werden, James set out from Paris on the 21st of April, 1652. A few grooms and servants followed in the rear drawing two mules, that bore his camp-bed and supplies. It mattered little that they were all his possessions, and that fighting in Flanders meant hardship and danger. He was eighteen, and it was spring.

CHAPTER II

SOLDIER OF FORTUNE

'A prince of high spirit, who has now had experience in the art of war.' – *Venetian Papers.*

IN 1652, when the Duke of York joined the French army, his cousin King Louis XIV was still an exile from his own capital. The spark, which set alight the civil wars of the Fronde, had been the suspicion that the Queen-Mother, Anne of Austria, was the mistress of Mazarin, the Italian Cardinal, who monopolised the conduct of affairs. Louis was only fourteen, but he was already beginning to resent his mother's control. Very gradually, as his personality began to make itself felt, the tide of national feeling turned in his favour. But, when James volunteered in his cousin's cause, the war was still primarily a civil dispute with the issue in the balance. Midway between the religious wars of the sixteenth century, and the revolution of 1789, the Fronde bore a superficial resemblance to the constitutional struggles in England and the rebels claimed to stand for political reform. The selfish ambitions of great territorial nobles such as the King's uncle Gaston d'Orleans, the Prince of Lorraine and Condé, the rebel leader, and the ever present influence of Spain, ready to support any revolt in France, gave the Fronde its own peculiar character. But the eventual triumph of the young King was so complete that it repressed for more than a century the development of ordered self-government, which was the counterpart in political life of the revolt from tradition and authority in the sphere of religion. France became the epitome of cultured despotism, and Louis a glorious example to all monarchs. It was in France that the most impressionable years of James's life were passed, and Louis became his closest friend. When his brother was restored to the throne of England, the Duke of York urged and expected him to mould his country on the French pattern. Charles had wit and wisdom to achieve his own ends in his own way, but James, impercipient in all matters touching human nature, continued to the end of his life to look at England through French eyes, thinking in terms of a despotism and seeing in Louis's triumphs the justification of his own endeavours.

. . . .

The wars of the Fronde, sordid as they were in many ways, were enriched by the genius of the two opposing generals, Condé, the inspired rebel, and the prudent but tenacious Turenne. Both were Protestants, and James, staunch Protestant himself, was bound the more closely to his leader by this religious tie. Turenne was a scion of the house of Orange, and sufficiently akin to James in temperament for a true understanding to exist between them. Unperturbed by dangers and difficulties, the marshal forbore to run into needless peril but, believing that intelligence no less than courage should be the attribute of a good general, pursued his course in campaign or battle with quiet fortitude and painstaking honesty. The Duke's admiration for the good soldier under whom he served breathes through the memoirs, which he wrote of their four years together, memoirs characterised by a modesty and straightforwardness that make good reading in an age of florid diction.

They were days that were to stand in James's memory for all the adventure and confident achievement of youth. Four years cut out of life, fighting in northern France and Flanders, should not be hard for this generation to imagine. The mud of the trenches, the incessant rain and the merciless winds of March, coarse food and uncertain quarters, the terror of sudden death and the horror of mangled bodies, James writes of them all among the familiar names, Arras and the Somme, Cambrai and Bapaume: 'There was on the right a brook which comes from Roiset and falls into the Somme a little above Péronne. There was in front a little valley and on the side of the brook a water course which the cavalry could not pass without great difficulty; the nearest village was called Tincour or Buires.' It is an Englishman writing three hundred years ago, from the country whose quiet fields have been doomed so often to the nightmare of invasion.

Each winter he returned to Paris on leave. His reputation, as a soldier and a man of honour, grew with the rapidity that characterises fickle fortune, when she changes her frowns to smiles. But life out of the trenches was a complicated affair, and the Louvre was still a hot-bed of intrigue. The Duke received instructions from his brother, couched in authoritative terms, to beware of the pervasive Bampfield, and to keep Charles informed at Cologne of any designs upon England that might come to his knowledge. 'You must be very kind to Henry Bennet,' Charles commanded, suspecting the growing influence of Berkeley, the Queen's friend. The Duke endeavoured to give implicit obedience to his brother's instructions, but it was not always easy. Too often they conflicted with the wishes of his mother, who expected to have her own way, in Paris if not in Cologne.

Henrietta in 1654 was in a most pernicious humour. Henry of Gloucester had been allowed to leave England and join his family. His mother insisted on him coming to the Louvre. Charles was anxious, fearing that attempts would be made to convert the boy to the Roman Catholic faith. He instructed the Duke of York to take what precautions he could, and when he heard that his mother had had the effrontery to arrange for Gloucester to be educated by the Jesuits, he sent Ormonde, the loyal aristocrat, to Paris to remonstrate. Henrietta lost her temper and delivered an ultimatum to Gloucester, who at fourteen had proved himself apt in theological argument and as stubborn as every true Stuart. Either he did as she wished or she would never see his face again. Ormonde could keep him, she added scornfully, well aware that his purse had been emptied over and again in his master's cause. Henry was obdurate but unhappy, and next day being the Sabbath, he met his mother on the way to Mass and knelt, as was the custom, for her blessing. She refused to acknowledge him; her heart bitter and her head high, she passed on to find what consolation she could in the forms of the religion, whose spirit she had betrayed. Gloucester and the Duke of York sought consolation in their bewilderment at the house of the English Ambassador, where the Anglican service was celebrated. They returned to the Louvre afterwards, to find no dinner had been prepared for them. Ormonde came to the rescue and demanded an interview with Henrietta. But the Queen-Mother was implacable. When Gloucester, more wretched than he dared admit, went to his chamber for refuge, he found that his bed had been stripped of its sheets, a gesture that bore only one interpretation. His mother had finished with him. It did not enter the boy's head to submit; he had not forgotten his father's injunction, as he sat on his knee the day before Charles died: 'Let no-one turn thee into Papist or Puritan.' He left the Louvre, and went to a loyalist's house in the City. Ormonde pawned his jewels and his George: and a few days later set out with Gloucester to join the King at Cologne. James returned to the front, well-content to exchange the complications of human intercourse and of religious and political intrigue for the steady discipline and unquestioning comradeship of army life.

It was an ordered existence, which suited him admirably. He was not a dashing officer, but there was a passive courage about him which demanded respect. He had the great gift of concentrating whole-heartedly on the immediate job on hand, and he was intensely interested in the details of soldiering. Whether he were engaged in a siege or a forage party, reconnoitring the enemy's position or organising a midnight march, he acted with the same calm efficiency, that inspired trust and affection in the men he commanded as no mere brilliance could have done. He won their obedience by his 'gentle rule and overflowing courtesy' and was ready to share their hardships. At his sieges he spent a great deal of time in the batteries, condemning the inclination of many young officers to leave the routine work to the engineers. When a cannon ball struck between three barrels of powder close beside him, or a musket ball glanced off his boot, he recorded the fact that he had narrowly escaped death, but added that there was no time to be 'apprehensive of it'. When his lodgings turned out to be within the enemy's range and his fellow officers retired to safer quarters, he remained where he was, noting with satisfaction that he was not disturbed, since his presence so near the line was not suspected. At such crises the very insensitiveness, that was to harden in later years into brutality, stood him in good stead; it was typical that the only superior officer he disliked intensely was a very Gallic marshal, who lost his temper volubly at any opposition and expressed his opinion with more noise than clarity. Fortunately most of his associates were more congenial. They included a fellow volunteer and a brilliant soldier, the German Schomberg, now at the beginning of a great career, which was to end when he completed James's ruin at the battle of the Boyne. Now the two fought side by side in blessed ignorance of the future.

The war ran its course, in 1652 against Lorraine and the rebel princes in France, in 1653 against an invading Spanish army in the north and subsequently in Flanders. The balance of success was on the side of the French, largely because Condé's genius was hampered by the clogging formality of the numerous Spanish commanders, who refused to act without detailed orders from the correct source though the enemy were escaping under their very eyes. Moreover, the feeling in France itself was rapidly changing and the desire for peace and national unity gave Louis his opportunity.

Condé realised that the old devotion of the Paris mob was wavering, when in July 1652 his army was refused admission into the city, and was cooped up in the Faubourg of St. Antoine, before Turenne's attacking force. On that hot and sultry summer's day, the quiet suburban roads awakened to horror. In and out of the houses men fought hand to hand, losing and recovering by deeds of individual daring the barricades thrown up across the streets. In corners of gay gardens, men were trapped and butchered. From the neighbouring windmills, Turenne's guns swept the roadway, while King Louis and the Queen-Mother watched the carnage from an adjacent hill. The Duke of York was in personal attendance upon Turenne, and saw his friend Colonel Werden wounded by his side. The tragedy had a sudden end, when the gates of Paris miraculously opened to Condé's wearied troops, and inspired by the eloquence of La Grande Mademoiselle, the citizens turned the guns of the Bastille upon the pursuing Royalists. One woman's zeal had checked, though it could not prevent, Louis's ultimate victory.

There followed a winter of long route-marches in bitter weather. The frost was so intense that on one day 'thirty or forty of the common soldiers perished . . . for as soon as any of those which were not well clothed sat down to rest themselves, the cold seized them so that they could not possibly get up on their legs again'. Supplies were short and the staple food was cabbage-stalks. Exercising their age-long prerogative of grumbling, the men called it 'the Cardinal's bread'. As they marched across a treeless plain in the face of a bleak north-easter, or underwent the fatigue of a thaw in an uneven country of clay soil, they wondered why they were fighting Mazarin's battles.

But James, at the end of his first campaign and just nineteen years of age, endured the hardships as became him and was marked out by Turenne as a reliable officer.

Thereafter the war developed into a succession of sieges and counter-attacks. Turenne's relief of Arras in 1654 was the Duke's most vivid experience. In that year, as he records with pride, he became the youngest general officer serving in the French Army. He came back from the campaign, full of good stories. Of the soldier who bore a message from Arras wrapped in a ball of lead, which he swallowed for greater security. Having avoided the Spanish lines and reached Turenne, the messenger was at a loss to produce the message and all purges failed, till a fiery marshal moved that his belly be ripped open, whereupon fear produced the desired result. Of the tragic accident to a Spanish convoy, bearing gunpowder – a half-drunken trooper smoking a pipe of tobacco, a terrified officer whipping the pipe from his mouth and striking the man with the flat of his sword, and the trooper, enraged, firing his pistol at the officer, who saved himself by falling flat upon the ground, while death leapt from horse to horse as the powder bags exploded and no other remained alive of the stricken convoy. And lastly of the great assault on the Spaniards, who were besieging Arras. By a secret midnight march, Turenne misled the enemy, attacking where they least expected it. James withdrew from the troops, to see for himself that they were invisible. It was a night without a moon, and the men concealed their matches and moved forward in silent columns. As they reached the point of onset, the musketeers uncovered, and a breeze fanned their lights into abundant flame. The enemy's guns were trained upon the attacking line. A rumour arose that Turenne had been wounded and the men began to waver. With an unexpected flash of imagination, James saved the moment from disaster. He bade the band strike up a cheerful tune and behind the drummer, who was the first to fall, the troops pressed on to a hard-won victory.

During this campaign, James celebrated his twenty-first birthday. He could not go through such experiences unscathed. If Charles paid for the years of enforced and embittered idleness at Brussels and Cologne by a loosening of moral fibre and a sacrifice of his ideals, James, by going to the wars too soon, became hardened to the sufferings of others and careless of the sanctity of human life. None the less he enjoyed his soldiering, and looked upon it as the profession, in which in all likelihood he would spend the remainder of his days. But in 1656, he was bewildered and dismayed by the first of those strokes of bad luck, which so consistently and tragically undermined his confidence in life. His success had perturbed the Protector, who feared the effect of a Stuart doing romantic deeds within hearsay of London. When peace was made between Cromwell and King Louis, the former stipulated that James Stuart should not serve with the French armies, save in Italy. James, who loved his mother's sister the Duchess of Savoy, was excited at the prospect of attaching himself to her court and gaining fresh experience of war in the mountains, but his brother discomfited him, by demanding his presence at Bruges and ordering him to quit the French service, in view of a new alliance between the exiled Stuarts and Spain. James was on the horns of a dilemma. It needed no persuasion of his mother to stay his departure, nor the anxious flattery of the French politicians, conscious that 70,000 Irish troops at present in French pay would probably follow the Duke, if he enlisted under another flag. Yet his brother was King and his command could not be disregarded. In the summer he made a formal and forlorn visit to Madrid, but he only alienated his brother's new allies by hiding his feelings under a haughty reserve that out-Spaniarded the Dons. He returned to Paris to make his adieux. But when he met his chief again, it seemed impossible to break the happy association of the last four years. With Turenne's help, the Duke wrote to his brother a last impassioned plea to be left in France, to follow the career for which he was best fitted. But Charles's reply was an 'absolute order to repair to Flanders', and James, who always gave to his superiors the obedience he expected from those beneath him, instantly obeyed.

The Princess Royal also came to Bruges for Christmas, and shook her head over her brothers' wilfulness. They were scarcely on speaking terms! Charles, jealous of James without knowing it and temporarily suspicious of anyone pro-French, distrusted the influence of Sir John Berkeley and his nephews and was annoyed that the Duke had brought them with him to Flanders. James, always blind to questions of policy where his loves or hates were concerned, resented the coldness with which his friends were treated, and lost his temper in the King's presence when aspersions were cast upon them. Then he sulked, and more like a schoolboy than a soldier of repute, planned to run away. He told Berkeley to retire to Holland, and leaving Bruges on the strength of a shooting expedition, joined his friend, and defied his brother, declaring that he would go back to France. Charles lost his patience and vowed that the Duke would ruin him. But he gave way on the question of Berkeley's employment, and James returned in a subdued humour to Flanders. Such precipitate action in personal matters, so alien to the prudence which had made his reputation as a soldier, might well alarm those who had the Duke's interest at heart.

During 1657, the incessant fighting in Flanders continued. As a soldier of fortune, James enlisted in the Spanish Army. But warfare had lost its savour. The Spaniards irritated him. As soldiers they left undone so much that should have been done and, in their scrupulous formality, did a great deal that might well have been left undone. The *camaraderie* of the brilliant Condé could not compensate for the arrogance and inaccessibility of Don John, the Commander-in-Chief. Brave in battle but aloof in counsel, the latter disapproved of the democratic ways of Condé and the Duke of York, who mastered the details of siege or encampment instead of leaving the work to non-commissioned officers. Condé told James he would get used to it in time, but the younger man fumed when the health of the troops was undermined by an unnecessarily long campaign among the low-lying Flemish marshes. But the Duke himself kept fit and in spite of his complaints he had one joy, which grew steadily, the companionship of his younger brother Gloucester, to whom he gladly taught the art of war.

On June 14th, 1658, the battle of the Dunes was fought. The French were besieging Dunkirk, and at a council of war held on June 11th, Don John proposed, to bewildered and silent subordinates, that the main Spanish army should relieve the town by marching across the sand-dunes and attacking the unsuspecting French. The Duke of York, who had been absent from council, was sent ahead with two other officers to find a suitable place for the Spanish army to encamp. He went with a heavy heart, for he knew Turenne too well to expect him to play the role which Don John had allotted him, that of waiting in innocent inactivity to be attacked. James's foreboding was justified.

At eleven o'clock next morning (13th June) when Turenne saw the Spanish army among the sand-hills, he could not believe his own eyes. At evening he learnt from a prisoner that they intended to take the offensive. Without hesitation he ordered his own army to advance through the night, that he might steal his enemy's thunder and himself attack at daybreak. It was only what James had expected. In vain he had urged the Spaniards to call in the horse, which had been allowed to dispense on foraging excursions, and to expedite the supplies and ammunition which had not yet come up to the camp. At five o'clock next morning he espied the French approach. The Spanish Generals prepared, with unabated confidence, to resist. James was uneasy, but Condé met him with his usual nonchalance. 'Have you ever seen a battle?' he asked young Gloucester, and to the novice's excited 'never' he replied, 'Then in half an hour's time you will see how we shall lose one.'

The chance and circumstance of war and of diplomacy had so confused the issues that the two armies, facing each other across the Flemish dunes, fought under the flags of Spain and France but were in fact of diverse nationalities. French rebels under Condé, Scots and Irishmen and English loyalists fighting for the friends of the Stuart cause, whoever they might be, faced Turenne's veterans and the English regiments whom Cromwell had dispatched to help his new ally. The bitterness of party hatreds gave venom to the attack and sullen courage to the vain resistance. When the battle began, James with a handful of men had been detached from the other English regiments and posted to the rear of the Spanish right wing, among the higher sand-hills bordering on the sea. Here he witnessed the rapid advance of the Cromwellian troops, who outstripped their French comrades with an incautious zeal which might have cost them dear, had the Spaniards charged their flank. But Don John permitted them to reach unscathed the foot of the hill, whereupon his troops were stationed. He considered himself impregnable; no troops would face that steep ascent under enemy fire. But James watched with pride, and misgiving. The men below might be his enemy, but they were Englishmen; he could not wish and he did not expect any hill to daunt them. They came on under the leadership of Lieut.-Colonel Fenwick who at this juncture 'commanded his men to halt and take breath for two or three minutes that they might be more able to climb and do their duty'. Then with a great shout, they began the ascent. They had not gone many yards when Fenwick was shot through the body. The second-in-command sprang to the front, and led on the men 'who stopt not till they came to push of pyke'. The Spaniards were driven from the hill. Then James in the rear gathered such remnants as he could and attempted to charge the victorious English across the shifting sand. It proved an impossible task. Charles Berkeley was hit and James saved only by his armour. The Spaniards scattered in panic. James could only rally his own men, a bare handful of forty horse.

The two main armies had now come into action, but the undulating sand-hills hid each section from its neighbour, and accident and confusion soon replaced the ordered tactics of war. Condé on the left flank achieved a straight fight with his opponent but was gradually forced from the field. In the centre the Spanish regiments fired too soon and 'presently ran away', their English allies breaking also before Turenne's ruthless advance. On the right, James had enjoyed one gleam of success. The magic of his name, the cry that 'the Duke' was there, had stayed some fugitives, Spanish and English. As he put them in order a Don rode up, and asked him why he had not charged the enemy. James's succinct reply wasted no breath, 'I told him I had done it already but been beat.' He did not leave it at that. Cromwellian troops had wound their way through the sand-hills, lost to sight, and at this moment appeared on James's flank. The Duke charged at the head of his forty horse, the reorganised fugitives behind him, and the enemy were driven to the edge of the sea. 'Not so much as one single man of them ask'd quarter, or threw down his armes, but every one defended himself to the last; so that we ran as great danger by the butt end of their muskets, as by the volley which they had given us.' Both the Duke and Gloucester were in imminent danger. Nor could they achieve more than a momentary triumph. As they breasted the next hill, the troops saw that the main Spanish army was in precipitate retreat. James's little band broke up in disorder.

The Duke was left with a mere handful of English horse.

His next effort was a bold dash across the line in the hope of reaching Condé on the left. He was disgusted with the Spaniards, but he and Condé together might avert disaster. With his customary phlegm, he rode through the French lines. In the general confusion he was unmolested, Turenne's men and their English allies alike taking him for a Cromwellian officer. But he found Condé in flight, and his last hope gone. He too left the field. The battle of the Dunes was over, except in one small cavity among the sand-hills where, regardless of the tide of battle and the desertion of its own commanding-officer, an English regiment, the King's Own, stood firm on the ground to which it had been posted by the Duke. Its officers refused to surrender though the French assured them that they were alone on the field. Only when two of them had been led to the top of the nearest hill to see for themselves their isolation in defeat, did they consent to lay down their arms upon honourable terms.

. . . .

In the autumn of 1658, there seemed little prospect of a change in the Duke's immediate future. In the Pyrenees, French and Spanish diplomats flirted with each other and the idea of peace. But there would always be some war in progress, to serve as an arena wherein James might increase the reputation for good sense and gallantry, which already stood so high. Except for the constant irritant of his poverty, he had little to worry him. Then suddenly out of the blue came the news of Cromwell's death. The arch-fiend had gone to his own. England now would turn, with a gesture of relief, to her rightful King. On an impulse of joyous affection, James threw up his command and hastened to his brother at Brussels. To his excited fancy their troubles were already at an end. But nothing decisive occurred. Charles, counselled by Hyde who still urged caution and disparaged force, went incognito to

Spain, to see if his improved chances would extract some real help from his dilatory friends. The Duke joined his sister at Breda and indulged his propensity for plans and projects to the full. But the response from England was disappointing.

Cromwell's grip of the English nation had not been merely that of a tyrant. Real devotion to common principles and an honest desire to make a good job of ruling England, had won and kept him true adherents. The untiring mind and brave spirit of Thurloe, his right hand man, was not likely to waver because his master was dead. The Royalist plots of 1659 went awry, and only Sir George Booth's ill-starred rebellion gave a last proof of Cavalier devotion. On the coast of France the royal brothers awaited in secret the news of the rising; Charles at Calais, dubious of a course alien to Hyde's counsels, accepted defeat before definite news arrived and slipped away to the Pyrenees again, to see what advantage he might reap from the polite bickerings of France and Spain. At Boulogne, the Duke clung tenaciously to the hope of getting across to England, running narrow escapes of capture, and adding false alarms to real dangers. Once he was wakened 'with great knocking and bouncing at the door of the inn and going to the window, he heard as he thought the noise of soldiers . . . for so they were: but their business was not to search for the Duke, it was only to bring home the master of the house, who was dead drunk'.

A secret message from Turenne took the Duke post-haste to Amiens, where the marshal gave his former comrade amazing proof of his friendship. He offered to the Duke for his brother's service, not only ammunition and sailing-ships, but the regiment of foot which James had commanded when he served with France. In addition Turenne offered to pawn his plate to provide the necessary money. The glamour of the Stuart cause had stirred to romantic sacrifice even Turenne, the embodiment of hard-headed prudence. But the news came of Booth's defeat and the total eclipse of the Royalist hopes in England. The marshal regained his balance and held back the Duke, who regardless of reality, wished to hazard his life and his friends' fortune in a sudden descent on the Kentish coast. Ignorant of his brother's whereabouts, he feared he might have gone to England. He must follow and rescue him. Turenne calmed him. It was unlikely that Charles was in England; if so all the more reason for the Duke to preserve his own life. The high hopes of Amiens ended in the marshal lending James three hundred pistoles for his return journey to Brussels. There he awaited Charles's return in galling idleness; he solaced himself as best he could by making love to Anne Hyde, and when the spring of 1660 stirred him to action, in politics' despite, he accepted an offer from Spain to serve against Portugal as High Admiral of the Spanish fleet. Again his life had set into the old mould of a free-lance of the wars.

But within a month all was changed. Without the aid of European potentates and neither sullied by bloodshed nor imposed by force, the Restoration of the King was effected with an ease and unanimity so amazing as to appear miraculous. Yet though to the Stuarts and their counsellors it seemed a 'prodigious Act of Providence' it was the inevitable outcome of the drift of circumstance since the death of the Protector. Richard Cromwell, too mild a man to control an unsettled country and too honest to pretend to powers he did not possess, resigned his father's heritage, leaving England at the mercy of that Republican remnant of the Long Parliament, which was known derisively as the Rump, and a group of brilliant and ambitious army officers. From the latter, two figures gradually came to the fore. John Lambert emerged from a self-imposed retirement, growing tulips and gillieflowers in the sandy soil of Wimbledon, to barter his Republican principles in a gamble for dictatorship and to flirt with the idea of marrying his daughter to the Duke of York. But George Monck, in command of the Commonwealth troops in Scotland, was in closer touch with reality. For he was an ordinary man, in that he sensed the feelings and desires of ordinary folk, though his great ability and his unconventionality freed him from the inhibitions that constrict the actions of the average man. He realised that the chief need of his countrymen was not any particular political system nor yet any one man, but simply the blessing of peace. For the last twenty years England had been robbed of the quiet beauty of well-ordered days. Whether they were philosophers or country squires, soldiers or merchants, her people wanted security, freedom not to rule but to develop themselves and live their own lives against a background of sound government. Cromwell's very successes, in his foreign policy, had given an impetus to trade, which made the citizens of London especially voluble in their demands for a free Parliament, that a peaceful settlement might be effected, and they might continue making money.

In February, 1660, Monck acted. Marching south from the border township of Coldstream, where he and his troops were stationed, he reached London and at first belied the hopes his coming had aroused by obeying the dictates of the Rump, which refused to dissolve itself. But after an enigmatic week during which Monck, silent and shrewd and eternally chewing tobacco, became the mystery man of the situation, he invited himself to dine at the Guildhall and declared himself for a free Parliament. The citizens of London broke into an orgy of joy, and roasted rumps of beef at innumerable bonfires. The new Parliament met, and in Brussels the exiled court waited anxiously for Monck's next move. He had the reputation of being a staunch Republican, and an honest man. But he was Cromwell's political heir and an opportunist rather than a theorist. Republican though he had been, he saw that the King's return was the only satisfactory solution, and set to work to effect it as speedily as possible. Sir

John Grenville, a kinsman of Monck's and a scion of a loyal house, was sent secretly to Charles to recommend him to leave Brussels for Breda, a more neutral territory. There, acting on Monck's instructions and under Hyde's guidance, Charles issued that Declaration of Breda, which, by its moderate tone and its promise of liberty to tender consciences, stressed the elements of compromise and consent and made a peaceful Restoration possible. This declaration, presented to the new Parliament shortly after its assembly, evoked a unanimous invitation to return. On May 8th, Charles was proclaimed King in London. It only remained for the exiles to prepare for the triumphant home-coming, of which they had dreamt so long that they could scarcely now believe in its reality.

They gathered at The Hague, where their aunt, Elizabeth of Bohemia, rejoiced with her nephews in the happy turn of fortune. Their mother wrote from France that she would visit them in England as soon as it could be arranged and the Princess Henrietta, Charles's favourite sister, should accompany her. Charles himself was good-humoured and gay, as he had never been since his return from the tragedy of Worcester. It was as if a blanket had been rolled away from his soul. Characteristically, James could not express himself save in action. He went in state to Scheveningen, whither the English fleet had sailed to make submission, and there he was received as Lord-Admiral of England. Gloucester, who seemed to combine in his attractive person the charm of one brother and the courage of the other, went everywhere with the Duke, exciting favourable comments from the many English who had flocked into Holland on some slight pretext. Mary of Orange shared in her brother's joy with the same whole-hearted loyalty that she had manifested in their days of trial. The States of Holland, that had looked askance at her family in the bad days, now offered her brother generous gifts. It was wonderful to have money at last. From the Lords and Commons of England came a grant of £10,000. They kept the gold in a chest in the King's bedroom, and every now and then, they would run in and look at it and let the lovely coins run through their fingers. They would never be poor again!

A bout of atrocious weather delayed their departure, but at last it was possible to sail. The two Dukes returned to the fleet. Lord Montague was in command, a comrade-at-arms of Cromwell and Blake, converted now to reluctant Royalism. As a seaman, he knew his work thoroughly and was fortunate in the possession of an excellent secretary, an able though rather locquacious gentleman, Mr. Samuel Pepys. As secretary, Pepys shared his master's vague sense of hostility towards the Royal Admiral who might oust them from their job, but as a man he was proud and a little flustered to draw so close to royalty. He noted with pleasure York's yellow trimmings, and Gloucester's grey and red, and as he sat under an awning on the quarter-deck transacting business with the Duke, he was happy to find that in his official as in his personal capacity, he could approve: for the new Admiral showed some sound common sense. With the Duke, was his newly-appointed secretary, William Coventry, a quiet and well-bred man, whose reserve hid unexpected depths of ability and principle. It had been well for James, had that first hour of business been an omen for the future and had he always been assisted by such honest and clear-sighted servants.

They allotted each ship her service on the return voyage and then went down to a crowded and mirthful dinner. Next day, everybody came on board for a farewell visit: the King and his brothers, the Princess Royal and her solemn little son, even Aunt Elizabeth, frail but enthusiastic. They spent a happy morning, rechristening the ships, as if by the metamorphoses of the *Naseby* into the *Charles* or the *Bradford* into the *Success* they could wipe out the memory of the wasted years of tragedy.

It was time to sail. Mary said good-bye to her brothers. She would willingly have married Harry Jermyn and gone with them to England. She consoled herself with the promise of a visit, when troublesome affairs of State were settled. She would accompany her mother and Henrietta, and they would all spend Christmas together, the first happy Christmas for twenty years. So with assurances of future joy, defying the jealousy of the gods, they parted.

Amid cries of 'bon voyage' from a crowded shore, the 'happy return' began. The Dukes had left the King and gone to their own ships. All afternoon Charles paced the deck, talking freely and eagerly to those about him, recalling the hazards of his flight from Worcester now unreal enough to bear the telling. Everybody's heart was full:

> 'To see near a hundred brave ships sail before the wind with the vast cloths and streamers, the neatness and cleanness of the ships, the strength and jollity of the mariners, the gallantry of the commanders, the vast plenty of all sorts of provisions; but above all, the glorious Majesties of the King and his two brothers, were so beyond man's expectation and expression. The sea was calm, the moon shone at full, and the sun suffered not a cloud to hinder his prospect of the best sight, by whose light and the merciful bounty of God, he was set safely on shore at Dover, in Kent, upon the 25th of May, 1660.' [1]

Four days later, on his birthday, Charles rode into London 'surely the most pompous show that ever was, for the hearts of all men in this kingdom moved at his will'. Even John Evelyn, a quiet-souled man who maintained the decencies of life though kingdoms tottered, was shaken out of his usual moderation as he stood in the Strand and watched. 'The ways strewed with flowers, the bells ringing, the streets hung with tapestry, fountains running with wine . . . Lords and Nobles clad in cloth of silver, gold and velvet, the windows and balconies all set with ladies,

[1] *Memoirs of Lady Fanshawe* [Ed. 1829], pp. 137–8.

trumpets, music and myriads of people flocking': Evelyn beheld it all 'and blessed God'. Only, in secret places that would soon be discovered, the men who had killed their King awaited retribution, while in undisturbed retirement such men as Henry Cromwell or Milton, the old blind poet, sought elsewhere than in statecraft for a key to the meaning of life.

So Charles and his brothers came home to Whitehall. Throughout the summer they enjoyed themselves. Charles interspersed fits of early rising and ceaseless activity, with orgies of pleasure and lazy self-indulgence. James was less irresponsible. He meddled little in the difficult business of settling the many outstanding political and religious problems, which Charles and his advisers had to face. But his work at the Admiralty gave him just the scope he needed for his ability and enthusiasm. Had it been his lot to rule, his well-wishers might have felt anxiety. For he had shown already, by his obstinacy in face of opposition and his readiness to be duped by the counsels of more subtle and less honest men, that he lacked both the suavity of manner and quickness of thought which successful kingship necessitated. He lacked, more disconcertingly, that sensitiveness of spirit, which compensates many simple souls for any shortcomings in intellect or experience. But the Stuart characteristic of seeing only his own point of view had not yet hampered him. As an army officer, it had enhanced his efficiency. He could obey as well as command without questioning the wherefore of things. His honesty was apparent, and the world respected him. He made human contacts slowly and with difficulty, but once they were made, his loyalty was unassailable. He was in fact an ideal person for the position he was called upon to occupy, that of the King's brother, prince of the blood royal, man of action and servant of the State.

PART II

ACHIEVEMENT

CHAPTER III

ANNE HYDE

'The Duke of York . . . applies himself but little to the affairs of the country, and attends to nothing but his pleasures; but he is a young man of good spirit, loving and beloved by the king, his brother. . . . He treated us with great courtesy and offered to go in person to the war against the Turks if the opportunity should arise; a compliment which does not commit him in any way.' – *Relation of Venetian Ambassadors, 1661.*

IN the quiet days before the Civil Wars, a young lawyer and his wife lived in London, 'very comfortably and very joyfully'. He was a student by nature, devoted to his work and conscientious in the exercise of his duty, both as a citizen and as a family man. Yet, despite his learning and his rectitude, he was less grave than many, and a witty turn of mind and a cheerful disposition inclined him, as his chief relaxation, to cultivate the acquaintance of interesting men. His wife was a capable and motherly woman, who bore her husband in due course three sons and a daughter. Mrs. Hyde was content; her husband was doing well in his profession and was obviously regarded with respect by really distinguished people; her sons were normal healthy children, and little Anne, though inclined to be greedy over her food, was decidedly intelligent and of a gay and amiable character. Before the happy and united family, there stretched the prospect of many quiet years of useful life.

Then fate intervened with its usual disregard for the laws of probability. Edward Hyde, who had been elected a member of the Long Parliament, gradually came to the front in public life. Not only was he a close friend of Lord Falkland's, one of the finest though one of the least flamboyant personalities of the age. Nor was it merely on account of Hyde's fund of legal knowledge, his ability in debate, the probity of his character or the clarity of his thought. Others might equal him in these respects. Where he stood supreme was in his attitude to the problems of his age, which was in effect his attitude to life. By a conscientious and intelligent study of the question in hand, followed by a moderate decision put into effect with firmness and scrupulous honesty, Hyde had made himself what he was and thus he would have counselled Charles and Pym alike. Only in his abiding love for the Anglican Church, did he lose a tolerant understanding of his opponents' point of view. That devotion inspired him to risk all in the King's service, but that one streak of intolerance was to mar, eventually, the work he accomplished as statesman.

The Civil Wars came and went, and Hyde found himself an exile with the other loyalists in Flanders. He had done his best for a master who, alike in his strength and his weakness, was incapable of adopting Hyde's philosophy. For the moment he had little influence with Charles's gay-hearted and impetuous son. He was content to wait and to serve him faithfully. In 1649 he was sent on an embassy to Spain and before his departure he brought his wife and young children to Antwerp, where they could live in safety though straitened in circumstance. He returned after two years, to find that Anne had grown considerably, and that at fourteen she was becoming a good companion to her competent but overburdened mother. Almost immediately Hyde was called away to attend Charles II, and nearly four years elapsed before the family was reunited. Meanwhile, the Princess Royal had become acquainted with Mrs. Hyde, whose worth she quickly recognised. She offered her a house in Breda, which relieved her of the burden of rent. In 1654, Mary of Orange found another opportunity for a kind act. One of her maids-of-honour died of smallpox.

The Queen-Mother had asked to make the next nomination but Mary liked to manage her own affairs. She offered the post to Anne Hyde.

When Hyde's permission was asked, he very respectfully refused. Conscious of the irritation which his success evoked in men of more aristocratic though not necessarily of better birth, he bore himself with circumspection, failing to realise that an innate sense of his own superiority made his reserve closely resemble arrogance. He had excellent excuses for objecting to his daughter's promotion. He would not have anything occur which would increase the discord between Henrietta and the Princess Royal. Moreover, Anne was old enough now to look after her mother, and he preferred that his wife should not be left alone. But the Princess Royal insisted. In a quandary, Hyde did the only thing possible for a man to do; he left it to his wife to decide, confident that her opinion would coincide with his. Like many another husband, he received a shock. Mrs. Hyde was delighted with the idea of Anne being a maid-of-honour; the matter was arranged immediately, and Mrs. Hyde packed her bags and joined her husband, who was with the King at Cologne. Pleasant though it was to have a daughter to look after one, she preferred first to see a little more of the world on her own account.

Anne, in her new role, was a great success. She enjoyed herself in an attractive and unsophisticated way, and what she lacked in formal beauty she gained in her pleasant manners, her intelligence and the unspoilt freshness of her youth. She captivated the fashionable world of The Hague, in the guise of a shepherdess at a New Year's Ball. Men fell in love with her and found her provocative and sometimes indiscreet, but the shrewd common sense which she inherited from her mother kept her out of serious scrapes. The Princess Royal thought her a paragon, especially when she showed a spark of her father's literary ability and produced a character sketch of her royal mistress. The Queen of Bohemia loved her for her high spirits, and she even won the heart of the solemn child, William, enticing him to romp with her, when his mother was engaged in entertaining visitors.

Early in 1656, the Princess Royal decided to visit France. The Queen-Mother had deluded herself with the hope that young King Louis might fall in love with his cousin, the Prince of Orange's young widow, and Mary had spent more money than she could afford on a wardrobe that looked elegant at The Hague but dowdy in Paris. All she gained from the visit was the doubtful benefit of Harry Jermyn's acquaintanceship, a little man with large head and slender legs who by some strange fascination won the hearts of the beauties his handsome rivals failed to subdue. But for Anne, who accompanied her mistress, the visit had deep significance, for in Paris for the first time she met the Duke of York, home on leave and a most presentable young man. Of course they flirted and the Duke, always more susceptible to character than to good looks, was charmed with Anne's gay yet forceful personality. For underneath the natural light-heartedness of youth, was an innate dignity of bearing and a fund of quiet ability which made the lawyer's daughter seem no unfit companion for an exiled prince. The Duke was firmly convinced that he was in love; and he was a tenacious lover.

Nearly four years afterwards, James found himself in Holland, disappointed in the hopes and projects that had succeeded Cromwell's death. His brother's restoration appeared as remote as ever and a career of arms his own inevitable destiny. The flirtation with Anne, whom he met again at his sister's court, was renewed at first in a mood of boredom; but her wit and her spirit were excellent tonics, and her unfailing good temper made her a good comrade to a man, who longed to find in his sweethearts mental stimulus and spiritual fellowship as well as physical satisfaction. He gave Anne gladly the written promise of marriage for which she stipulated, and their love was consummated.

A few months later, the miracle of the Restoration had occurred. King Charles had come into his own again, and the Duke of York had sailed back with his brother to England. Sir Edward Hyde had accompanied him to undertake the task of transforming the miracle into an everyday workable system of life and government. His difficulties were colossal but he rejoiced that, at last, he could be at home again and resume the family life which had fallen into pieces twenty years before. But it was not to be the easy matter he envisaged, to turn back the clock, either in his personal or his political life. As soon as he was settled, he sent to Holland for his wife and daughter. Already he had in his mind a suitable match for the latter. It would be good for her to settle down after the dissipations of court life. Anne and her mother came home, but neither were eager to discuss matrimony. Anne seemed quieter than he remembered her, but she looked well and was even plumper than usual. Lady Hyde too was preoccupied, but they assured him there was no cause to worry and he left it at that, immersing himself in his exacting public duties. But Lady Hyde and her daughter were worrying, despite their protestations. They were doing their best to conceal the truth, which they knew must come to light eventually. For Anne had confided in her mother, when her timorous doubts became a certainty. She was pregnant. She had for consolation only a scrap of paper, and the belief that her lover was an honest man.

Honest the Duke was in a somewhat laboured way, but he had been educated in a lax world. Less joyously promiscuous than his brother in matters of the heart, his vigorous manhood urged him to sexual indulgence whenever he was denied other strenuous activity. As a youth on leave from the wars, he had begat a child of one of his mother's waiting-maids, a girl called Jane, of whom he still thought with affection and eventually recalled from France to educate with his own legitimate children. The intrigue with Anne had stirred him deeply and satisfied his mind as well as his body, but it had been to him a happy episode, though in a moment of madness he had risked its perpetuation. In the summer of 1660 he forgot it. Ogling his brother's mistress through the farce of Matins at Whitehall, sauntering in the Park with young Gloucester and his cronies, sailing down the river through darkness pierced by music and the blinding flash of fireworks, the Duke savoured to the full the gaieties of that brilliant year. The God of Whitehall was Pleasure.

Like the others, of course he must find a mistress. His choice fell on Lady Southesk, a woman of greater experience than virtue, whose husband was absent in Scotland when the flirtation began. The liaison was terminated in a manner almost farcical, which first gave to James's *amours* that touch of the ridiculous, exploited by the courtiers who had no respect for persons in the sacred cause of wit. It was said that one day the Duke visited his mistress accompanied for appearance's sake by Richard Talbot, the lively Irishman who was one of his closest friends. Talbot awaited the Duke's pleasure in an antechamber, the window of which looked out upon the street. Good-natured and incurably absent-minded, he watched the passing crowds and noticed with amusement a coach draw up at the door below. From it descended Lord Southesk, whose suspicions had been aroused since his return from Scotland. Southesk had been Lord Carnegie when Talbot had met him last in Flanders, and unconscious of his change of title and his relationship with the fair lady within, 'Welcome, Carnegie, welcome my good fellow,' Talbot cried, forgetful that he was supposed to be on guard. 'Do you likewise wish to see Lady Southesk? If this is your intention, my poor friend, you may go away again, for I must inform you the Duke of York is in love with her and I will tell you in confidence he is in her chamber.' Southesk could say nothing in his rage, but in dangerous silence withdrew to meditate a foul revenge. Talbot considered the joke too good to keep to himself, and retailed it to James, with a glee that changed to puzzled irritation as he realised that the Duke was not amused.

It was a sorry essay in gallantry and James, who was worthy of better things, was still savouring the sordid taste of it, when Anne Hyde visited him in secret. At sight of her, her comely health and her clear eyes, his old love returned unabated. She told him that their child might be born in a few weeks' time, and reminded him of his promise to marry her. He vowed that he would redeem his word and driven by the impetus of his emotion, precious in its unwonted intensity, he went to the King and told him the whole story. James knew that he was no longer a free agent, and that he could not marry without the King's consent, but, were it withheld, he declared that 'he would immediately leave the kingdom and must spend his life in foreign parts'. Not for the last time, Charles cursed his brother's conscience.

The King would have been yet angrier, if he had not been amused. He admired Anne's pluck in putting up a fight for the rights of her unborn child, and above all he wondered how her father would take it. In arrogant isolation, Hyde faced, unmoved, the dissatisfied Presbyterians, who resented his monopoly of power and the insolent Cavaliers, to whom his morals made him more than half a Puritan. His defence against their assaults was his incorruptible loyalty and his honest service. If his daughter married the King's brother, their hostility would be pointed with a venom that would add a sting to their attacks he might find it hard to withstand. Charles's sense of humour was tickled. He commissioned Ormonde and another to break the news to the Chancellor, under the pretence of seeking his advice. Interrupting the interview the King found Hyde in an agony of rage and grief. His eyes were swollen with the angry tears he had shed. His corpulent figure shaking with nervous exhaustion, he strode about the room, calling his daughter a strumpet and threatening to turn her out of doors. He counselled the King wildly to send her to the Tower, to pass an Act of Parliament enabling him to have her head chopped off. 'He is mad,' said his friends, and so he was for the moment, unless he were play-acting. It would certainly be just as well for his critics to know how angry he had been. However, he allowed the King to soothe him with kindly words, and still muttering that His Majesty was too lenient he went home 'to sleep upon it', ordering his daughter to keep her own room.

But no domestic incarceration could raise an insuperable bar between the two ardent lovers. The King was content for James to do as he pleased, and gave his grudging consent. The Duke confided his secret to young Ossory, Ormonde's son – the very man for a romantic escapade. Somehow they gained access to Anne, and secretly at midnight on the 3rd of September, she and the Duke were married. It was a date of evil omen in the Stuart calendar, but with the gay bravado of youth they challenged fortune; Ossory gave the bride away, and the Duke's chaplain officiated. Then the lovers kissed and parted, and the secret visitors crept from Anne Hyde's chamber. She could sleep quietly now; her child would be born in wedlock. Officially Lady Hyde knew nothing of what was happening. She was not ambitious and might well fear for her child as for her husband, the deceitful prizes of rank and fortune. But she was a woman and a mother, and her child's happiness and honour were at stake. No doubt she knew what had occurred and successfully prepared her husband for the shock of the coming disclosure. Those about them noticed that the old people treated Anne with unusual respect during the ensuing month. The incredible truth was dawning slowly upon the one-time lawyer and his wife: the child their daughter was about to bear might one day be King of England.

Anne's whole being was centred in hope and thanksgiving upon her approaching confinement. But the world pressed in upon James, and fear of the world's opinion, its scorn and its amusement, rendered the act of avowal which should have followed his secret marriage more difficult with every passing day. A rush of affairs claimed his notice and seemed to excuse the welcome postponement, while family ties, never lightly abrogated by a Stuart, were drawn more closely that autumn by renewed and overwhelming tragedy, which silenced any utterance that would have grieved and alienated those of his own blood. So James kept silent. Silent before the world though rumour spoke, and as the secret spread his enemies scoffed and his friends were troubled at the hasty action which had ruined him. Charles Berkeley now Earl of Falmouth, beloved of both the royal brothers, as devoid of principle and brimful of affection as in the unregenerate days in Flanders, could not grasp that true feeling had impelled the midnight marriage. The Duke, he meditated, was over-conscientious and ought not to suffer through a life-time for a peccadillo in youth. He must be freed of this intriguing female, who had ruined his peace and his hope of good-fame in a world in which princes did not marry lawyer's daughters. Only one way could Falmouth envisage of disentangling his master. He must be shown that the girl was not worth his consideration, and the marriage must be annulled. The Princess Royal was due to reach England on the visit so joyfully arranged in the spring. The Duke had gone down to Dover to meet her and Falmouth looked to her help to bring his plan to fruition.

It was mid-September, when suddenly the serenity of early autumn was shattered by a gale that presaged the coming of winter storms. The Duke remained inactive at Dover till the Princess Royal could make the passage from Holland. A chance of fortune momentarily set him remote from action and, confused, he waited upon circumstance. Something happened, but not what he expected, something that made him forget his own dilemma. A messenger arrived from London; his looks foretold him the bearer of bad news. Henry Duke of Gloucester had sickened of smallpox; already, he was dead! James returned post-haste to town, in time to witness his brother's obsequies. Two days later on September 23rd, he and Charles sailed down the Thames to welcome their sister to England. In the old days they had been inured to tragedy, but fate's wanton cruelty, in striking down the very one among them who had been the epitome of joyous and courageous youth, robbed them of all defence against grief save their affection for each other. Perhaps the fierceness of Mary's protective love for James excused in part her wrath at hearing of his entanglement with her former waiting-maid. Wounded vanity that she had been duped, when they flirted before her eyes in Holland, and the uncharitable righteousness of one woman regarding the moral lapse of another gave added force to her anger. Falmouth found her a ready and unscrupulous ally.

The Queen-Mother who had been told the news by letter, had replied in strains of indignant dismay, and announced her intention of coming to England at once to arrange the annulment of the marriage. In October the Duke went with the Fleet to Calais to convoy his mother and the Princess Henrietta across the Channel. All the trappings and the finery of the Lord-Admiral of England could not divest him of the feeling that he had flouted his parent's authority and was in disgrace. His mumbled excuses appeased neither her temper nor his conscience. For he was no longer the happy and confident bridegroom. Falmouth's devilish ingenuity had done its work. He had spread it abroad that Anne was no better than she should be, and that the paternity of the child she carried was doubtful in the extreme. Calling upon Jermyn and Talbot to support his words, he assured the Duke that all alike had enjoyed his Anne's promiscuous affections. Warming to the task, the conspirators embroidered their tales with circumstantial details of the waiting-maid's indiscretions, disgusting but disconcerting. The Duke, to whom a fit of honest rage would have been a godsend at this crisis, failed to send the courtiers about their business in scorn and indignation that would have steeled his mind to unbelief; he worked himself up instead into a state of wretched uncertainty, a passion that had once been fresh and lovely wavering in the balance against the asseverations of trusted friends, and the knowledge wrested from the gaieties of the summer that virtue seldom visited the purlieus of a court. At this juncture, Anne's son was born, at Worcester House in the Strand, where her father lived. In the event, her parents fought for their daughter's honour with bourgeois tenacity. The highest ladies in the land were invited to be present at the confinement; as she grappled with the pangs of her first labour, a bishop bent across her bed, and asked her solemnly whose child she bore. From the abyss of her pain, she answered unflinching that James, Duke of York, was the father of her child.

This was the state of affairs when the Queen-Mother reached London. Throughout November and most of December, the business and pleasures of the court continued unabated, saddened by the fresh wound of Gloucester's death, but stimulated by the presence of Princess Henrietta, radiant with the youth and the charm which linked her and King Charles in close companionship.

The weeks passed and the gossips on the Exchange grew tired of shaking their heads over the Duke of York's misalliance. But Falmouth's insinuations did not cease, nor the Duke's misery abate. Tormented by the thought of having loved a whore, he found himself conscious of relief that he could rid himself without remorse of the encumbrance his impetuous marriage had imposed upon him. And so, ashamed, he realised that he too was unfaithful in spirit, and his anguish was renewed. The King ignored his vacillations. In like case he himself would have openly fathered the child, without a thought of marrying the mother. And no one would have thought the worse of him! He showed his belief in Anne's character, by sponsoring her son, and with one of those generous impulses that have endeared him to posterity, he chose this moment to create Hyde, Earl of Clarendon. Charles recognised and appreciated an honest man, but James, through some defect in his rigid nature, some inability to get in touch with his fellow-creatures, lacked the faculty of judging men. Those whom he liked he trusted, and he was at the mercy of their ambitions or their whims. This, rather than any vice, was the secret of his failure, and it was this which went near to making his marriage a tragic mockery. He worried himself ill. Then Falmouth relented. When the Duke had taken to his bed, dispirited and unable to resist some local infection which inflamed his eyes, his friend decided that if he cared so much it were folly to flout him. Falmouth confessed the slander he had circulated. James was overjoyed. He wrote to Anne declaring his eager wish to see his son, and the simple phrase proclaimed her victory. The King was informed, and the Queen-Mother was browbeaten into acceptance of the inevitable. She stipulated that Anne should remain at Worcester House, 'for,' she declared, with a flash of the old spirit, 'if that woman should be brought into Whitehall by one door, I would go out of it by another and never come into it again.' Four days before Christmas, the Duke publicly acknowledged Anne Hyde to be his wife, visiting her in state at her father's house while the Chancellor stood respectfully behind his daughter's chair. The Princess Royal was not present; it would have needed a temper more humble than hers to watch with equanimity her former maid-in-waiting, take precedence of her by virtue of her marriage. She had a good excuse for staying away; she was not feeling well. Here was Christmas at last and she was hot and feverish, sickening for some malady – she dare not question further. The doctors, who had been accused of neglecting Gloucester in his last illness, hovered about her in fearful solicitude and aggravated by excessive bleeding the mild attack of smallpox which developed. On Christmas Eve, the Princess began to sink and her quick tongue, stilled at last, faltered at the approach of death, revealing her share in Falmouth's shameful slanders. When Christmas Day dawned, she was dead. The Queen-Mother shivered under the grey skies of England, land of ill-omen that had robbed her of husband and of children; she was homesick for France and the security of the convent life where she had found peace. There was a plain talk with the Chancellor, after which she grudgingly acknowledged his daughter and extracted from him with a flash of Medici guile a promise to pay her debts. Then the Queen-Mother departed, taking with her the reluctant Princess Henrietta, destined to marriage with the most vicious man in France. The two brothers were left alone: power and pleasure, the easy conquest of women, the hard-won triumphs of politics or the consolations of religion, in these they could indulge at will, but the joy that does not count the cost, the exuberant happiness of youth, vanished with the tragic ending of the year, that had begun in the ecstasy of home-coming in May.

Anne Hyde had become first lady of the land. In due course she took up her residence at Whitehall, and idle rumours and unsavoury jests wavered into silence. Her gratitude to James was unaffected and intense: however he might fail her in the years to come, he had done her 'too much honour' in making her his wife. Her humble appreciation of his action, and her forgiveness of Falmouth at his request, best indicate the magnitude of the sacrifice he had made in the eyes of the world. For her part, she was determined not to prove unworthy. Her quick intelligence, the solid strength of her character, and the reserve which the year's suspense had imposed upon her open nature, alike came to her aid. She made no false step, avoided all affectations in speech and manner and by a quiet dignity of bearing, won for herself a unique and respected position in the little kingdom of the court. She conducted her domestic affairs with skill and prudence, organised her household well and chose her maids with care, imposing upon them a modicum of good behaviour. She herself was a model of propriety and good sense. Even after the King's marriage with the Portuguese princess, Catherine of Braganza, the new Queen's retiring ways and her lack of English prevented her from undermining the importance of the Duchess. Instead, poor deluded Catherine found her sister-in-law a source of strength and comfort, her cheerful, homely courage, a refreshing antidote to the artificial wit of the Restoration court. Charles liked the Duchess but was rather frightened of her; the Duke demurred to her judgment and respected her ability. They lived comfortably together bound by mutual sympathy and steady affection. But the old passion was dead, killed less by the weight of years than by the doubts and strictures which had tarnished the romance. From a gay beginning it had struggled through to a subdued conclusion. Had James been wiser in judgment and one whit more unselfish in his love, he had made a niche for himself by his marriage in the incurably romantic heart of the average Englishman. But ill-luck, in this as in every enterprise, dogged his footsteps, and his own imperfections disenabled him. Men remembered not love triumphant and the respect due to a man of honour, but a prince befooled, making grudging acceptance of unescapable fact.

The child, whose inopportune birth had stirred the gossip of court and city, died in May, 1661, not regretted overmuch since his doubtful legitimacy would cast a slur on the heir-presumptive to the throne of England. In the autumn Anne was again pregnant, but this time she bore a girl-child christened Mary, in memory of the Mary who had died too soon. The child was sent to Twickenham to live with her grandparents Lord and Lady Clarendon, and in that sedate and strictly Protestant environment grew out of a babyhood into a sweet but solemn little girl. After her grandmother died and her grandfather was disgraced, Mary, made conscious at six of the mutability of life, went to live at Richmond Palace with the other royal children. Docile yet reserved, she was passionately moved, less by human relationships than by her religious devotions, more real to her than any earthly politics, and by an intense love of the beautiful English country, in which her secluded youth was passed. The Duke, a kind and considerate father, never knew her as intimately as he did his second daughter, Anne, who was born in the year of the Great Plague. She was a plain child, with her mother's plump figure, and bulging eyes that caricatured the prominent features of her grandfather King Charles I. But she had his lovely hands also, and a beautiful voice which redeemed her plainness. James loved her and romped with her, and sent her to France to live for awhile in the household of his sister, Henrietta of Orleans. After the latter's death she returned to England, a comfortable and good-natured if rather unimportant young person.

Save as pawns in the game of diplomacy, when they attained marriageable age, princesses were of small account. It was different with their brother, James Duke of Cambridge, born in 1663. Of him his father was inordinately proud. His coming gave significance to his marriage and peace of mind to the Duchess. Before the child could walk, they made him Knight of the Garter, and commander of a regiment of Guards. Upon his princely household, James squandered the money that his brother spent on his mistresses and his laboratories. The years of his babyhood, which also witnessed the Duke's triumphs as Admiral of the Fleet, were years of content for James and his Duchess. She took up her writing again, and studied with interest the meticulous journals, which James had kept of his military experiences in France. She planned to write his life, thus to glorify alike her ability and her affections. In body, mind and spirit she was satisfied – almost! To be at once the greatest lady in the land and a woman of brains had its delights and triumphs. She derived enormous pleasure from the joys of the table, and lost all pretence to a decent figure in consequence. But she retained her influence over the Duke. Because he himself was handsome and slow of thought, he always preferred good sense to good looks in his women-folk, and he was tremendously impressed by his wife's brain and character. To her he turned in his difficulties whether political or religious and tracts on theology found themselves in strange companionship with the flighty maids-of-honour, the card-tables and the rich food of the Duchess's household.

In all save his love affairs, said the gossips of court and city, James was 'led by the nose by his wife'. Unfortunately it was just those love affairs, and the Duke's inability to be circumspect in the conduct thereof, that bruised Anne's peace of mind. That her husband should be unfaithful was only in accordance with the custom of the time; that he should win the reputation of being the most 'unguarded ogler' of the day and make himself the laughing-stock of the courtiers by following a defiant young beauty 'like a dog', offended his wife's innate sense of dignity, and roused her temper in addition to grieving her heart.

For the Duke could take nothing with a light hand, in marked contrast to his brother, who skimmed over the surface of life and avoided the wounds which his clarity of vision might have inflicted upon him by the habit of laughter and the selfish virtue of detachment. In his *amours,* as in his politics and his religion, the very earnestness of James's desires roused an instinct to resist in perverse humanity whether wayward beauty or discontented subject. A healthy animal whose sexual impulses were strong and uncontrolled, he did not seek merely for physical satisfaction in his love affairs. Charles declared in amused dismay in later years that his brother's mistresses must be imposed upon him as a penance by his priests: they were as 'ugly as sin'. For one to whom human fellowship came easily as a gift of the gods, it was impossible to comprehend the Duke's yearning for mental companionship. In restless flirtations in the years immediately after his marriage, in renewed companionship with his wife after his son's birth, and in the attractions of an established mistress, when broken health and a tired spirit robbed the Duchess of the last of her charms, James sought in vain in woman's society for the spiritual satisfaction as well as the physical thrill, which he had won for a few brief years, fighting under Turenne. He never learnt the secret of his failures – that self-centredness which rebuts sympathy and stultifies the compelling force of desire. In one thing, at least he was happy; the illegitimate children he begat lived to stand by him in the years of his misfortune, more loyal to the father who had loved them than the daughters born in wedlock.

James was not by nature a philanderer, or a neurotic. Honest, stupid, reserved, he felt a certain lack in the unsympathetic and superficial acquaintanceships of court. He filled the gap not only by the pursuit of women, but by the astringent joys of the hunting-field, of which like his father he was passionately fond, and by the satisfying activities of his job as Admiral. On the whole, he was happy. For though self-centred, he was not self-conscious, nor of sufficient imagination to be sensitive. But none the less a consciousness of imperfection did mar his intercourse with women, as a sense of sin, which his brother apparently lacked, marred his physical pleasure in them. Yet he was too conventional to impose upon his erotic nature a self-control of which he might have been capable, had fashion decreed restraint.

For in essence it was a question of convention. We have

more in common to-day with the Restoration age, than most of the intervening generations. We can understand only too well the disillusioned spirits and the tired minds of those who came home, middle-aged, after the war, and the zest for pleasure at all costs with which the younger men and women challenged life, that now once again flowed freely and happily, immune from the horrors of exile or sudden death. Old philosophies had broken down, saintliness had proved itself hypocrisy, so much blood had been shed in the name of religion, that a bewildered generation found itself uncertain in belief, questioning the authority of 'Thou shalt not . . .' which cramped without explaining existence. On every hand knowledge poured in, stimulating interest and mocking restraint. Only by living to the full, indulging oneself in every experience, could one enjoy worthily or begin to understand the amazing, the baffling, the tragic irony that was life. The splendid autocracy of France, dominating the world through the personality of her King, the romance of the East Indies and the faint beginnings of Imperialism, the establishment of the first banks, the growth of journalism, the philosophy of Locke and the scientific discoveries of Newton, all these new ideas and forces were coming into play and men rode without an anchor the storms of a changing world. In an age brimful of life and movement, barren only in a robust moral code and firm convictions of right and wrong, it was inevitable that men in their personal relationships should break away from the discipline of a controlled sexual life. In part, it was reaction from the conventional correctness of Charles I's court and the repellant spiritual pride of too-triumphant Puritanism, but a new set of customs soon grew up which made it fashionably correct for men of high degree to indulge their appetites. Pepys, a man with a keen sense of appearances, was perturbed to see the Duke making a fool of himself, even de Grammont, a rake *par excellence* was disgusted when the æsthetics of romance were disregarded. But provided vice was conducted in a well-bred manner self-indulgence of the sexual instinct was considered as venial at Charles II's court as self-indulgence of the gambling instinct is considered by many to-day.

Those who saw more deeply thought differently. Widespread over England, based on common sense and sound finance as well as on the high hopes of romance, there was no lack of happy marriages, wherein physical union was sanctified by affection and trust, born of duties shared and common interests. Such idylls as that of Richard Baxter and his wife form a pleasant contrast to the petty squabbles of Mr. and Mrs. Pepys. And there were churchmen brave enough to reprove and punish their King. But the tone of the court was copied very definitely from that of France and the French attitude to sex was adopted by the upper classes with much else alien to the English temperament.

But in surrendering without restraint to their bodily desires, the King and Duke and their associates neglected one inescapable fact, that abuse brings retribution. Indulging themselves to excess, they ruined their splendid bodies. Nurtured in hardship, they could stand more than most men, yet Charles died before he was fifty-five, and James wore himself out to such an extent that at the crisis of his reign he was incapable of clear thought and prompt action. It was rumoured that for a time he suffered from a venereal disease, but apart from any such tragic complications (which the health of his illegitimate children seems to disprove), it is manifest that the broken King of 1688 lacked the stamina and courage of Turenne's Duke of York. Something more than the passing of years is needed to account for the change. He himself writing in old age at St. Germain attributed his downfall to God's wrath at his sexual sins, and there was truth in his conviction, for in undermining the physical health and vigour, which had made him a good soldier and a brave man, he had ruined the best side of himself, that might have re-inspired the loyalty his political mistakes had lost.

Nobody in 1661 could blame the Duke for falling in love with the adorable Miss Hamilton, for the greater part of the young men at court, eligible or the reverse, would have had to plead guilty to the same charge. The Duke of Ormonde, an aristocrat to the finger-tips, good friend to Clarendon and in turn shocked and indulgent with the King, was the *paterfamilias* of a large household of sons and daughters, nephews and nieces, the Butlers and the Hamiltons. They lived together at a 'large and commodious house near the Court'. Good to look at, quick of wit, charming in an easy-going Irish manner, unconventional and full of laughter, they kept within the bounds only because they respected their father and because of the essential goodness which springs from happy hearts. 'Miss Hamilton,' the loveliest of them all, eventually married her brother's friend, the gay rogue from France, the Count de Grammont. But first she broke innumerable hearts. In those early days the Duke of York would return to Whitehall at the end of a long day's hunting, and find her either with the Queen or the Duchess. 'There it was that not daring to tell her of what lay heavy on his heart, he entertained her with what he had in his head; telling her miracles of the cunning of foxes, and the mettle of horses, giving her accounts of broken legs and arms, dislocated shoulders and other curious and entertaining adventures, after which his eyes told her the rest, till such time as sleep interrupted their conversation. . . .'

The Duchess was not alarmed, for she esteemed Miss Hamilton and saw that she was only amusing herself with a mild flirtation. She was more perturbed when James embarked on another love affair, surprising the courtiers by assiduous attention to Lady Robartes, one of those beautiful women who fail to be attractive. Her husband according to the courtiers was 'an old snarling troublesome peevish fellow', who made his wife miserable by following her about. In other words, he was a rather disgruntled Presbyterian who objected on principle to being cuckolded. He soon put an end to the Duke's approaches by bundling his wife into Wales. James for a while was disconsolate, and confined himself to the chase, a sport in which he distinguished himself as he could not do in the arts of love.

It happened soon after this that an attempt was made to intermingle politics and *affaires de cœur* in true French fashion. The talented and wayward Earl of Bristol hated Clarendon, with the bitterness of the brilliant failure towards the man of lesser genius and greater character who has 'arrived'. He caballed with Henry Bennet who was as devoid of principle as himself and made no claim to brilliance, but who had a tenacity of purpose, so far as his own advancement was concerned, which carried him over many obstacles. While Bristol flaunted the Catholicism, which he had adopted too late in exile to benefit himself but to which he had the honesty to adhere, and plunged into an hysterical attack on Clarendon for which neither King nor country were prepared, Bennet made friends with Lady Castlemaine, the King's mistress, and wormed his way into the office of Secretary-of-State. Sir Edward Nicholas, an old man, who in an official career of over thirty years had lost no man's love and done no unworthy thing, retired willingly to the quiet of contented age; but for Clarendon Bennet's triumph, coupled with his rise to the peerage as Earl of Arlington, marked the first breach in the Chancellor's defence. Had his enemies been united, he might have been seriously alarmed. But Bristol's envy was now directed against Arlington. The latter's alliance with the King's mistress attracted his attention. Could Castlemaine, whose greedy beauty dominated the court, be ousted from the King's affections, the time-servers who fawned upon her would be supplanted. Under the ægis of the new mistress, Bristol himself would ride into power. The necessary instruments were ready to hand in the persons of two lovely young relatives, the Misses Brooke, whom he introduced to the King's notice at a series of hilarious midnight parties 'which always led to other enjoyments'. When the success of his scheme seemed assured, he received a sudden check. The imperious Castlemaine realised what was on foot, and stirring in her lazy arrogance enthralled Charles once more, and put an end once for all to Bristol's midnight diversions. Arlington stole his enemy's thunder, and many years later by just such a trick established himself in the royal confidence, by sponsoring the French beauty de Querouaille, when Charles had wearied at last of Castlemaine's enticements. Bristol as usual had failed through acting at the wrong moment.

Charles soon forgot his transient fancy for Miss Brooke. Nor for the nonce was his brother more constant than he. James had been fascinated by Margaret Brooke, the younger of the two girls, and was arranging for her inclusion in the Duchess's household, when his attention was diverted by the advances of Lady Chesterfield, the blue-eyed flirt, who was Miss Hamilton's cousin and daughter of the Duke of Ormonde. She ogled him shamelessly on public occasions, and the Duke proved an easy victim. Her husband began to be uneasy. The court, at the moment, was suffering from an epidemic of 'guitarery'; 'you were as sure to see a guitar on a lady's toilet as rouge or patches'. There was an Italian at Whitehall, an expert musician, who had composed a saraband, which caught the fancy of the court. The pages whistled it on the back-stairs; the ladies strummed it in their boudoirs; the very clerks of the secretary's office hummed it over their dispatches. The Duke, a better exponent than most, played it adequately and visited Lady Chesterfield, ostensibly to try it over on a fine new guitar she possessed. The Earl found them together and lost his temper. He dashed the precious instrument upon the ground, and left his wife in tears and the Duke dumbfounded. When the rumour of this new flirtation spread, Margaret Brooke was disconsolate. She had just been married to an elderly husband, Sir John Denham, the poet, a rake whose unstable genius made him an uneasy companion for a young wife. Lady Denham had spirit and no scruples; she determined to get rid of her rival and set about it with an ingenuity worthy of a better cause. One day in the late autumn of 1662, as the Queen played at cards and the court thronged about her, the Duke and Lady Chesterfield, close together in the crowd, attracted Margaret Denham's eye. She soon saw to it, by significant gestures and whispered words, that the attention of others should be directed to their indiscreet behaviour. There was almost a public scandal, for by an unseemly flirtation where all could witness it, the Duke had offended against the code of a court which disregarded vice in private, but, like all morally unsound societies, paid strict attention to the conventions of public behaviour.

The Duchess, stirred out of her usual placidity complained to the King, and relaxing her hold upon herself, poured out to her father the misery her husband's infidelities occasioned her. Lord Chesterfield acted promptly. His wife was packed off to his country house in Derbyshire, with such alacrity that 'sending one's wife to the Peak' became a proverb at court.

Margaret Denham had won the first round. But it was Anne not she who reaped the benefit. James was thoroughly ashamed of himself, and was ready to make amends to his wife as publicly as he had offended against her. In the New Year, he attended a performance in her company at the theatre in the Cockpit, and Mr. Pepys who was present noted with the average Londoner's abhorrence of emotional display that the Duke and Duchess 'did show some impertinent and methought unnaturall dalliances there, before the whole world, such as kissing of hands, and leaning upon one another'. There followed the Duchess's three years of happiness; her son's birth and babyhood, and the naval war with Holland which attracted the Duke's energies to more worthy purposes.

In the late summer of 1665, James and his wife made a progress in the North of England, arranged partly for political reasons, partly to keep away from the plague-stricken capital. For Anne it was a triumphant journey. They visited the city of York, and the Duchess was approved as 'a very handsome woman with a great deal of wit'. When the Duke left her to attend the parliament in Oxford he issued instructions that she was to be treated with the same respect as if he had been present. It was amid the subsequent ceremonies that folk noticed for the first time the assiduous attention paid to her by Henry Sidney, 'the handsomest man in England'. The Duchess was 'not unkind to him but very innocently'. She had had her share of admiration since her marriage but hitherto had always kept her head. But no woman, least of all a plain one, could resist a flirtation with so beautiful a creature, and if he were also rather stupid, that made it none the worse for one whose brains enabled her to command the situation. Anne was the least malicious of women, but she could not prevent a quiver of triumph, when the Duke heard of her conquest and with male inconsistency was inordinately jealous. Sidney, on some pretext or other, was banished from court, and for some days the Duke and Duchess were not on speaking terms. On the whole things were going well for Anne, and the birth of another son in the course of the following year completed her content.

But a presage of tragedy came with the fall of the year. For the first time, James took a public mistress, succumbing to the blandishments of Margaret Denham who was at court again, more irresistible than ever. The affair soon passed beyond the bounds of a passing flirtation. On October 8th, 1666, Pepys at Whitehall watched the Duke take Lady Denham aside, and talk to her with a proprietary air which alarmed him. Anne refused outright to make the woman a lady of her bedchamber, but in spite of the Duchess's resistance Margaret's position was soon established. Even William Coventry, fastidious, well-bred and incorruptible, thought it no shame to visit her, to such an extent in the crooked morals of the time did the status of *maîtresse en titre* confer respectability. Then suddenly in January, 1667, Margaret Denham died. Rumour, busy as usual, averred that she had been murdered by a drink of poisoned chocolate. Some, indiscreet, murmured that the Duchess might have done it. But public suspicion soon fastened on the husband, and angry crowds besieged Sir John Denham's house. He was a strange creature; his wit and gaiety had delighted an earlier age, his excesses had astounded even his contemporaries, and now in his old age he had known love and been betrayed. With 'slow and stalking gait', with piercing eyes that 'looked into your very thoughts' he confronted the hatred of the mob, and lost his reason. The King was hard put to it to avoid the discomfort he barred at all costs, when Denham visited him one day and poured upon him wild and sacrilegious talk, identifying himself with the Holy Ghost and displaying his tortured mind and heart to the uneasy court.

For the Duke's sake, the scandal was hushed up, and the thoughts of the Duchess were already elsewhere. For the children were ailing. The infant prince, Charles, Duke of Kendal, died in April. His elder brother the Duke of Cambridge was at death's door. Summer came, laden with health and promise, and the child recovered; in anxious joy he was carried into the Park, that fresh air and sunshine might complete the cure. From St. James's, too near to the city to be safe from the pestilence as the heat increased, he was taken to the quiet security of Chelsea. The Duchess breathed freely again. The strict diet which had been imposed upon the child was removed, and he was allowed to eat what food he wished. In an age ignorant of the rudiments of hygiene the licence was fatal. He fell ill, and sank with alarming rapidity.

> 'Kendal is dead and Cambridge riding post.
> What bitter sacrifice for Denham's ghost',

wrote the satirist Marvell, with his pen envenomed in politics and ignorant of a mother's torment. Within a few weeks, the child was dead. In September the birth of another son, the third to bear for a brief time the title of Duke of Cambridge, brought a mockery of comfort, but he was a sickly child who could not be expected to outlive infancy. Two little girls were born and died in the last two years of the Duchess's life. The loss of her mother and her own increasing ill-health, as cancer of the breast gradually developed, her inability to save her father, banished in the end from the land he had served so faithfully, wore down in turn the courage and good-humour that had been Anne's assets in life. And meanwhile the Duke took another mistress.

The Duchess had acquired a new group of maids-in-waiting. To one of them the Duke had been attracted. Frances Jennings, a lovely coquette, gently repulsed his approaches, flirted atrociously with the clumsy and devoted Talbot, lost her heart to Jermyn, who meant to subdue her and found himself in love, and eventually married one of the ubiquitous Hamiltons. Her blonde and haughty beauty was in marked contrast to the pale and angular features of Arabella Churchill, her companion maid-of-honour. Daughter of a loyal and impecunious family, Arabella and her young brother John, had been taken into the Duke's household, about the time of the journey to York. To that period, Hamilton in the *Memoirs of the Count de Grammont* dates the beginning of James's infatuation. It was, he says, at a Greyhound Race 'a diversion practised in England upon large downs, where the turf eaten by the sheep is particularly green and wonderfully even', that the Duke and Arabella were in conversation, when the latter's horse shied and bolted. She was thrown, without serious injury, but the Duke hastening to her assistance, was struck by her courage and tantalised by the grace of her figure. Whether the incident occurred or not (and if so it probably belonged to a later date), James's interest in Arabella grew, stimulated perhaps by the contrast between her plain but striking personality and Margaret Denham's fatal beauty. By 1668, Arabella had become his mistress, and early next year Pepys, with his usual appetite for well-spiced gossip, heard from one of the Duke's servants 'that he was going to his master's mistress Mrs. Churchill with some physic, meaning, I suppose, that she is with child'. By her, James had four children, the second of whom was born in 1670 in France, where Arabella had judiciously retired for her confinement. Returning at the age of seven, James Fitz-James, later Duke of Berwick, was educated for the profession of arms; a career that brought him glory and the world's respect began, at the siege of Budapest, in the year that his father came to the throne of England. His brother, Henry, Duke of Albemarle, born in 1673 eventually became a cleric, and both of Arabella's sons, the one as a marshal, the other as Grand Prior of France found in their adult years, recognition and friendship in the country that had always been James's spiritual home.

Arabella was installed in a house in St. James's Square and received an annuity from the Duke. Her brother John, who had the good looks his sister lacked and character into the bargain, had been the Duke's page and had received of James's bounty the desire of his heart, a commission in the 1st regiment of the Guards. Destined to great deeds, his first achievement was a disreputable if amazing *amour*. For a short period he carried on a successful intrigue with Barbara Villiers, the Countess of Castlemaine, between whom and her royal lover a surfeit of sexual passion, undignified by any true affection, had inevitably bred irritation and boredom. John Churchill's escapades were scandalous but transitory; he put his whole heart into his profession and a genuine love affair saved him from the fatal attractions of court life. As for his sister, after some seven or eight years the Duke's devotion wavered. Arabella, not complaining of a fortune which on the whole had treated her well, received a generous pension, married a certain Colonel Godfrey, and passed out of history. James's last mistress, Catherine Sedley, took up her residence in St. James's Square.

So, by degrees for James, women had become a habit. The first absurd yet honest strivings after perfection in his love affairs, had died away with youth, but he continued to break the seventh commandment with an uneasy consciousness of sin, that he could never stifle. For he was not by nature a vicious man, and the scandal-mongers of the day have given a false prominence to his intrigues, in their desire to mock his clumsiness. In the first twelve years of his brother's reign, there was something which counted for more in his life than any lady's love. That was the organisation of the British Navy, the unfailing satisfaction of hard work and the joy he experienced when he set out to serve England on the deck of the Admiral's flagship.

CHAPTER IV

LORD-ADMIRAL OF ENGLAND

'Up, and to the Office....' – Pepys *Diary, passim.*

WHEN the Duke of York fell in love with Lady Chesterfield, and King Charles stirred to uneasiness the hearts of his loyal subjects by flaunting his passion for Castlemaine in the face of his young bride, Samuel Pepys condemned but excused their indulgences: 'it is the effect of idleness, and having nothing else to employ their great spirits upon.' The efficacy of hard work as a means of attaining felicity had been preached by the Puritans in their zeal for the kingdom of God on earth. It was the tragedy of James's manhood that he lived in an age which revolted from this theory of a disciplined life, so that before long rottenness and slackness permeated not merely the courtiers with their empty social round, but the public services and the whole body of the nation; the better elements were disgusted and the apathy of the 18th century succeeded the enthusiasm of the Ironsides and the Cavaliers. James himself was a man bound to suffer more than most in this decadent atmosphere. His limited imagination and his physical energy disenabled him from finding refuge in flights of fancy or an ascetic philosophy. He was an ordinary man who needed for his best fulfilment a settled task, which would evoke his powers of decisive action or meticulous study. He had obtained it under Turenne, and in spite of his infidelities, the first decade after 1660 was less disastrous to him than to some, because he obtained it to a certain degree in his work as Admiral. It was for this reason that the sacrifice of his office for the sake of his religion in 1673 proved so great a tragedy.

His position as prince of the blood royal was no sinecure. The government of the realm was still regarded as the King's personal affair, in the conduct of which he took the advice in council of those of his subjects he thought fit to consult. But the result, in 1660, of including in the Privy Council the leading Presbyterians and the surviving Cavaliers had been to create an unwieldy body of some forty members, which tended to split into various cliques and committees. In these smaller units the real decisions of policy were reached, to be ratified later in full council. And whether it were the official subcommittees of trade or of foreign affairs, or the unacknowledged group of intimates – Hyde, Ormonde, Albemarle and the rest – with whom the King consulted, 'the Duke' was always present. He pulled his weight not merely because of his position, but because of his reputation as a man with strong views and courage to uphold them.

There were certain anomalies in his relations with his father-in-law. His brother's Restoration was based on Clarendon's philosophy of patience and moderation. In the generous treatment of all malcontents, except those directly concerned in the trial of Charles I, in the equitable settlement of old questions of feudal rights and land tenure, in the absence of any attempt to restore the autocratic system of government which the Long Parliament had destroyed in the first session of its existence, Clarendon showed himself a statesman and a realist. Only in one thing was he reactionary. The Church for which his friends had died must be restored in the fullness of its power. In Clarendon, the loyalties of youth combined with the growing rigidity of age to strengthen his resolve and blind his vision: at a time when a gesture of true Christian charity might have healed the wounds of a hundred years, the Church of England failed and by the penal code, which bears Clarendon's name and sullies his memory, perpetuated dissent and drove into unwilling hostility many of her noblest sons. The Duke regarded Clarendon with esteem and true affection. He had moreover a keen sense of 'family' and felt it behoved him to support his father-in-law, when a greedy gang of adventurers combined with those who truly opposed his policy to question his virtual dictatorship. But mentally they had little in common. James was a thorough autocrat. The French conception of kingship dominated his theory of government. The growing claims of Parliament to control the executive, as yet neither glorified by success nor justified by philosophy, were not merely alien to his temperament but appeared to many as to himself contrary to law and reason. The philosopher Hobbes, though he had introduced the dangerous idea of contract as the basis of kingship in contradistinction to that of divine right, had not queried the absolute power of Kings. John Locke was still a youth, associating with those who were to work out in practice the democratic ideas for which he was to provide the philosophy. For James, it was sufficient that his father had been murdered by rebels, and that if they were given half an opportunity, malcontents abounded who would readily murder his brother and himself. This temper of James's mind, manifested frequently throughout his brother's reign and growing more marked as opposition checked and thwarted him, this uncompromising faith in a King's right to have his own way, was responsible for his eventual failure to almost as great an extent as his religion. His natural bent, stressed by the influence of France and his military experience caused him to introduce the tactics of the sergeant-major into the Council Chamber. He had naturally little sympathy with Clarendon's *via media*.

On one point alone, he was more tolerant than the Chancellor. He approved the persecution of schismatics because he regarded them as potential rebels, but already there was an uneasy stirring in his mind; during his campaigns he had lived in friendly relationships with every colour of

Christian, and he knew in his heart of hearts that no one branch of the Holy Catholic Church had the monopoly of the sons of Christ. Even here then he could not agree enthusiastically with Clarendon. In one respect he did influence his father-in-law. Linked to his belief in autocracy and his memory of his soldiering days was an abiding love for France and for his cousin, King Louis. He was not a man who gave his affection easily, but Louis had won it and kept it through all the mists and misconstructions of politics. Charles was Louis's ally for what he could get out of him. James was his friend. It may have partly been through his influence, that Clarendon in his foreign policy to his own undoing supported the interests of France.

The settlement of England was the immediate concern of the Restoration Government, and in the New Year of 1661, the first breach occurred in the unanimity with which Charles had been acclaimed. A band of Anabaptists led by a certain Venner, a fanatic uncompromising in his hatred of mitres and crowns, declared themselves for Christ and prepared to master London. The rapid pace at which the New Model was disbanding and the absence of the King, who was escorting his mother to the coast on her return to France, gave a shadow of hope to their wild designs. For a few days, the rebels hid in the woods of Highgate; then they marched boldly into the city, scattering dismay in Cheapside and taking refuge in a house in Wood Street when the trained bands proved too strong for them in the open. The Duke, not yet himself again after the tragedy of his sister's death and his hapless love affair, was convalescent at Whitehall, when news was brought of the revolt. Attended by some twenty horse and a crowd of excited nobles, stimulated by the gust of danger blowing through the decadent court, the Duke rode against the rebels, but the danger was over by the time he reached the city. Venner had held out in Wood Street, defying his besiegers until somebody suggested that the house should be entered from the roof, and by this means the rebels were mastered. Inspired by the force of their bitter enthusiasms and in the temper of martyrs, wretched but unafraid, all but one refused to surrender, and more fortunate than their leader died in the exhilaration of the fight. Venner was kept alive with difficulty to suffer a traitor's death. The populace resented the premature revolt, mere froth on the deep waters of thankfulness with which the return of peace and prosperity was still regarded. It was decided to maintain some of the regiments that had not yet been disbanded, and Monck's men, remembering the Scottish village whence their fateful march on London had begun, remained in being as the Coldstream Guards. It was the only result of the rebellion, but it may have served to root more deeply in the Duke's still impressionable mind the belief that no ruler could afford to loose the rein and that a small but trustworthy standing army was part of the essential equipment of a king.

During the next decade there was no further rebellion, but the activities of malcontents gave a spice of danger to existence, and the later acts of the Clarendon Code emanated from fear rather than religious principle. In the deliberations of council, when the problematical questions of land-settlement and religion had been dealt with, the King's marriage, the sale of Dunkirk to the French and the growing hostility of the United Provinces in turn engaged attention. In the latter, the Duke was particularly concerned, both as head of the Navy and on account of his personal interest in trade and colonisation. The economic rivalry of England and Holland had been strong enough to drive the two Republics into war, even in Cromwell's time. Now this rivalry was accentuated by the Stuarts' dislike of the oligarchy, led by the de Witts, which controlled Dutch politics and excluded the young Prince of Orange from the power his family normally exercised as chief magistrates in the state of Holland. The brothers' love for Mary, strengthened by her untoward death, the memory of the loyal friendliness of her husband in the most hopeless days of exile, impelled the King and Duke to watch over their nephew's interests and combined with more material motives to incline them towards the inevitable war. It broke out early in 1665 after years of friction. In 1663 the Dutch had been grievously affronted by the foundation of a Royal African Company of which the Duke was Governor. It purposed to trade with the coast of Guinea, hitherto a monopoly of the United Provinces, and certain lands were seized and trading stations established. The Duke also planned to send ships to Brazil, a scheme which the anxious Coventry urged should be proceeded with 'on solid foundations, that so catching at a shadow we lose not the substance of which his royal Highness hath no superfluity'. In the event, Sir Robert Holmes's expedition to the west had results of greater magnitude than any financial profit, for sailing north in 1664, he occupied without opposition the Dutch settlement on the Hudson, changing the title of its capital New Amsterdam to that of New York, in honour of the Duke. The morals of the adventurers who built our Empire were often rough and ready; Holmes seized New Amsterdam some months before war had been declared, but the peace treaty of 1667 confirmed the British occupation. Thus, the chance of war determined Anglo-Saxon dominance in the United States of the future. In his interests in America and in the schemes which first brought England into contact with Africa other than in the nefarious slave-trade, James was finding a worthy outlet for the inveterate love of 'designs', which had characterised him since a boy. Hope of financial gain may have been the chief underlying motive; but gain had also inspired Hawkins and Drake, coupled with the impossibility of staying at home when an adventure was on foot. James had to stay at home, and bedraggle his bold spirit in faction and intrigue, which blinded posterity to these early ventures. Had his end been happier, they might have won his name a place of honour among those who had faith in England's future overseas.

There were two curiously contrasting strands in James's nature, on the one hand the love of action, on the other a *penchant* for the detailed analysis and co-ordination of facts to which his copious memoranda and the journals of his early days bear witness. If the former characteristic made him a good soldier and a dangerous king, the latter assured him success as an administrator. In the years between 1660 and 1673, the development of the British Navy became with increasing force the interest and passion of his public life.

They were vital years. When Elizabeth fought with Philip of Spain, the coasts of England had been defended by a small number of royal ships, assisted with enthusiasm by privately-owned craft supplied by nobles, merchants or fishermen. The Queen, through the Lord-Admiral, controlled the fleet. But during the first forty years of the 17th century there was a development in the science of government no less interesting and fascinating than the more strident political changes and the romantic clash of King and Parliament which overshadowed it. Changing their theories to fit the facts in typical manner, the English began to realise that the administration was no longer a personal affair of the King's servants and lieutenants, the corollary in the sphere of the executive of the financial fallacy that the King must live of his own, but that office equipment and a trained bureaucracy were necessary for the efficient conduct of a department of State.

But the process was only half-completed when the civil dispute broke with tragic discord the continuity of England's progress. Meanwhile Charles I's genuine efforts to develop his navy, led to an increase in ships and in commitments, without any corresponding development of the machine of administration. Cromwell by his establishment of a Navy Board, the members of which enjoyed fixed salaries, bequeathed to his successors the embryo of a department of State, and at the Restoration a compromise was effected here as everywhere. The Duke of York became Admiral, with the old powers and duties, but he was advised and assisted by a Navy Board consisting of four officers of the Admiralty, Treasurer, Comptroller, Surveyor and Clerk of the Acts and three extra commissioners, one of whom remained at Chatham to keep an eye on the building of ships. The general instructions issued by the Duke in 1662 were based on those of his father's Admirals and were too conservative to meet the exigencies of the situation. During the succeeding years, the Admiralty, not without serious growing pains, developed steadily, in the face of almost insuperable difficulties. For the Navy was no longer a small fleet, aided by volunteers; it was a great and growing service, an instrument of policy and England's chief engine of war. James and his colleagues had not merely to face a chronic state of debt but to administer a growing concern and engage in a naval duel, at the same time that they were endeavouring to create an adequate organisation. Treasury and Secretariat were faced with similar problems and developments but without the extra strain which the war with Holland supplied in the case of the Navy, or the fear of such spectacular results of failure as the invasion of the Medway. That James and his associates did fail is neither surprising nor blameworthy, save to the extent that the peculation and corruption rife in the ranks of lesser Admiralty officials mirrored the general slackening of moral fibre, which had contaminated the whole nation. It is to the Duke's credit that in the main the system he established with the help of able subordinates remained unchanged until the beginning of the 19th century, and that the hard-won victories to which he led his beloved ships prepared the way for the glorious history of the future.

The Duke's chief asset was the honesty of his secretary, William Coventry, who became a commissioner of the Navy in 1662, and the genius of his Clerk of the Acts,

Samuel Pepys. It was Coventry's zeal for good management which set fire to Pepys's interest and industry. At first, the latter, who was just making his way in the world, was inclined to fashion himself on his social superiors, and those with whom he came in immediate contact in his new house at Seething Lane were not particularly edifying. Sir William Penn, whose son, the Quaker of the future, was still a vigorous young man enjoying the world and the feeling of his own ability, was an easygoing gentleman, able enough on the battle-deck but inclined to think that short working-hours and good fellowship were the perquisites of civil life. Sir William Batten, his colleague, was a degree more coarse and less capable. But Coventry was a man of different calibre. Most elusive of that fascinating group of men connected by ties of blood and marriage, the Forsyte clan of the Restoration, to which Shaftesbury, Halifax, Sunderland and the Sidneys also belonged, William Coventry lacked the spiritual power which makes the hero and the martyr, or if it be twisted awry, the criminal. He was eminently well-bred, in the best sense of the word, shrinking instinctively from the coarseness and the extravagances of a generation that had lost its balance. Like his brother Henry, who after an embassy in Sweden was to do yeomen service to the King as Secretary-of-State, he was a born administrator, loving exactitude for its own sake, incapable of dishonesty in word or deed, deriving from hard work and the mastery of files and minutes the satisfaction others found in heavy drinking or the conquest of a woman. Both of the brothers were bachelors, as one would expect; passion was an unsteadying force they preferred to leave unplumbed. That William was capable of loyal affection, his love for his nephew showed, and George Saville, who was to become the famous Earl of Halifax, owed much not merely to the advice and admonition but to the heartening companionship of his uncle. For his master the Duke of York, Coventry also had a real respect and affection, though characteristically, when reason asserted that he should oppose Clarendon, he severed his connection with the Duke in order to pursue his duty thoroughly. Fortunately, James was an honest enough man to appreciate his motives.

Coventry entered the Navy Board 'resolved to do much good and to enquire into all the miscarriages of the offices'. Very soon he and Pepys recognised in each other congenial spirits. Together they had accomplished much in the way of improved organisation and reduced debt, when the Dutch war and the devastation of the Plague upset all human calculations and plunged the Admiralty again into confusion. But Pepys worked on, with a doggedness that amounted to heroism. Once his interest had been stimulated he found a thrill not merely in the immediate job of making both ends meet (and a little for himself into the bargain if it could be done to the King's advantage), but in a study of the whole panorama of naval history. Working late at the office produced a delicious glow of virtue and an excellent excuse for less admirable relaxations afterwards.

Pepys – and the Duke – had three main difficulties, lack of men, food and money. The latter of course occasioned the former. The cause of dearth was twofold. Not even the Cavalier Parliament of 1661 was free from the traditional parsimony of every House of Commons, and in effect the executive was doomed to inefficiency until the legislature had found some other means of controlling it than that of keeping it in a chronic state of poverty. Not till the system of cabinet and party rule emerged at the turn of the century was the problem solved. Parliamentary grants, in Charles II's reign, even in the enthusiasm of war were inadequate, and not merely because of their paucity but also because the Admiralty was already so cumbered with debt. For, in familiar words, credit had gone awry; money was misbehaving. In a time when the advances of science and the reviving trade of the nation produced no shortage of the goods of the earth, there was no corresponding facility in methods of distribution, and no credit to be obtained except from one or two financial magnates whose terms of interest were prohibitive. The government departments had no means of raising ready money. It was impossible to get rid of the rogues who grew fat in the King's service because there was no cash with which to pay the wages due to them; while even officials of standing had such inadequate salaries that in the Duke's own words, they succumbed 'to a compliance with others, gaining one shilling to themselves by losing ten shillings for the King, and then by falsehood becoming slaves to their inferiors, for fear of discovery'.

Such being the state of affairs, it was natural that corruption was rife in the Dockyards and among the victuallers. The practice of doctoring old rope and selling it as new was one of the small vices, to combat which Pepys spent many days in practical study of hemp and tar as well as in writing memoranda. Not without profit to himself, he made new and advantageous contracts for the supply of timber to the fleet; he spent a whole day from five in the morning till three in the afternoon writing, without refreshment, on the subject of ships' pursers, and he investigated the serious question of victualling, declaring that 'Englishmen, and more especially seamen, love their bellies above anything else. . . .'[1]

In view of the possibility of semi-starvation, and the probability of being discharged with a 'ticket', redeemable at a future date instead of wages, it was no wonder that the right sort of men were not forthcoming. The press-gang worked briskly but without discrimination; 'pitiful pressed creatures who are fit for nothing but to fill the ships full of vermin', was one report of the fruit of its labours, in the autumn of 1664. Trained men were always scarce, and in December, 1665, it was noted upon an order of the Duke's 'to impress five able shipwrights within the borough

[1] For Pepys's efforts in this direction see Bryant's *Pepys*, vol. I, p. 277.

of Arundel' that 'after diligent search none could be found abiding within the said borough'. There was of course the usual rush of volunteers when the fleet was actually about to sail against the Dutch. Only the shrewdest heads realised that while the efforts of the zealots at Tower Hill had put the affairs of the Navy into some order it was a different matter to withstand the strain of war.

Prayers for the success of James and the fleet he commanded were said in the churches of Edinburgh as early as November, 1664, while in the Isle of Wight, in December 'Nothing is talked of but the King's wisdom and greatness, the gallantry and conduct of the Duke of York and the meanness of the Dutch. All are willing to part with their money and most to fight.' The spirit had not entirely evaporated by the second year of the war when Sir Thomas Clifford reports from the *Royal Charles*: 'all are cheerful and in good heart and make themselves merry with the newcomers. There is a dancing master and two men who are or feign themselves mad and make very good sport to a bagpipe.' But Pepys paints another picture in his references to the wretched seamen begging for bread, who were stranded in the streets of London in the summer of 1665. Once ashore in the pest-ridden town, they were not allowed to re-embark. On September 24th of that year Pepys describes how he 'went to a blind alehouse at the further end of the town, to a couple of wretched dirty seamen, who, poor wretches! had got together about 37 lb. of cloves, and 10 lb. of nutmeggs and we bought them of them – the first at 5s. 6d. per lb. and the latter at 4s. and paid them in gold; but Lord! to see how silly these men are in the selling of it, and easy to be persuaded almost to anything. But it would never have been allowed by my conscience to have wronged the poor wretches. . . .' A fortnight later he 'did business, though not much, at the office, because of the horrible crowd and lamentable moan of the poor seamen, that be starving in the street for lack of money, which do trouble and perplex me to the heart, and more at

British Museum]

JAMES, DUKE OF YORK,
AS COMMANDING OFFICER OF THE ARTILLERY COMPANY

From the portrait by William Vaughan

noon when we were to go through them, for then above a whole hundred of them followed us; some cursing, some swearing and some praying to us'. If some deserted to the Dutch, one could scarcely blame them.

James, as Lord-Admiral, was harassed by yet another difficulty, in which his subordinates, who struggled with the shortage of money and supplies, could do little to assist him. The rivalry between the old sailors trained in the Commonwealth wars and the gentlemen who adopted the sea as an attractive career when the court had wearied them, required constant vigilance on the part of the Duke if serious consequences were not to ensue. Lord Sandwich, who as Sir Edward Montague had sailed at the head of the Republican fleet to bring home the King in 1660, hated Prince Rupert, who still bore the impress of great deeds done in the King's service. Albermarle, old but dogged, regarded the Duke, his junior but his superior, with sullen and critical resentment. In the lower ranks the same cleavage showed. Hotheads were not wanting who urged that Cromwell's sea-captains should be displaced since otherwise the King would not be master of his own fleet. Fortunately the Duke was too good a seaman to contemplate so drastic a cure. He admired the craftsmanship and had no fear for the loyalty of the 'tarpaulins'; on the other hand, he appreciated the necessity of training thoroughly the young gentlemen who followed him to sea. The midshipman, who has played such a happy role in the annals of the British Navy, thus came into being, and from the Duke's efforts to persuade his unmanageable friends to treat the sea, not as a chance adventure but as a serious profession, there developed the proud tradition of education and efficiency among the officers of the senior service.[1]

[1] According to Tedder this innovation of the Duke's 'had more far-reaching effects' than all his other reforms put together. His *The Navy of the Restoration* is an excellent guide to this subject, and is the source upon which this section is based.

Through the years of experiment and effort up to the outbreak of the Dutch War, in the crisis and failures of the war years and in the renewed effort and reorganisation that succeeded the speedy peace, Pepys's admiration for his chief steadily increased. At the Navy Office on Tower Hill, in the Duke's closet at Whitehall, where James discussed business in the process of dressing or retiring for the night, and in joint expeditions to the dockyards at Woolwich, to the fleet at Portsmouth or the Chatham shipbuilding yards, the master and servant had much opportunity for further acquaintance. At first Pepys was critical, repelled by the unpleasant affair of James's marriage and noting when he first went up with Mr. Coventry to the Duke's bedchamber that 'in his night habbitt he is a very plain man'. He did not dance as well as the King, a small detail that prejudiced a man like Pepys. Moreover Lord Sandwich was Pepys's patron and he could not therefore be sure of Mr. Coventry's friendship and the Duke's approval. But as these latter became manifest, the energetic Clerk of the Acts devoted himself with satisfaction to co-operating with superiors as keen as himself, while maintaining his friendly relations with Sandwich. Even the latter was favourably impressed by the Duke's honesty of purpose.

'And here,' writes Pepys on April 29th, 1663, 'speaking of the Duke of York and Sir Charles Berkeley, my Lord [Sandwich] tells me that he do very much admire the good management and discretion and nobleness of the Duke, that however he may be led by him [Berkeley] or Mr. Coventry singly in private, yet he did not observe that in public matters, but he did give as ready hearing and as good acceptance to any reasons offered by any other man against the opinions of them, as he did to them. . . .'

'My Lord tells me that he observes the Duke of York do follow and understand business very well, and is mightily improved thereby,' Pepys added, six months later. He himself was delighted by the Duke's friendly recognition, and he was compensated for the slight notice that was taken of his new periwig when he wore it at church one Sunday, by the fact that next day when the Navy Board met 'the Duke . . . told us that Mr. Pepys was so altered by his new periwig that he did not know him'. This pride in his relationship with royalty, and the respect he bore the Admiral as of one good workman to another developed steadily into genuine affection, so that when he heard that James was to sail against the Dutch in 1665 and saw him trying on his buff-coat and hat-piece covered with black velvet, he could only write, 'It troubles me more to think of his venture than of anything else in the whole war.'

Others too thought well of the Duke. When John Reresby, a Yorkshire squire, came to court in 1666 he went to James to remind him of an earlier promise of an office within his gift. 'I remembered you for all you were not here,' the Duke answered, 'and your business is done for you.' 'And at that time, to speak the truth,' adds Reresby, 'no prince was observed to be more punctual to his promise.' It was this quality of reliability in a drifting generation, which endeared the Duke to all who were brought in close contact with him. With it was allied a modesty, in itself proof of his genuine worth. In defiance of the generalisation that no man is a hero to his valet, Coventry instanced his master as the bravest man he knew while admitting his limitations. 'He is more himself and more of judgment is at hand in him, in the middle of a desperate service, than at other times . . . and though he is a man naturally martial to the hottest degree, yet a man that never in his life talks one word of himself or service of his own, but only that he saw such or such a thing. . . .'[1] Thus, James set out to sea at the head of an English fleet, a man of thirty-one in the prime of his life, rejoicing in the service he could do the State and respected by all for his virtues of honesty, modesty and

[1] This is certainly corroborated by the tone of his extant memoirs.

courage. When the battle broke it had been well for him if the cannon ball which killed the friend beside him had not spared the prince, before the years had dulled his virtues so that honesty appeared stupidity, courage deteriorated into brutality and in place of modesty, there was despair.

James went down to Portsmouth in November 1664, to take command, and through his indefatigable zeal managed to complete preparations and to set sail two days after Christmas. 'Less resolution or less concernment for the King's service than that of his R.H.,' wrote Coventry, 'would scarce have carryed anybody to sea in such weather.' There was no sign of the Dutch fleet and James returned after a few days at sea. In March war was formally declared, and on April 30th the fleet sailed again, adequately manned but badly victualled. After watching the Dutch coasts for some weeks the Duke had to return to England for fresh supplies, as some of the ships had only one day's beer on board, as great a calamity as any that could befall a British crew.

On May 30th, the fleet set out for the third time, and meeting the colliery ships sailing down from Newcastle pressed into service the crews of pugnacious northerners, always excellent material and never averse to a scrap. The Dutch had sailed from the Texel and were offering battle off Lowestoft, but though the opposing fleets were roughly equal in men and ships, the English were spoiling for a fight and had gained cohesion in the previous cruises, while the Dutch divided into seven squadrons were hampered by disaffection in the ranks and mutual mistrust among their leaders. As dawn was breaking on the morning of June 3rd, the English fleet, running before a steady breeze from the south-west, passed the Dutch on the opposite tack, the latter endeavouring to encircle the enemy so as to have the advantage of the wind. The White squadron, under Lord Sandwich, led the English van; the Duke on the *Royal Charles* kept well to windward with the Red squadron and thus prevented the Dutch from attaining their object; Rupert in the rear was Admiral of the Blue. It was James's pride, typical of his methodical mind that now for the first time the English fleet was acting as a unity 'fighting in a line and a regular form of battle', to which end he had tutored his officers carefully during the preceding months. In Cromwell's time they 'minded not any set order and their victories were still more owing to their valour than method'. It was the corollary at sea of the work of organisation which he had initiated at home. The fleets tacked again, manœuvring for position, and about ten o'clock in the morning the Duke gave the signal to bear down upon the Dutch. The two fleets engaged, and in full noontide the noise of the guns, the shrieks of the wounded and the glare of the burning ships turned the quiet beauty of the cloudless day into a thing of horror.

The Duke sought out the ship which carried van Opdam, the Dutch commander-in-chief. 'Nor did these two Admirals leave plying one another most furiously for some hours, till the Dutch began to give way.' Word came that Sir John Lawson, a rough and honest seaman, was mortally wounded. His ship perforce fell off leaving the *Royal Charles* dangerously exposed. On the quarter-deck, James, happy in action, urged on his men. By his side stood Falmouth, the companion of his soldiering days, best-loved if at times most injudicious of friends. Two others were with them, Lord Muskerry a brave and experienced soldier and young Mr. Boyle, a courtier-volunteer, acquitting himself well on his first active service. A shell landed on the quarter-deck. The noise rent the air and died, the smoke cleared, and the horrified spectators looked to see their Duke the inevitable victim. Miraculously, he stood, unhurt, bespattered by the blood and brains of his three companions, whose remains terribly mangled lay about his feet. He said nothing, but continued the work on hand.

'I owe more tears
To this dead man than you shall see me pay.
I shall find time, Cassius, I shall find time.'

So, in the words of Brutus, he might have mourned his friend. But first the battle must be won.

The Dutch were slowly diminishing their fire, and about two in the afternoon, James ordered another broadside to be delivered into van Opdam's ship. On the third shot the Dutch flag-ship blew up. 'At which terrible sight the Enemy's fleet all gave way, and ran for it putting right before the wind.'

The sea was alive with Dutch seamen, who flung themselves out of the burning ships; the Duke approved his men's efforts to save them when they could. Severe though his nature was it had not yet been twisted into cruelty, and when an English captain fired 'without order, against the custom of war', at three enemy vessels that had struck, James in his anger ordered a court martial which the wretched man's death from wounds alone averted.

And now the demon of ill-luck which haunted the Duke entered into the game. Victory was assured, but a prompt pursuit of the fugitives might transform their defeat into a rout. Full sail was set towards the Dutch coast, and when darkness fell and James retired to his cabin, the enemy was still in sight. He had ordered watch to be kept and the pursuit to be maintained that with the morning the remnant of van Opdam's fleet might be overtaken and destroyed. Then, dressed as he was he flung himself on his bed and slept the dead sleep of mental and physical exhaustion. Until morning, nothing could be done.

He was mistaken. In attendance upon him was a certain Henry Brounker, a man of mean courage whose nerves had been badly shaken by the horrors of the day. The fact that he had promised the Duchess on their departure to do his utmost to prevent the Duke from running into unnecessary danger gave him all the excuse he needed for a piece of effrontery that saved his own skin but nearly ruined his master's reputation. Returning to the deck, he bade the Captain shorten sail, implying that he carried orders from the Duke. The Captain, amazed, refused to obey. Brounker approached the Duke's lieutenant, who compromised with a request for more definite instructions. Brounker crept down to the cabin, but forbore to enter. He reappeared above boldly reiterating the Duke's pretended order. Perhaps Harman, the lieutenant, had lost his nerve also; two hundred men had been killed that day on the *Royal Charles* alone. The flag-ship shortened sail; the Captain fumed but dared not utter his suspicions of treachery. When later the fleet returned to harbour, he approached the Duke and tried to voice his doubts but the uneasy fear lest Brounker spoke the truth entangled his tongue, so that he welcomed an interruption that called the Duke away and said no more. The rest of the baffled fleet had of necessity to follow their flag-ship's lead, and by daybreak the Dutch were out of sight in the safety of their home waters. Full sail was set again on the *Royal Charles* before the Duke reappeared on deck, bitterly disappointed that the enemy fleet had escaped but knowing nothing of the tragic farce of the night-watches until rumour began its work in the months ahead. Then there was a public enquiry, and Brounker, dismissed by James from his household offices, found it convenient to travel in France. The fact that the Duke did not punish him more severely may be compared with his forgiveness of Falmouth in 1660, and his yet more regrettable disregard of the vices of Sunderland in later years. In his passionate desire for the personal affection he found so hard to win, he was ready to forgive any iniquity to one who seemed to love him.

So by ill-chance in 1665, the Dutch fleet reached harbour, defeated in a hard-fought battle but only crippled sufficiently to render them desperate and therefore dangerous. But to England the news of victory came undimmed by the presage of future ill; and the Duke of York was the hero of the hour. For almost the last time, in a life that hitherto had had its fair share of acclamation, he rode through the streets of Portsmouth to the plaudits of the crowd, read in the news-sheets tributes to his valour, and was voted by the Commons of England, assembled in Parliament at Oxford the sum of £120,000, 'in token of the great sense they had of his conduct and bravery'.

Yet even in this hour of triumph, circumstance was against him. The dread hand of pestilence held the city of London in its grip. The King was at Hampton Court; all who could had left the stricken town. Of those who were left, Death took his implacable toll, the number of victims rising week by week from two hundred and more in June to over seven thousand in the third week of September. Trade was paralysed, while the rest of England waited in the stupor of despair for the scourge to overwhelm it. Money, short before, was almost unobtainable, but Samuel Pepys remained at Tower Hill, saddened by the sight of the starving seamen, yet succeeding, by a miracle wrought through dogged energy, in fitting out a new fleet to sail in September against the unbeaten enemy. 'You, Sir,' he wrote to Coventry, who had sailed on the *Royal Charles* and returned infused with unaccustomed vigour, 'took your turn at the sword, I must not therefore grudge to take mine at the pestilence.' As usual it was those who worked hard and worried least who escaped infection and Pepys walked unscathed through silent streets that seemed accursed, that stank with decay and were only touched with life where some man of God went quietly on his way, saving souls in the very jaws of death. In the years of busy expansion and complicated governance after 1660, the English Civil Service was born, and in this hell of plague-stricken London it received a baptism of fire. When Pepys kept the machine of the Admiralty working from Tower Hill and the clerks at the Post Office drenched their letters in vinegar, so that contact with the outer world might be maintained and the sanity of the citizens be saved by a semblance of normality, a great tradition was begun of unspectacular but selfless labour, unshaken by the chances of politics or circumstance.

A new fleet sailed against the Dutch, but James was not in command. The shell on the quarter-deck had given the King a nasty shock; the heir-presumptive must not be allowed to risk his life again. In vain, the Duke argued; Charles was adamant. He had lost a brother too recently to view such a prospect with equanimity; moreover in the unsettled state of the country the death of the heir might be a serious matter. James was dispatched to the North of England, whence came rumours of incipient rebellion; it was better to be there than wasting time at Hampton Court, cut off alike from Navy Office and the sea. The royal agents in Yorkshire had reported that all would probably be quiet 'unless after harvest when the poor have spent their money. If ill-success at sea happen, trade being stopped by the sickness they may be wrought upon to make disturbances.' James, fresh from his naval victory, was the very man to quieten the ruffled northerners. He did his task successfully, making adequate arrangements for raising forces should there be revolt and pacifying the more well-known of possible malcontents. In particular he made an effort to see Lord Fairfax, the aged and disillusioned soldier, who had led the New Model to its victories and found Cromwell's dictatorship as distasteful as Laud's tyranny. His daughter had married the Duke of Buckingham, when the latter was playing the role of Presbyterian champion, and she had found little joy in her spouse. Fairfax met James, and was treated with such kindliness that he 'overcame his ordinary difficulty in speaking, and discoursed rationally and pleasantly, pleased at His Royal Highness's usage, which it is not hard for the Duke to afford to a man of courage so eminent'. With a tact which James might have used in later years, he won the old man's confidence by taking his loyalty for granted, and declaring that if needful he 'should call on him for assistance'. Coventry returned south with the feeling that 'if London do not lead the dance, in this distracted time, the country will not stir'.

During the next two years, distractions grew apace. Neither in the autumn of 1665 nor in the four days' battle of June, 1666, did the English fleet win a decisive victory. Louis XIV, distrustful of his cousin's navy, made a temporary alliance with his Dutch neighbours. Meanwhile the chronic shortage of money gave a quality of nightmare to Admiralty business. It became increasingly clear that it would not be possible to fit out a fleet for the summer of 1667. Folk began to murmur against the Chancellor, who was building a magnificent residence for himself in the pleasant thoroughfare of Piccadilly, and the Duke, working hard, hunting as often as possible and visiting Lady Denham 'at noonday with all his gentlemen in Scotland Yard' was uneasy in mind and restless in body. Then of a sudden came a fresh calamity. One morning in September, 1666, Samuel Pepys burst into Whitehall, dishevelled and dismayed but not disenjoying the exigency which excused such an unceremonial approach to royalty. The City of London was in flames.

The fire had broken out in a bakehouse in Pudding Lane in the early hours of Sunday, September 2nd. By way of Fish Street and St. Magnus's Church it spread to the low-lying streets and the wharves by the riverside. The King and his brother sailed down from Whitehall, to find that the flames, driven by a strong wind and fed by the tarred ropes and the oil in the Thames warehouses, were roaring on their way, unchecked by the pigmy efforts of the city authorities. The Lord Mayor was distracted. Dispatched to him with a message from the Duke to pull down houses as fast as he could and requisition the aid of any soldiers he required, Pepys found him in Cannon Street, 'like a man spent, with a handkerchief round his neck, crying like a fainting woman "Lord, what can I do? I am spent, people will not obey me. I have been pulling down houses but the fire overtakes us faster than we do it."' Individual citizens were concerned only in saving their own belongings, and the narrow streets were thronged with coaches laden with chairs and china, barrows piled with household goods, pans and pots jumbled with precious silver in a confusion that mirrored the terror of their distraught owners. The booksellers and silk-merchants of Paternoster Row stored their possessions in the vault of St. Faith's under St. Paul's, and many a volume of value and interest was lost for ever when on Tuesday, September 4th, the cathedral collapsed in ruins burying the church beneath it. The river was thronged with boats, overladen with goods and jostling each other in mid-stream, as if those who had taken refuge on the water could not tear themselves away from the awful fascination of the burning town. Only the paupers and the pigeons stayed till the end in the dark corners which by habit they had made their own, till the flames scorched their rags and their feathers and drove them out, dazed and miserable.

On Monday, the Duke was constituted General, and took over the complete charge of the distracted scene. By his 'example and princely courage, he put fresh heart into those who fought the flames, and by his calm authority allayed the panic, that was on point of breaking out'. The work of pulling down houses continued, and renewed efforts were made to supply the workmen with adequate implements. At Temple Bar, Clifford's Inn, Fetter Lane, Shoe Lane and Crow Lane, a constable was stationed with a hundred men, guarded by thirty foot-soldiers and 'a careful officer' to prevent disturbances. Three gentlemen were to attend each post and to distribute a shilling 'to any diligent all night'. More workmen were brought in from the country to relieve them next morning. There were to be five pounds of bread, cheese and beer at every post.

Two companies of the trained bands were to prevent looting by standing on guard over people's goods in Lincoln's Inn and Gray's Inn Fields. All day and night the Duke and the King rode up and down, urging on the workers and exposing their persons to risks of flame and falling timber. But in spite of all, the fire spread rapidly and bridged every gap that was made. By Tuesday evening it had nearly reached the Tower. Pepys and his friends were on anxious watch by the Navy Office, supping 'in a sad manner but merrily off a shoulder of mutton without any napkin or anything'.

He and his associates were convinced that only by a free use of gunpowder could a sufficient breach be made in the narrow streets to stay the flames. The sound of explosions told them that the Duke had followed their advice. It seemed that the house in Seething Lane was doomed and Pepys prepared to abandon it, when to his amazement in Tower Street the fire was stayed and from the steeple of All-Hallows, Barking, the Admiralty officers looked down safe but dismayed upon the saddest sight of desolation they had ever witnessed. By Wednesday the flames were well under control; there remained the wretched sights of women 'drunk as devils' on sweetened beer, of ruined citizens who had lost their homes and most of their possessions, of the squirming body of a cat and the unutterable misery of the stricken town. 'You would have thought for five days it had been Domesday from the fire and cries and howling of the people.' Rumours were rife that the Dutch and the French were about to land! But nothing happened. By next Sunday it was raining, and the last embers were quenched. Folk went to church as usual, and on Monday morning began to tidy up their houses, such as still possessed them. The Exchange opened among its ruins and not one merchant was broken. The spirit of the nation was expressed in one writer's comment. 'The King and his people will be able to weather it out.'

Indignation against the suppositious incendiaries and a determination to make the best of a bad job helped the people to recover their nerve after the Great Fire, just as a British lack of imagination and dogged courage had enabled them to face the terror of the Plague. But a new disaster was in store for them, which by its very shame came near to breaking their spirits. In 1667, British plenipotentiaries were discussing terms of peace with the Dutch at Breda, since at Whitehall the Lord Treasurer, an old man faced with difficulties too great for his declining years, had declared that there was no money left to fight. The Duke, who would have liked a parting-shot at the enemy, urged that by hook or by crook a fleet should be fitted out, but his objections were overruled and the ships of the Navy were anchored in the Medway, while a Dutch fleet sailed the seas unchallenged. On June 8th, 1667, the quiet country air of Bethnal Green was disturbed by the sound of distant guns. Rumours ran apace, and while Albemarle fortified Gravesend and courtier-volunteers hurried with no specific purpose into Essex, the mutinous seamen refused to tow the ships into safety. The Dutch landed at Sheerness, and on the 12th, broke the chain that had been erected across the Medway and sailed in among the abandoned vessels. Some were sunk and others captured, among the latter, the Duke's flag-ship the *Royal Charles*. The insolent and triumphant foe sailed out to sea leaving behind them an outraged people. Fear, a very real fear, of invasion had impelled the citizens to raise the trained bands and wait the event in anxious watchfulness, but it was shame, rather than fear that overwhelmed them. The hand of God was turned against England; the licentiousness of the court, the vain-glory of the prelates and the corruption of lesser men had been punished by calamities, unparalleled in the memory of a generation that had been nurtured in civil bloodshed and seen the execution of a King. To save at least a fraction of their self-esteem, a scapegoat must be found.

Clarendon, the Lord Chancellor supplied what was required. Against him, politicians fulminated and courtiers intrigued; his old associates tired of his arrogance while the King resented his scoldings and his patronage. Honest men like Coventry, adventurers like the greedy but irresistible Castlemaine; Henry Bennet, Earl of Arlington, an eminently useful man; above all Buckingham, most irresponsible of all the Villiers breed, combined to persuade Charles to dismiss his aged servant. The people of England, quick to forget the services of a lifetime, saw only the costly pile at Piccadilly, and in ribald rhyme charged the Chancellor with the triple responsibility of 'Dunkirk, Tangiers, and a barren Queen'. Political reverses, personal animosities and the sincere criticism of those like Downing and Carteret, who saw the need for urgent reform in the governance of the country, combined in an irresistible wave to drive Clarendon in turn from office and from England. His wife's death and his daughter's ill-health combined with his own disgrace to shadow his closing years, but his indomitable spirit rose above despair and he set himself to write his histories, immortalising by his pen the men whom he had loved and turning the years of exile into an old age of marvellous fruition.

For James, it had not been easy. Though they had little in common in their politics, loyalty impelled him to speak in his father-in-law's defence. Yet if he did so, he would offend his brother. For once in his life the Duke was lucky. When the Commons impeached Clarendon in the autumn of 1668 and the Lords debated the impeachment, James succumbed to a welcome attack of smallpox. By his enforced absence his difficulty was solved. He recovered from his illness without apparent ill-effect, and plunged into two or three difficult years in which as head of the Admiralty he faced the hostile criticism of the new brooms of the Treasury Commission appointed in 1667, while as a Privy Councillor, he suffered but disapproved the *volte-*

face in policy which led in 1668 to a triple alliance between England, Sweden and the Dutch. Louis XIV's aggressions had alarmed the Protestant powers, and this treaty, which the faith and the zeal of Sir William Temple brought about one Christmas in a few days' hurried visit to The Hague, was the beginning of the inevitable process which ended on the battlefields of Blenheim and Ramillies. James hated it, both because as a seaman the Dutch were his traditional enemy and because he regarded Louis XIV as his friend. But Charles, surfeited with his pleasures and interested in politics now Clarendon's grip upon the State had been removed, was coquetting with the Presbyterian element in his council. In consequence a rift appeared between the King and the Duke.

An eye-witness reported that 'the King, destitute of council is jealous of all men that speak to him of business . . . but he is afraid of the Duke of York and yet neglects and incenses him'. Mischief-makers were not lacking to indicate to James how great an interest Charles was taking in a bill under consideration in the Lords to enable a divorced person to re-marry. If the King divorced Catherine and married again and had an heir, James and his infant son would be excluded from the succession. Others averred that Charles might legitimatise a bastard, such as young James Crofts who had just come over from France. The King had married him to a rich heiress and made him Duke of Monmouth; he stood covered in the royal presence, and Charles spoilt him to his heart's content. But so did James, and their mutual fondness for the lad and the Duke's impeccable obedience to the King's authority ended the strain between the brothers.

And then a change in the King's temper brought them closer than they had been for years. It began with the visit of another illegitimate son, a young priest, Pierre de la Cloche. He was the child of the King's first love for the daughter of a loyal house in Jersey. There was a fragrance in the memory that touched a sentimental chord in

Charles. Pierre was an apostle of his Faith, and urged his father to save his soul, now that the gaieties of the Restoration had been darkened by the disasters of leaner years. Charles was something of a *poseur* and the idea attracted him. He wondered what his thorough-going Protestant brother would think. To his surprise he found that James was working along the same lines as himself and had gone much further; his mother's church was drawing him very close, so that reluctantly but of deliberate choice the Duke had decided to abandon the faith for which his father died.

CHAPTER V

THE FAITH

'First draw his Highness prostrate to the South,
Adoring Rome, this label in his mouth –
A vow, nor fire nor sword shall ever end
Till all this nation to your footstool bend.
Thus arm'd with zeal and blessing from your hands,
I'll raise my Papists, and my Irish bands;
. . . Prove to the world I'll make old England know
That common sense is my eternal foe.'

– Marvell – *Advice to a Painter.*

'Note that this day the Duke of York arrived at Court from the fleet in perfect health, to the great joy of King and kingdom, after the many dangers to which, during the war, he had exposed himself, in common with the meanest seaman.' – *Domestic State Papers*, ? June, 1672.

IN nothing is the gulf between ourselves and our forefathers more clearly fixed than in our attitude to eternal things. We can understand, even if we condemn, the sexual extravagances of the Restoration court. The philosophy that glossed the vicious indulgences of a group of young people, determined at all costs to have a good time, would evoke a response in many of our own unanchored generation. But the heights and depths of the religious faith of the Stuarts are alien to an age which has acclaimed the virtues of tolerance and good works at the expense of worship and other-worldliness. How can we explain a people who preached Christ and denied charity? How reconcile the trumpet-notes of the Shorter Catechism; 'What is the chief end of Man? To glorify God and to enjoy Him for ever,' or the beautiful simplicity of Bunyan's old women 'sitting in the sunshine, talking about the things of God' with the practice of burning witches or twisting men in the Boot, or, in the more 'tolerant' south, with the persecution of the conventiclers or the death of innocent men for fear of a Popish Plot?

In a sense there is no explanation. The growth of a wider humanity was a gift of the Spirit to later centuries; in this one thing at least, we can thank God and believe we have progressed. But the persecution of the 17th century was not entirely caused by a lingering barbarism; the methods might be unchristian, but the aim at least was due to the fervour of the average Christian's belief. All true faiths must evangelise, and the passing years have not brought us only gain. Since it ceased to be a dangerous thing to be a Christian, the Church's power for good has often been lessened by the apathy of its nominal adherents. Of this, there was little in Stuart England. In his old age, when James saw the military preparations of his friend King Louis, he reflected 'how very few amongst this great and formidable army think of their duty to the King of Kings' and since an eternity of misery or happiness would soon supersede this world's passing show, those who neglected their spiritual welfare were little better than 'so many mad men'. From this point of view, the salvation of one's soul and of one's neighbour's must be the matter of paramount importance in life. Better to be cast out, persecuted and killed, here and now for conscience' sake, than burn everlastingly in Hell hereafter: better to drive one's brother into conformity than watch him cast away eternal life. This conviction of the imminence of eternity did not result in an ascetic remoteness but in a vigorous infusion of theology into every corner of life. Thus there emerged the blending of religion and politics characteristic of the century. And thus fear entered in with its attendant vice of cruelty, and the victors persecuted the vanquished lest they should rise in revenge. After 1660 the sectaries were the suspects, everyone of them a potential rebel; gradually after 1670, the balance of suspicion was transferred to the old enemy of the Roman Catholic faith.

Cromwell had honestly believed in 'liberty to tender consciences' provided that unorthodox opinions were not dangerous to the State. But this very proviso defeated his good intentions, and the persecution of prelacy, which was synonymous with malignancy, was legalised by his authority. But in his administration of the laws the Protector seldom interfered with peaceful men, whatever their faith, who seemed to him 'to have the root of the matter in them'. The Cavaliers, however, who formed the overwhelming majority of the House of Commons elected in 1661, were spurred on by the consciousness of many petty injustices as well as by their real devotion, to re-establish in full glory the Church for which they had suffered.

By promising a revision of the Prayer Book, and offering bishoprics to some of the leading Presbyterians, yet more by exerting himself to listen to an occasional Presbyterian service, Charles showed that he wished to fulfil the promises he had made at Breda. But he lacked the moral force that would have nerved him to undergo the discomfort of disagreeing with his people: he let them have their way, with regret tinged with cynical amusement. Nor at this crisis did the bishops of the Church show the breadth of mind that, if it had not achieved comprehension, might at least have prevented persecution. They returned from years of exile, whole-heartedly happy to be again in their beloved England among the congenial company of other learned men. Many of them threw the greater part of their energies into renovating their cathedrals, those glorious witnesses to the majesty of the Divine. The wars had dealt hardly with the churches; sacrilegious hands had defiled them, the lofty aisles had stabled men and horses; and from the towers had issued not the challenge of the bells but the guns of the enemy. Patiently and thankfully the bishops restored the houses of God. They forgot that the spirits and minds of men had been scarred no less deeply; that the bitterest toll of war is not the corpses left on the battlefield, but the hatred, the disillusion, the crooked laughter that is left in the wounded hearts of the survivors. They themselves could not go scathless. Revolting from the sins of their opponents, they lived fully and zestfully in the truth of the saying, 'The fruit of the spirit is joy'. 'Serve God and be cheerful', was their motto. But in spite of deep scholarship and exemplary lives, spiritually they lacked something, these older men, Sheldon, Gunning, Morley, which their successors Ken and Tillotson recaptured. It was just this surrender of spiritual power which the world demanded from them as the price of their success, which made impossible that tremendous essay in charity and understanding which might have bridged the gulf between them and the Presbyterians.

In the spring of 1662, a year too late to have much chance of success, a conference was held at the Palace of the Savoy, between the bishops and the leading Presbyterians. Had the former not shown their consciousness of insuperable difficulties by an irritating tinge of condescension, and had Baxter not possessed the defect of his virtues, too great a facility in words and a very human and lovable impatience with the defects of other folk the meetings might have borne more fruit. As it was, when he realised the absence of any true will to succeed, Baxter the chief Presbyterian spokesman gave run to his polemical skill at the expense of his statesmanship and Christian charity. In May the Bill for Uniformity passed the House of Commons, and turned the prolonged discussions at the Savoy into little better than a farce. The new Act imposed the revised Prayer Book upon all incumbents, and ordered them to read it in their churches before St. Bartholomew's day. It was not till late summer that the work of revision was completed, so that the dissenting clergy had to make their vital decision without time for due consideration. Yet to many, one reading sufficed to show that a comprehensive church could not be built upon this foundation. Enriched by the inclusion of some beautiful new prayers, our most precious heritage from this century of lovely language, and denuded of most of the Laudian innovations, the revised Prayer Book stood firmly in the position midway between Romanism and Puritanism that the Church had held at the end of Elizabeth's reign. No change was made in customs, such as the use of the Cross in baptism, that seemed to the Presbyterians of vital importance, and on this dogma of baptismal regeneration more than on any other single question the ideal of comprehension came to grief. Perhaps, in spite of many tragic results, it was as well it happened so, for a united Anglican and Presbyterian Church, strange as yet to the thought of toleration, might have crushed out of existence the independent sects, the Baptists, the Congregationalists and the Friends, who could claim among their number, Bunyan, Calamy and Penn, the flower of 17th century Nonconformity.

On August 24th, 1662, over two thousand clergymen of the Church of England gave up their livings, and the salaries attached thereto, rather than offend their consciences. They went, in no spirit of defiance but sick at heart for the Church they were loth to leave. Pepys tells us how a crowded congregation listened to Dr. Bates on the last Sunday that he preached. He took for his text the words 'Now the God of Peace . . .'[1] and pleaded with his people to understand an action that for the moment seemed more like a desertion than an heroic measure. 'It is not my opinion, fashion or humour,' he said, 'that keeps me from complying with what is required of us; but something, after much prayer, discourse and study, yet remains unsatisfied, and commands me herein. . . .' The Church was immeasurably impoverished by the loss of so many honest men. Charles made a last effort to redeem his word by issuing an Indulgence in the following December, but Clarendon assured him that it would be impossible to legalise in the present temper of Parliament. Weary of the whole business, the King let it drop. By a series of cruel

[1] *Hebrews* xiii, 20.

laws, dissent was harried out of the towns, conventicles were forbidden, and the exclusion of Nonconformists from the Universities barred them for a century and a half from the higher learning, and did much to give them that sense of social inferiority which embittered their spirits for generations.

Happily, such severity defeated itself. In thought and conversation men familiarised themselves with the idea of toleration. In its own time, it came. But so deep were the wounds wrought by the hatreds and suspicions of this time of tribulation, that only in our own day have common action in the cause of right and the binding force of common adversity united the churches of this land in a renewed hope of harmony and in a true sense of the fellowship of the Spirit.

It was natural that such a man as the Duke of York, deliberate, painstaking, and like most of his contemporaries enormously interested in the life around him, should have directed his attention to this problem of religion. Nor was it surprising that his enquiries resulted as they did. He was bound, if he took his faith seriously, to become either a Catholic or a Calvinist. Both creeds were rigid, logical and thorough, as he was himself. He had nothing in common with the Church of England, at its worst a medley of contradiction and confused symbolism, at its best the embodiment of sweetness and light, opening its arms wide to all believers. James could not become a Calvinist, because the political outlook of Calvinism was so essentially different from his, though it is significant that the Presbyterians had hopes of his support as late as 1667.

But the Duke was an autocrat to the very bone, and the discipline of the Catholic Church, as well as the decisiveness of its doctrinal utterances made an unanswerable appeal. When exactly he joined the Church of Rome is uncertain. In the early days of exile, the love they bore their father's memory bound Charles and James to Protestantism, and the vigour with which they resented their mother's attacks on young Gloucester's faith showed that it was no mere case of lip-service.[1] Yet in later years, James looked back upon his first exile as the gift of a Divine Providence, which had enabled him to learn something of the Papists. 'I began to be sensible by experience that I had wrong notions given me of the Catholic religion.' On one occasion he lodged at a Flemish convent, and was stirred by the gentle entreaty of a nun, who bade him pray that 'if he was not in the right way, God would bring him to it'. It was this chance encounter which first brought home to him the possibility of not taking his Protestant faith for granted. But it was in memory afterwards rather than in the zestful present that he was affected by the influences of the years abroad. For some years before and after 1660 he was content to live, without questioning very closely the opinions in which he had been brought up, and to which he felt it a point of honour to adhere.

But as life became less easy, when his children died and he fell out of love with his wife, and his work at the Admiralty was criticised not extolled, he began to think again about eternal things. And the first fact that struck him was the facility with which his Protestant friends maligned the Catholics. He had fought side by side with Romanists in France and Flanders and he knew that they were often brave and honest men. He had seen converts to Catholicism abandon their vices to lead exemplary lives. There was little sign of the Protestant gentleman of his brother's court, sacrificing their pleasures for their religion. He himself was no better than the rest, and he wondered if he were a Catholic whether he would find in that faith some power to resist the temptations of the flesh, which continued to overwhelm him. Why had the Anglican Church broken away from Rome? He read his history, to find that the main cause of cleavage had been apparently an English King's determination to satisfy his lust. He

[1] See his *Papers of Devotion*, published by the Roxburgh Club, and edited by Mr. Godfrey Davies.

considered theology. Was the doctrine of the Mass, more or less believable than the sacramental system of the Anglican communion? His logical mind arrived at the conclusion that the only alternative to Catholicism was the Socinian heresy. For the arguments against transubstantiation applied equally to the doctrines of the Incarnation and the Trinity, and the whole basis of Christianity was destroyed 'by believing nothing that does not agree with our senses'. Probing deliberately into the debatable subject of church-government, James read Hooker's *Ecclesiastical Polity*. So cogent did he find the reasoning in episcopacy's defence that he went further than the learned author and admitted the sanctity of the apostolic succession.

By now the Duke was anxious for human companionship in the lonely furrow which he ploughed. He showed Hooker's volume to his wife. The Duchess, poor thing, anxious to please her husband, declared herself equally impressed. She had obtained much comfort, for some years, from the practice of private confession, and Morley the Bishop of Winchester had acted as her spiritual adviser. It was a Popish practice. James was interested to find that they were feeling their way to the same conclusions. They studied the Scriptures together, and found definite authority for the papal claim that Christ had left in St. Peter's care the seed of an infallible church. At this stage, it seemed to them that only by challenging the authenticity of the Bible, could they deny the authority of Rome. To a Christian of the 17th century, such a possibility did not arise, though James spent many further hours of study on the problem.

Had he been a private subject, he would now have seen his way clearly, and would have ended at one stroke his religious doubts and his material prosperity, by applying for admission to the Roman Catholic Church. But he knew that as the heir presumptive to the throne he had other responsibilities. As yet no bigot, he would have been content to leave the externals of his life unchanged. Could he join the Church of Rome, he asked a Jesuit confessor, while continuing the formal attendance at Anglican services, which the State required of him. The Jesuit said, no; the Pope, on appeal, echoed the denial. Secret adherence to the Faith was inadmissible. Had not that been Peter's sin when the cock crowed thrice? One must not be ashamed of the true religion.

This was the stage which the Duke had reached when his brother disclosed to him his own religious doubts. For once, Charles seemed to be more precipitate than James. Early in 1669, the Duke was invited to a secret meeting to consider the possibility of re-establishing the Catholic faith in England. He met there Lord Arundel, the head of the Howard family, Bellasis, a knight of tried loyalty to the King and the ancient faith, and most surprisingly, Sir Thomas Clifford, the young man who was doing so well at the Treasury. James realised he had not been so alone as he imagined. But the practical difficulties were very great. Charles had kept free from the thraldom of a single chief adviser after Clarendon's fall, and the heterodox selection of privy councillors who share his confidence according to his moods were no easy team to drive down the path of resolute and dangerous endeavour. William Coventry, the best man among them, had already withdrawn from the political arena. Buckingham, who thought him a prig, had caricatured him in a topical comedy, and Coventry showed a human but unexpected streak of vanity in losing his temper and challenging his rival to a duel. As a result he found himself inside the Tower. But genuine disappointment at the lack of any real improvement in administion did more than pique to dishearten Coventry and he was clear-sighted enough to realise he would never be happy at court. He withdrew into the country, more blessed than most in finding happiness in little things, instead of breaking his heart in the struggle for fame and power.

Bored with Presbyterian half-measures, which he found as dull as Church-and-State Cavalierdom, Charles seriously considered the attractive possibilities of a Catholic autocracy. His son had returned to his seminary, but another more potent than he weighted the scales. Henrietta, Charles's younger sister, now married to the Duke of Orleans, was even more lovely and charming than in girlhood, so that King Louis himself realised the prize he had lost and consoled himself with a friendship that mingled political intrigue with true sympathy and affection. Through Henrietta, whom Charles called Minette and the world called Madame, Charles and Louis made their plans, and letters outlining the 'Grand Design' passed between France and England. Minette threw into the scheme the whole warmth of her impulsive nature, starved in her unhappy married life; Louis played his part shrewdly but not entirely insincerely; Charles allowed himself to believe that for love of his sister for once he was going to be heroic. But his sense of the incongruous was tickled by the agent Minette sent to England, the Abbé Pregnani, who combined a zeal for astrology and chemistry with other accomplishments. In foretelling the result of the Newmarket races so inaccurately that young Monmouth lost his pocket-money, the Abbé was unfortunate, but over the test-tubes in the Royal Laboratory, he succeeded in some delicate and satisfactory diplomacy.

Still wavering between possible alternatives and enjoying the feel of his own hand upon the helm, Charles allowed his Presbyterian advisers to submit a scheme for religious comprehension to the House of Commons in the autumn of 1669. Its unfavourable reception and the immediate framing of a second Act against conventicles showed that as things were, the religious situation could not be changed by legal methods. The French intrigue now went on apace. With Louis's aid in men and money, Charles would re-establish the Catholic faith and make himself independent of Parliament; while in return he would assist Louis in his forthcoming struggle with the Dutch. And this, thought Charles rejoicing in subtlety, might hoodwink his Protestant councillors. For them a dummy treaty should be prepared, in which the French payments and the French soldiers would appcar as nothing worse than the concomitant of the alliance against Holland. Even Ashley, that renegade Roundhead, would rejoice in the chance of another tussle with the Dutch to wipe out the disgrace of 1667.

The negotiations culminated in Madame's visit to England in the spring of 1670. Orleans resented his wife's influence at Louis's court and restricted her leave of absence, so in order to make the most of every precious moment Charles and his court moved down to Dover. There for three weeks the King and his sister revelled in each other's company. In the riot of merry-making, even Rupert mellowed, Buckingham fell head over heels in love, and Monmouth won yet further good opinions by his natural and infectious gaiety, Before Madame sailed, the secret treaty had been signed by Clifford, Arlington and Arundel on England's behalf, while Ashley put his name to the faked treaty in all good faith, and Buckingham following suit prided himself on being supreme in the King's councils. The Duke of York to whom merry-making did not come easily was detained in London till some days had passed; on reaching Dover he regretted the inclusion of the clause in the secret treaty promising English help in a Dutch War. He saw that such a complication would probably wreck the whole scheme and that the religious project would slide into the background. Nothing could indicate more clearly how deep an impression his religious enquiries had already made on James, that his hatred of his old foes and his shamed memory of their ships in the Medway were forgotten in his zeal for a crusade against Protestant England.

The King said good-bye to his sister, and returned to the gaieties of Whitehall with unaccustomed heartache.

A few weeks later came news of Minette's death. There were rumours of poison, which Charles knew were unlikely to be true, yet he guessed that her husband had killed her, not crudely by murder but by breaking her spirit. His petty torments and his vice had worn her out, the joy and the responsibility of her visit to England had stimulated and exhausted her and an acute chill had done the rest. Charles mourned her with all the sincerity of which he was capable; to fulfil their last secret compact became for the moment a debt of honour and of love; he even went so far as to give audience in secret to the Papal Nuncio in the presence of the Duke of York and Arlington, who smuggled the dignitary into the Royal presence by a private passage from the secretary's office. But as the months passed, the first enthusiasm dwindled, the King's vision cleared as his emotions cooled; he saw that he had almost made a fool of himself. He did not at once discard the secret treaty. There was a thrill about it, a hint of danger, a joy in tricking Ashley and Buckingham, as exhilarating as an evening with Castlemaine or Nell Gwynne. But henceforth it was a game to be put aside as soon as the novelty wore off, or things became too uncomfortable. For the Duke it remained a supreme adventure.

Charles was finding it increasingly difficult to steer his course among the conflicting counsels of the small group of privy councillors, who tended to monopolise the work of government. By a curious chance their initials spelt the word CABAL, long a term of opprobrium and now attached to them in scorn by an increasingly hostile nation. Two at least of them, Clifford and Ashley, were sincere men. Clifford was the soul of honour. The son of a Devonshire squire, he had been brought into public affairs by the patronage of Lord Arlington, when the latter needed the help of bright young men in his efforts to undermine the Chancellor. But Clifford soon outstripped his patron. He fought at sea in the Dutch wars with a daring which endeared him to the Duke of York, who found much that was congenial in his subordinate's cool courage. Clifford was a man who as a matter of course put his best into everything he did. At the Treasury he showed ability and industry, and as a courtier his rectitude and his pride marked him out as exceptional and therefore attractive to the somewhat jaded Charles. Arlington had come to hate him for he had proved no puppet who would dance to his tune. Clifford made no secret of his Catholic leanings, and immersed himself with all the enthusiasm of his fiery temper and serious bent of mind into the schemes of 1670. While they were maturing, he devoted himself to his financial duties which won him at length the supreme honour of the Lord Treasurer's staff, and to collecting the works of art in which he found his highest joy. An honest man and a talented, his character was marred by a natural arrogance, which took into no account either the hostility of a courtier or the deepest feelings of a nation.

Arlington on the other hand had little pride and less courage. But he was undoubtedly clever. He had the knack of turning all he possessed into assets: his Dutch wife, who predisposed the Dissenters in his favour, the friends he had made as ambassador in Spain thereby causing the Catholics to regard him as reliable, the scar on his face earned in the civil wars that made him *persona grata* with true-blue Cavaliers. He exploited the scar and a Spanish formality of address to win himself the reputation of a mystery man; at times it was useful to have an excuse to watch the way the cat was going to jump. Yet Arlington was not merely a politician with a taste for intrigue, though he caballed in turn with Castlemaine, Coventry, and the Papal Nuncio, and would have greeted the Devil himself, if thus he could advance his position without risking his skin. He had gifts and the virtue of diligence, and he did the same work for the Secretariat of State that Pepys and the Duke were attempting at the Admiralty. As a politician he had little to his credit not even the courage of his convictions, but as an admirable administrator he deserved well of Charles and of the State.

Given an alternative choice of action, Arlington would in all likelihood have done what he thought was right, provided no benefit accrued to himself from the other course: Buckingham, from sheer devilment, would probably have done what was wrong. But he was very fascinating and the best companion in the world. La Belle Stuart, who found the pose of childishness a considerable help in a wicked world, used to stop playing with her dolls and disturb the courtiers she had trained to build her castles of cards, to send them to look for Buckingham if he were not there to amuse her. And Mary Fairfax, his wife, pining for the Yorkshire garden where Marvell had tutored her and written his immortal rhymes, would shrug her shoulders in despair and go and call on the Queen, two women whom fate had used abominably and who had sinned in nothing save lack of charm. Buckingham's excesses angered even Charles, and occasionally he would find himself sojourning in the Tower. But the King could not do without him for long. They had been brought up together in the nursery at St. James's, where Charles I had heaped upon the children of his murdered favourite the benefits that were the outward sign of an unforgettable love. It was not as politician but as friend that the King petted and punished and forgave the wayward brilliance of this absurdly amusing courtier. He would imitate Clarendon's dignity, James's clumsy wooing or Castlemaine's tempers, till the onlookers were helpless with laughter; in the laboratory he would become of a sudden a serious and intelligent student; at the Council-table, he would pose on the strength of his marriage as a champion of the Presbyterians, a force to be taken into account. 'Everything by starts and nothing long,' he was a typical product of the Restoration court, a man of ability, at times approaching genius, who accomplished nothing of worth in the world through lack of moral stamina and honest affections.

Ashley, his political colleague in the Cabal, became Earl of Shaftesbury in the spring of 1672. He had more than his fair share of the ideals that Buckingham lacked. His passions were as strong as Clifford's; his talent as an organiser as great as Arlington's. Buckingham himself could not exceed his lack of scruple in obtaining what he wanted. Like them all he was ambitious with the fierce, vindictive urge of one reminded by constant bodily pain how brief the time at his command to garner immortality. He had been one of Cromwell's secretaries; but like many another honest man, in its time had welcomed the Restoration. His practical ability, greater than that usually associated with intellectual brilliance and visionary fire, had won him by degrees a leading place in the councils of the King. The political background of his youth naturally inclined him towards sympathy with dissent; and his enthusiasm for the future of England as a trading and seafaring nation made him the champion of the merchant classes, who had suffered most from Clarendon's persecution. A measure of toleration and uncompromising hostility to Holland were for the present the chief planks of his political platform; but it was Shaftesbury's tragedy that in his zeal for the idea of the moment he betrayed his past enthusiasms. Regardless of the means by which he reached his end, he welcomed in place of legal toleration the exercise of the prerogative in favour of dissent, and in his association with the Cabal government, belied his own past record and his future creed of ordered liberty and the supremacy of the law. He was a ready tool for Charles's Catholic friends, provided he guessed nothing of the intended re-establishment of the Romanist faith. On that point he was as prejudiced as those middle classes whose cause he sponsored. If he thought he had been tricked, he would be dangerous. He meant to go far, and heaven defend those who stood in the way. Meanwhile, untempted by the sexual extravagances of his colleagues, as incorrupt as Clifford whom he disliked intensely, Shaftesbury walked alone among the crowded court. Charles recognised his ability but distrusted him:

> 'Yond Cassius has a lean and hungry look;
> He thinks too much: such men are dangerous.'

But Parliament, who was growing restless, would be helpless under the flood of his heartfelt oratory. If only for that, he must be advanced. In strokes of genius, Dryden hymned for all time:

> 'A fiery soul, which working out its way,
> Fretted the pygmy body to decay,
> And o'er-informed the tenement of clay.'

Different alike in his physical bulk, the coarseness of his mind and his enthusiasm for autocracy, was Lauderdale the ugly Scot whose erudition and caustic wit was a striking contrast to his ungainly speech and non-existent manners. A Covenanter in his youth, he was now an Episcopalian by expediency, but the Presbyterian slough was difficult to cast and he welcomed the King's talk of a change of religious policy. He had an army in Scotland which Charles might well use if his southern subjects were recalcitrant. He was the worst possible influence on the Duke of York, who reacted at once to this talk of an armed force, and was attracted both by Lauderdale's bluffness that might be mistaken for honesty, and his shrewd wit which appealed to the Duke in contrast to his own slowness of thought.

Two years of political finesse intervened between the visit to Dover and the only active steps Charles took to put into effect the clauses of the ill-starred Treaty. The temper of James's life was subdued by calamity; death played the ground-bass through the uncertain months. His mother had died in France in 1669; the news had been brought to the royal brothers as they hunted in the New Forest. Erratic in temper though she had been, they remembered in death only her vivid and loving self. James, who had been a difficult child, for that very reason had been her favourite son. She had gone, and a year later, her youngest child had died also. Charles and James were left alone. Behind them lay the memory of dangers shared with the others, and all the strength of Stuart clanship bound them by invisible bonds, which no divergence of opinion or character could shatter. At crises in the future as in the past they could not fail each other. Those who later caballed against the Duke, relying upon the surface friction often apparent between him and Charles, forgot that holding them together were the hands of those who had gone, their murdered father, the mother who had been a gay princess, Elizabeth and young Gloucester, Mary and Minette.

At the end of 1670, James told the King that his wife had been reconciled to Rome. Her father had written to her from exile, agonised by his daughter's desertion of the Anglican faith, 'the best-constituted church and the most free from error in Christendom'. 'You will,' he declared, 'bring irreparable dishonour on your father, and your husband and ruin on your children.' But Anne Hyde was facing eternity; neither pleading nor argument affected her. On New Year's Eve she was taken seriously ill and suffered intermittently throughout a miserable spring. A girl-child, born in February, 1671, did not live, and Edgar, the baby Duke of Cambridge, was rapidly losing strength. Anxiety for him lessened Anne's powers of resistance. In March, there was some improvement in both the invalids and the doctors held out hopes of their recovery, but on the last day of the month the Duchess died.

Early in the morning, in a private visitation, she had been fortified by the rites of the Catholic Church. Later a Church of England divine was sent to offer her consolation, and if possible, to wring from her an admission that she still adhered to the Anglican faith. But, to his credit, he attempted little when he saw the Queen sitting by her friend's bedside and had been briefly told by James that his wife had become a Catholic. Death was present in the chamber and it was no time for wrangling. Anne was impatient of his approaches, recalling, perhaps, how once before in her pain a bishop had leant across her bed and questioned her. But the agony of her first labour had ended in joy: this agony bore her into darkness. Could the secret rite of unction she had undergone sustain her in her final need? She struggled for faith, and as her failing life dimmed the pain of her body, her mind was pierced with grief and terror and she called for the man, who once had loved her, like a child calling for his mother in the night. With a last cry of anguish, she faced the unknown. 'Duke, Duke, death is terrible; death is very terrible.' And so she passed.[1]

Three months later, James's only son died at Richmond. He was buried at night; the body was brought privately by water to Westminster, and there he was interred 'with the rest'. It was a sad ending to the romance that had begun at The Hague twelve years before. For the Duke, it meant the end of his sense of security. In spite of his infidelities, Anne had given him a background, a feeling of someone in tune with himself from whom he could derive guidance or consolation. Her death and the failure of the Grand Design initiated at Dover marked the end of his years of achievement. For the rest of his life, he was alone amid crowds; one who learnt to hate because he had been soured by hatred. But his wife, in her death, had at least shown him clearly the next step he should take. If he made the requisite sacrifice and adhered openly to the faith he believed to be true, he might find sanctuary from the blows of fortune and power to live a changed life. He proved brave enough to make the sacrifice, but some lack in him of grace or self-forgetfulness prevented him from emerging sane and sweet from the struggle the sacrifice entailed.

In the spring of 1672, the King acted. On March 15th, he issued a Declaration of Indulgence, suspending the

[1] See the account in *Burnet's History*, I. 156–7, *et alia*.

ecclesiastical laws and permitting freedom of worship. Anxious critics were not slow to point out that while Protestant dissenters were ordered to apply to the secretary's office for a licence for their chapels, Catholics, who were allowed private worship, needed no licence and were not subject to control. But it was not only fear of religious change which troubled the nation, with it went dislike of so extensive a use of the prerogative. Old Commonwealth principles stirred uneasily under the veneer of post-Restoration royalism, and the very people who benefited from the Indulgence were most keenly conscious of the challenge to Parliamentary supremacy. With joy, they welcomed their co-religionists from the prisons that had held them and the long-suffering congregations, that could now stand in the open, were never again crushed out of existence, but their joy was subdued and their hearts were anxious, as the summer came and went and by a renewed prorogation Charles postponed meeting the Parliament that might legalise but would more probably denounce his action.

Two days after the Indulgence, England declared war on the Dutch, who were already preparing for a French invasion. In May, for the last time, James sailed out at the head of an English fleet. He was delighted to learn that the Dutch were already at sea under de Ruyter, to him 'the greatest commander of his times'. All the doubts and the tragedies of the last few years fell from his tired soul, as the burden fell from the back of the Pilgrim, of whom the Tinker Bunyan wrote in Bedford gaol. He bent his whole mind to the glorious task on hand, in the last carefree moments of his life.

Through the mists and sand-banks at the entrance of the Channel, the two fleets manœuvred in hope of an engagement. The Duke proved himself no great strategist, for his power as a commander lay rather in the influence of his dogged courage, than in any subtle generalship. By retreating into Southwold Bay to revictual, he let himself be trapped. He had been joined by a French squadron, and had wished to stand out to sea, but he allowed himself to be over-persuaded by the Captain of his flag-ship. Once in the bay, the French and English officers fraternised with a blind eye to the danger of sudden attack, while York and Sandwich shared uneasily in the uncongenial day of pleasure. De Ruyter did not miss his opportunity; at two o'clock on the morning of the 28th of May, the alarm was sounded; the Dutch were upon them and half their ships were out of action in the Bay. It was a tribute to the spirit of the English fleet that such as could stood out in battle array, and in spite of heavy losses, more than held their own. James was on board the *Prince*; when she was put out of action he transferred the Admiral's flag and his presence to the *St. Michael*, where his heroic example inspired a resistance so unshaken that at last de Ruyter drew off his fleet and ended the uncertain fight. But while the battle still raged, the *St. Michael* foundered; jumping into a small boat, James was rowed across to the *London*, a perilous voyage under enemy fire that lasted three-quarters of an hour. Sandwich in like straits refused to leave his ship, and lost his life in a despairing effort to re-establish a reputation that his Cavalier critics had attempted to tarnish.

James, returning to Whitehall, was greeted as the hero of the fight. Pæans of praise delighted his unaccustomed ears, and the florid versifiers acclaimed him:

'. . . When your feet shall bless our English ground
Our thankful hearts as in all duty bound
With shouts of joy may echo and resound.'

The fates, however, did not permit him to crown his campaign with a great naval victory. In council, he urged a vigorous offensive but Rupert and Shaftesbury opposed his plans. The summer was wasted in a fruitless pursuit of the Dutch East India fleet, but when in the autumn the English returned to harbour, ridden with the scurvy, it was only by an appeal to his subordinates that the Duke vetoed his opponents' suggestion that now three months too late was the time for a pitched battle. His dislike of Shaftesbury, antipathetic to him in his whole personality, was now aggravated by a craftsman's irritation with a bungler, who had made him spoil his job.

Shaftesbury's influence was supreme. In November he was made Lord Chancellor of England. The necessity of funds for the war would require a meeting of Parliament in the spring, and though Charles had given up all idea of a public restoration of Catholicism, he still hoped by an alliance with the dissenting classes for whose interests Shaftesbury stood, to prevent an attack on the Indulgence and so gain something for the prerogative from his experiment in political intrigue. Shaftesbury was a good Chancellor. His enemies admitted that seldom had justice been executed so ruthlessly and so impartially. He enjoyed the work and his ambitions had been realised beyond his highest dreams, but his restless spirit was not at peace. He sensed the existence of schemes in which he had no share, in the mysterious caution of Arlington and the meteoric advancement of Clifford. He had obtained an inkling of the King's preference for the Catholic faith, though he was still unaware of the secret of Dover. Clifford had become Lord Treasurer a few days after his own appointment, at James's instigation and to Arlington's disgust. Thus another cleavage was made in a cabal already at cross purposes.

It was a bad moment for the government to be divided. There was much for Parliament to criticise. Surprisingly, the Dutch had not been beaten. Pressed by the English at sea, with Flanders overrun by the French and invasion imminent, their very existence had been at stake. 'No man can conceive the state of Holland in this juncture, unless he can at the same time conceive an earthquake, a hurricane and the deluge.' But the Dutch were at their best in such an emergency. They cut the dykes, that the flooded fields about Amsterdam might encircle their capital with safety. And they thought of the great days of William the

Silent. The House of Orange had saved them then and it might save them again. There was a William of Orange still, who had reached man's estate. Let him lead them from despair to victory! A great wave of feeling swept over the country, before which politicians and potentates were powerless. The politicians, going with the tide, approached the English Government. If William of Orange were restored to power, would England treat for a separate peace with Holland? Arlington and Buckingham visited the states to see what could be done. They were mutually so jealous that for the moment they were inseparable!

Soon after their return, in August, 1672, William's chief political opponents, the de Witts, were set upon and murdered by the mob, who forgot years of honest work in an orgy of hatred at the oligarchs' insolence and the guilt of their failure. The upheaval of fear and disorder that followed could only be allayed by the restoration of William to the office of chief magistrate and leader of the Dutch armies. For him the de Witts' murder had been most convenient. He did not enquire further about it, for he was a cold-blooded youth who succeeded in combining a sincere, if narrow, religious life with cynical readiness to benefit when he could from the passions and treacheries of lesser men. His uncles in England had a sentimental regard for him as their sister's son, at which he must often have smiled, and his restoration to power took the heart out of the war so far as the King of England was concerned.

In addition to a disappointing war, the Commons were sure to attack certain unconventional financial expedients which bore the mark of Clifford's impatient temperament. In the spring of the year, the Council had authorised a stop of the Exchequer, which postponed the payment of interest on the loans borrowed from the goldsmiths. A considerable amount of ready money was thus raised, and how to find ready money was so overwhelming a difficulty for Stuart governments that an occasional ingenious device was not entirely blameworthy, but it was at best unorthodox and was not likely to escape attack. And above all there was the Declaration.

For the dangers inherent in the religious position had been made apparent by the end of 1672. James had had time to think things out, while he cruised upon the high seas. He had returned, invigorated in mind and body, with the clear eyes of a seafaring man, determined to put an end to the hiatus which his spiritual sojourn in the wilderness had imposed upon his life. The doubts which had still lingered at the time of his wife's death had not exactly been solved, but had ceased to exist while his mind lay fallow during the stress of action at the head of the fleet. Christmas was approaching, and the King urged him to attend Communion in state, as was customary upon that day. For some time James had omitted to take the Sacrament. Charles felt that a formal attendance on Christmas morning would allay the growing suspicion of the nation. He employed every subtlety of argument upon his brother, when he realised to his amazement that the Duke did not mean to comply. It was useless. James would not argue. But when Christmas Day came, and the King took the Sacrament, attended by the Lords of the Council, the gentlemen of the bedchamber and the officers of State, young Monmouth went with him, the son who could never be King, but the Duke of York, his brother, was not present. The incredible rumour leapt through the city, and the merchant of the quiet ways, who prayed each week at the dissenting-chapel in Holborn, was no less alarmed than his jovial neighbour, who attended the church of St. Bartholomew. Both alike ate his festive goose, with an unexpressed foreboding darkening his Yuletide. It was true: the heir was a Roman Catholic. They dare not surmise what eventual horror of persecution or revolt that fact foretold.

When Parliament met in February, the King played his strong suit. 'I shall take it very ill to receive contradiction in what I have done,' he stated with uncompromising vigour, 'and I will deal plainly with you. I am resolved to stick to my Declaration.' In the Lords, Shaftesbury poured out the full force of his eloquence, in a great war-speech beginning with the ringing words 'Delenda est Carthago.' But the Lords were not impressed; with the Commons they were hot upon the trail of the Indulgence. In Macaulay's incomparable phrases, 'the most opposite sentiments had been shocked by an act so liberal done in a manner so despotic. All the enemies of religious freedom, and all the friends of civil freedom found themselves on the same side.' Nor did the critics waste time in words. The Commons voted a supply of near a million pounds which would enable Charles to restore England's financial prestige and bring the war to a worthy conclusion. But the grant was suspended until the religious question was settled. A resolution was passed by a considerable majority denying the King's right as head of the Church to suspend ecclesiastical laws, and addresses were submitted to him urging him to recall the Indulgence. Concurrently a bill was introduced into the Commons, 'for preventing Dangers which may happen from Popish Recusants and Quieting the minds of his Majesty's good subjects'. It enacted that every government official should deny the Catholic doctrine of the Mass and take the Anglican Communion before entering upon his appointment. The crisis had come. In view of such a drastic measure it was evident that the Indulgence and the policy it stood for could only be upheld by force and an abrogation of constitutional rule. If this should be attempted, the armies raised to assist Louis against the Dutch and Lauderdale's Scottish troops would be available to crush opposition, while the equivocal attitude of the Protestant dissenters gave the venture a possibility of success.

Another than Charles might have risked it. He had vowed when Parliament met that he would stick to the Declaration, and he hated giving in. But not only were his convictions less potent than his desire for ease; he had too keen an appreciation of reality and too genuine a respect for solid English common sense, to derive any satisfaction from opposing his people's unanimous will. James was different. There was no elasticity in his principles and he saw only disgrace in surrender. Alone of the Stuarts he was an autocrat by nature. His grandfather's shrewd pedantry, his father's conventional morality, his brothers' sense of humour debarred each in turn from being happy in the role of tyrants; James could conceive no other form of kingship.

His only staunch ally in the Cabal was Clifford, whose conversion to Catholicism had become a matter of common talk, the malicious declaring in derision that he had set his heart already upon a Cardinal's hat. Clifford was in mental agony as he urged resistance. If the King gave in, the Test would pass. Then the Lord Treasurer could only save his career by deserting the Duke and his religion. Clifford's ambition and his honour were fighting a bitter duel. Lauderdale, a bully by instinct and reasonably certain that he would be able to save his own skin in emergency, agreed with the Duke and the Treasurer. But Buckingham was frightened. Shaftesbury was uncertain, and Arlington advocated surrender. His words at the Council-table as usual shrewd and to the point had their effect, but he had no intention of trusting to mere words. He was terrified. He would not be happy till the hare-brained scheme initiated at Dover was scotched beyond hope of survival. The Test he surveyed with equanimity, for he desired Clifford's downfall only one whit less eagerly than his own safety; both might be endangered if a fit of Stuart obstinacy attacked his capricious sovereign. He would take no risks.

Arlington knew the best way to the King of England's heart. Castlemaine's day was over. At Dover, a vivacious maid-in-waiting in his sister's suite had attracted Charles's roving eye. A few months later, Louise de Querouaille had returned to England and it was at Lord Arlington's country-house at Euston that she had stayed until her unexpected scruples had been overcome. After a mock-marriage with the King she had become his acknowledged mistress and was created Duchess of Portsmouth. Louise considered herself no strumpet like Nell Gwynne; she thought of herself as *maîtresse en titre*, entitled to respect, and as Louis's unofficial ambassador was prepared to interfere in politics. Charles, who refused to have his love affairs organised, smiled at her pretensions and never let her rule him, but her wit and her intelligence made fast the bonds in which her beauty held him, and a wise politician stood well with 'Madam Carwell'. To her Arlington appealed in his quandary. It was clearly to the interest of the French King that Charles should be at peace with his Parliament, so that supplies should be forthcoming for the still inconclusive war. Louise agreed: and within a few days a secret message from Louis was whispered by his fair envoy into Charles's ear, its peremptory tones softened by her blandishments. The King's mind was made up. On the evening of the 7th of March, 1673, a year after it had first been issued, Charles called for the Declaration to be brought to him in council. Standing apart for a moment from the drama which he had created, he looked round on his anxious and expectant ministers, on Rupert expiating the battles of his youth in an old age of loyalty to the people of England, on Shaftesbury puzzled and ill at ease, while Arlington whispered in his ear a hint of the secret treaty at Dover to change the Chancellor's dubiety into the flaming hate of a man who has been tricked, at Clifford and the Duke, their backs against the wall, refusing to believe in their imminent defeat.

With the resolve that never again would he be mastered by emotion Charles broke the seal of the Declaration! That which might have cost the lives of men, had become a scrap of worthless paper.

Clifford fought a last round against the Test. When the bill came up to the Lords, still the more important centre of Parliamentary debate, he spoke with vehemence against the measure, emulating Shaftesbury's Latin oratory, as he uttered the words of opprobrium 'monstrum horrendum ingens'. But Shaftesbury spoke on the other side and to those who listened he spoke with more authority. Clifford was a suspect Catholic and the Duke's man.

The Test passed, and at the end of the session, it received the King's assent. Every Catholic in the King's service, from the Admiral of England downwards, must choose between his religion and his job. The citizens of London, their interest stimulated by proximity to Whitehall, by the close interaction of politics and trade and their incurable Cockney curiosity, watched the drama of public life as they watched a cock-fight or a football match. 'What would the Duke do now?' The answer soon came. On June 15th, 1673, James sought an audience with the King and with tears in his eyes surrendered his signs of office as Lord-Admiral and Commander-in-Chief and Warden of the Cinque Ports of England.

The fleet went out to fight the Dutch with Rupert in command. The men were sullen and the officers insolent. In three uncertain battles they failed to outmatch de Ruyter, and the war ended as indeterminately as its predecessor. Pepys and his associates continued the task of reformation and organisation at Tower Hill. But the Duke was debarred from the work, which had been the most beneficial influence in a life meant for action. His enforced idleness soured his nature and a wanton streak of cruelty debased his character. This deterioration was gradual and was checked at first by the excitement of his second marriage and the fact that he still succeeded in influencing politics through his presence in council and his friendship with Lauderdale. But the process, which the cruel attacks of the Whigs completed in 1679 and 1680, was begun by the Test of 1673. To most men, with the years comes the realisation of failure, of the inconceivable fact that they are much as other men, faced with the obligation to make the best of poor achievements. Then, two things can establish them, their faith and their work. James, grievously disappointed at the failure of the Grand Design, was denied the solace of work. Nor did the faith for which he had made the sacrifice, give him that abiding sense of joy and peace, the gifts of the indwelling Spirit, which have empowered the lives of many who suffered for their religion. 'He rideth easily who is carried by the grace of God.' But the mistakes of all parties, the political doctrines of the Jesuits under whose influence James fell, and the embittering effect of unchristian persecution had made his religion a cause to be championed rather than a cross to be endured; a system to be established by designs and secured by force, rather than a source of quiet and abiding comfort. Perhaps because it was thus secularised and soiled it failed to give him the power to change his life, for which he had hoped. Sexual indulgence still made an overpowering appeal to him; he still failed as completely as before to sympathise with the underdog or to envisage any other way than force for dealing with another point of view. The religious zeal of a priest, superimposed on the mentality of a military officer, produced a curiously contradictory personality, which the intellectuals satirised and against which the progressives railed. But he had been honest in an age when honesty was not a fashionable virtue. Whatever sins James committed in later years, however justifiably the people of England turned him off his throne, they have done him less than justice in forgetting that at the prime of his life, he had to make the choice between a small sin and a great sacrifice. Charles did not hesitate to practise the nominal conformity which his position required. All the arguments of expediency urged the same course on James. Without hesitation, he did what he thought was right, and no threats of exclusion, no exile, no danger to his life or throne ever made him waver.

The Lord Treasurer Clifford was a man after the Duke's

heart. His conversion was yet little more than hearsay and his ambition was common knowledge. The curiosity was intense as to whether he would conform. One Sunday a rumour ran round the town that he was about to attend Communion. The crowds gathered to catch a glimpse of him. He did not appear. Instead came the amazing news that he had lain down his staff of office. Some muttered that he had 'warped to Rome' a long time since; others such as his good friend Evelyn were confident 'he forbore more from some promise he had entered into to gratify the Duke, than from any prejudice to the Protestant religion'. He retired for a month to Tunbridge and there his friend hastened to visit him, knowing how reluctantly Clifford must have yielded his life's ambition. Breaking for once from pleasant formalities into a genuine expression of feeling Evelyn wrote later in his memoirs: 'This I am confident, grieved him to the heart, and at last broke it; for though he carried with him music and people to divert him, and when I came to see him, lodged me in his own apartment and would not let me go from him, I found he was struggling in his mind. . . .' As men and animals will when they are sorely hurt, Clifford turned to his own country. Coming up to town, he gathered together the pictures he had collected with such loving care and said good-bye to his friends, with the sad prophecy: 'I will never see this place, this city or court again.' Then he went down to Devonshire. Near to the prosperous town of Chudleigh, at Ugbrooke where his forefathers had lived, he had built a house of fine proportions, through whose western windows he could watch the distant hills of Dartmoor. Eastward the ridge of Haldon, with its regiment of pines, hid him from the valley of the Exe. There in the place he had made beautiful in the days of his worldly success, he fought for peace of mind and lost the battle. Life held no more for him: he would challenge eternity. One morning his manservant, dismissed from his master's presence in a manner that seemed to him unusual, returned in anxiety to the bedchamber. The door was locked. A blurred shape showed through the small keyhole. The man broke down the door, horrified fear giving strength to his arm. Clifford hung by his cravat to the tester of his bed. As the manservant cut him down, he vomited blood. Instantly he rallied, and as his eyes fell on the beauty of tree and sky without he smiled and spoke: 'Well: let men say what they will, there is a God, a just God above.' In that faith, he died.[1]

Clifford died; but the Duke lived on. At once less sensitive and more confident than his friend, he endeavoured to wrest from an uncertain future the victory that the years after Dover had denied. For no soldier can fight and believe in defeat, and James as a soldier meant to fight it out. Conscious of his own rectitude, he could not under stand, that others who opposed him had religious principles for which they would make sacrifices, and political beliefs that were more than shibboleths.

[1] See John Evelyn's *Diary*, 18 Aug. 1673; on whose testimony the story of suicide depends.

PART III

STRIFE

CHAPTER VI

MARY OF MODENA

'Poor Princess! born under a sullen star,
To find such welcome when you came so far!'
– Marvell – *Advice to a Painter.*

'White-liver'd Danby calls for his swift jackal
To hunt down's prey, and hopes to master all –
Clifford and Hide before had lost the day;
One hanged himself and t'other ran away.
'Twas want of wit and courage made them fail,
But O[sbor]ne and the Duke must needs prevail.'
– Marvell – *An Historical Poem.*

LIFE goes on in spite of man's occasional despair. The individual, emerging from a crisis, finds to his somewhat rueful amazement that he must and can engage as before upon ordinary affairs. The day's routine enfolds him in its narcotic spell, until such time as he is whole again and, in experience's despite, plans once more for the future. So it was with James, Duke of York. His Christmas denial of the Anglican faith in an age when kingdoms were weighed in the balance with a Mass, had been the visible sign of years of spiritual tumult; the surrender of his public offices in the summer of 1673 turned the key upon the past. The events of that spring had shown that neither ease nor glory but the hard path of isolation and suspicion lay before a Popish prince. And deliberately, James had chosen the way of sacrifice.

Yet when the autumn came, the full tide of life flowed in again. James had been a widower for over two years, and the question of his second marriage had been debated for some time in diplomatic circles. The uncertain state of Europe, alarmed but as yet impotent against the threat of Louis's domination, gave to the English alliance an artificial value. Unlikely to accomplish much in military exploits on the Continent, her naval strength and the weight of her diplomacy might make all the difference between triumph and frustration to Louis, between resistance and surrender to his victims. Archduchesses of Germany and Italian princesses, nominees of the Emperor, protégées of France made a goodly array of fair women, from whom the Duke could make his choice of a second bride; as early as November 1672, his friend Charles Mordaunt, Earl of Peterborough, had set out for Innsbruck to negotiate the match which appeared the most attractive and to ask for the hand of the beautiful Austrian duchess, Claudia Felicitas. To the King's mind, it was high time his brother re-married for he had already given him some uneasy moments. Arabella's sway was weakening, and soon after his wife's death, the Duke had involved himself in a flirtation with Lady Bellasis, a woman of no outstanding charm, with whom James was so infatuated that he actually gave her a written promise of marriage. The King's innate dignity as well as his sense of humour was outraged by this repetition of the folly of 1659; at the age of forty, it was time for the Duke to cease behaving like an emotional young man. It was made clear to the lady concerned that the paper must be destroyed. James recovered from his love affair, and remembered he was a prince. Peterborough went on his embassy. But Claudia Felicitas was not for the Duke. The negotiations foundered on a clause familiar to modern ears; the Emperor required a guarantee from England that she would give armed assistance if the states of Germany were attacked by France. Charles, though he was not averse to frightening Louis by an independent alliance, had no wish to offend him to such a dangerous extent. The problem of how to carry full weight in European councils, without sacrificing Englishmen to the age-long jealousy of France and Germany in a futile war, was already a vital concern of the English government. On this occasion, the difficulty solved itself. While Charles was still hedging, the Empress died and the Emperor put an end to diplomatic inanities by marrying Claudia Felicitas himself.

Peterborough spent the summer touring Europe, interviewing with non-committal tact various possible ladies. The Duke objected to the sound of some of them; one possessed an intriguing parent whom the Duchess of Portsmouth refused to have in England; it was an ambassador of confused mind and jaded nerves who came to Modena in July 1673. There was a girl there, called Mary Beatrice d'Este on whom the choice of his capricious master seemed at last to have fallen.

In the days of Italy's grandeur, when the supreme intellects of a re-awakened world thronged her cities and did not flinch from challenging the mystery of the Universe; when those who glorified God with their hands made lovely the places of their earthly sojourning, and the poets adventured in the spirit as other voyagers sailed the uncharted seas, the house of d'Este had not been unworthy of its place in the hierarchy of Italian princes. When disaster fell upon the country, and moral instability wrecked a brilliance that had become superficial by decay, the princes of d'Este suffered with their fellows and a secularised Papacy seized their capital, Ferrara. The Duke of Modena, head of a younger branch, intrigued with France and shared in welcoming the foreign invaders, who for the next three centuries were to give to Lombardy the horrors of continuous war and disillusion of the spirit. But when the Earl of Peterborough came to Modena, he found a town still prosperous and erect in the knowledge of its own vitality. It lay among fertile fields in a low-lying plain in the very centre of northern Italy, while over the roofs towered the fine cathedral as over the country hung the shadow of the Papacy. The young Duke played, like a child with toy soldiers, with a live army of gorgeously apparelled men; his uncle Rinaldo d'Este played with politics and craved a Cardinal's hat; his mother, a woman of wisdom, ruled her family and Modena.

Mary Beatrice, the Duke's sister, was not yet quite fifteen; and though her tall slim figure gave her an older air, the gentle hesitation of her bearing proclaimed her inexperienced youth. 'She will suffice' thought Peterborough when, after many set-backs, he was allowed to meet her. He noted her pale complexion and her mouth too large for beauty; but he forgot any formal defect of feature in the perfect oval of her face and the loveliness of her eyes. Under the heavy crown of her jet-black hair, the dark eyes shone with a light and sweetness that moved the courtier to uncustomary emotion. He felt in them some power that physical beauty alone could not give, a force that had in it something divine: 'power to kill and power to save'. Of the quick wit, the warm affections, the deep religious feeling and the Italian craving for beauty and joy that lay behind the quiet exterior, as yet he could know nothing; but he had immediate proof of the strength of the young girl's character. When the purpose of his embassy was revealed to her, she firmly declined the honour. She had never heard of the Duke of York, and to her, England was an unknown and barbaric land. She had vowed herself to a convent, 'to another sort of life, out of which she could never think she should be happy'. Why, she cried, should she be forced against her inclinations into a marriage, into which many others would delight to enter? Tears came into her eyes as she repeated that 'there were princesses enough in Italy, that would not be unworthy of so great an honour, and that from the esteem they might have thereof would deserve it much better than she could do'. In Peterborough's own words, 'the Earl began to be a little peek'd'.

In the ensuing weeks he had reason to be seriously perturbed. Mary Beatrice's reluctance proved to be no mere tactical manœuvre; the persuasions alike of her mother and of the agents of Louis of France left her unmoved; one who had promised herself to a life of spiritual devotion did not so easily forgo her vows. All the emotional turmoil of adolescence combined with a natural fear of leaving the country of her birth, with an unexpressed repugnance to the suit of a middle-aged widower and with a true religious vocation, to steel her against the commands and exhortations of her friends. But there was one more august than they who had not yet spoken. The greatest potentate in Christendom bent from his throne to plead with the girl princess. The Pope wrote to Mary Beatrice, and told her God's will. Not for her the calm of the nunnery and the sacraments of prayer and praise; England had deserted the ancient Faith; by her, England must be reconverted. 'We therefore earnestly exhort you . . . to place before your eyes the great profit which may accrue to the Catholic faith in the above-named kingdom through your marriage, and that inflamed with zeal for the good which may result, you may open to yourself a vaster field of merit than that of the virginal cloister.'[1]

There was no alternative, and the Princess submitted. She was a curious child, whose generous temper impelled her to give abundantly whether in love or hate. The well-meant severity of the mother, whom she adored but who had always disparaged any excessive display of affection, drilled her and her brother into an obedience, only to be obtained at a price. In endeavouring to shape her daughter into the mould of a perfect princess, the Duchess Laura had twisted awry a lovable but wayward nature. Mary Beatrice never forgot the meals of her youth, when she refused to drink her soup and her mother battled with her till she complied. To her, they had been purgatory, ending only when she left the table in tears to find solace in the more comfortable presence of her kindly governess. When the Princess was nine, the governess left in order

[1] This account of the marriage negotiations is based on Haile's *Mary of Modena*. Mrs. Strickland includes the details of Mary Beatrice's youth in her *Lives of the Queens of England*.

to enter a Carmelite convent. The force of the little girl's grief alarmed even her Spartan mother, and eventually it was arranged that she should continue her education at the convent. The quiet serenity of souls dedicated to Christ made an irresistible appeal, in contrast to her own hot conflicts and disordered will, and her girlish passion for her governess and the young aunt who was also intended for a religious life made it natural for Mary Beatrice to wish herself a nun.

Her mother watched her uneasily. Her clean-cut pagan renaissance mind knew too well how much a princess needed the virtues of courage and self-control. It gave her no pleasure to refuse her children sweets, or to exact prompt obedience to her least command. One day the training would stand them in good stead; in that assumption she went on, and in the realisation of that truth Mary Beatrice thanked her in her heart, when she had storms to weather that would have broken any who had not been disciplined in youth. Yet no severity, nor the example of a princely reserve could instil into her the necessity of disguising her emotions. She wept with abandon, when the pressure of her friends and the Pope's command had extorted her reluctant consent to her betrothal. After her marriage by proxy on the 30th of September and the tiring series of feasts and rejoicings which ensued, when the time arrived for her departure from Italy, she collapsed in a paroxysm of tears and temper that would have disgraced a child of seven. Nervous exhaustion and homesickness, rather than any reasoned grief, had overwhelmed her, and when after two days misery for all concerned, she had wearied herself into acquiescence, she turned to her mother like a tired child and refused to leave home, unless she would accompany her. As Regent of Modena, the Duchess was needed at home, as a mother, she rejoiced at a last chance of helping the child who was growing away from her so rapidly. On October 5th, the Princess's fifteenth birthday, the royal party left Modena and journeyed through Savoy and southern France to Paris. The excitement of finding herself a young person of importance, of seeing King Louis himself and receiving visits of state from noble ladies of the court, proved an effective cure for the misery of the very young and very human bride, but she had been through too much to stand the strain and excitement of the journey and fell sick of dysentery, thus delaying her passage to England and possibly laying the seeds of the ill-health that was to darken much of her later life.

The Duke of York anxiously awaited her arrival. Throughout the early autumn an enraged Parliament had protested against the Catholic match and had been prorogued and rendered innocuous by a King, insulted at the suggestion that the marriages of royalty were in any way the concern of the common people. But in the streets of London they were burning effigies of the Pope, whose bastard, they cried, had fathered Mary of Modena. Unconscious alike of the coarse jibes of the proletariat and the honest disapproval of 'the better sort of citizen', Mary Beatrice reached England on November 21st. On the sands of Dover the Duke her husband awaited her; upon her landing 'she took possession of his heart as well as his arms and was thence conducted to her lodging'. The marriage contract was ratified in the presence of the Bishop of Oxford, and five days later the royal couple reached London by sea.

The King came down from Whitehall to meet them on the river and with a few gracious words won the heart of his new relation. 'He was always kind to me,' she said, years afterwards. She had need of his kindness at first. She was shy and disappointed. She had been told that the Duke was handsome, but the new fashion of the perruque seemed to accentuate his lined and angular features. They bore the marks, not only of the mental struggle of the previous spring, but of the smallpox from which he had suffered six years previously. He was too old for her and too diffident in speech; her chatter seemed impertinent in his presence, and he treated her more like a playfellow for his daughters than as a wife. But Charles made her happy, responded to her southern gaiety and wit, and yet paid her a respect that gave her confidence; she felt that she could easily have fallen in love with him! Charles himself was charmed by her innocence and her ingenuous youth, amused by her refusal to wear rouge, and impressed by the calm dignity of her behaviour in the maelstrom of court jealousies and intrigues. He was also determined that the public hostility to the marriage should not be reflected in the treatment of Mary Beatrice at Whitehall. The presence of her mother did not simplify matters, and at first some Protestant dames were inclined to forget Christian ethics in their eagereness to express disapproval. 'Most of our great ladies have been rude in their behaviour to the Duchess of Modena, who when she was allowed to sit in the Queen's presence caused many of them to hump and withdraw themselves.' With such as these, Mary Beatrice could not hope to achieve popularity. The undisguised piety of her religious observances condemned her in their sight. But the King's favour assured her recognition, and after her mother returned to Italy her position improved. At St. James's, the customary home of the Duke and Duchess, her levees were well attended and Charles himself began to make use of her apartments for those brief but pertinent discussions with French Ambassador or wavering statesmen, by which he liked to conduct his political affairs.

Early in 1674 James took his bride for a royal progress, to show her the spring in Southern England. At Windsor in the lush beauty of summer and in the open stretches about Newmarket when the autumn came, Mary Beatrice soon found that her new life was far from being the exile she had feared. She derived a growing pleasure from the company of her stepdaughters, and they repaid her impetuous affection with a comradely regard. But perhaps she never knew them as well as she thought she did. They were so different from herself. Mary was as English as she was Italian, reserved where she was impulsive, conventional and controlled when she ached for colour. Yet this they had in common. Mary Beatrice was made for love and only in abandoning herself fully to the service of the person or the cause she loved could her nature achieve fruition. Mary expressed her emotions more quietly so that perhaps they would only appear under the pressure of external events, but her happiness also would depend on her chance to love and serve. Anne was little more than a dumpling schoolgirl, not long returned from France; the first stirrings of adolescent emotion were in her case to be centred on one of her stepmother's waiting-maids, young Sarah Jennings, the sister of the beauty Frances. Anne never grew beyond that first infatuation.

James was very fond of his daughters, and Mary Beatrice realised that she had not been fair to him. Each month she grew to like him better. His apparent strength and his obvious honesty seemed to provide a frame for her own grace and fire; the certainty of his political convictions and his courage in the face of opposition enabled her to admire and respect him, and their common religion steadily bound them together. There were not wanting those who thought it their duty to inform the Duchess of her husband's irregular *amours*. She was very innocent of the world, and at first she was heart-broken. She reproached her husband in impassioned words; though it needed no rebuke to stimulate his sense of sin. But as she grew accustomed to the fashions of the court, Mary Beatrice grew, not to tolerate, but to forgive even her husband's vice, while he for a time controlled himself with better success than usual, pleased with his bride and passionately desirous of the children that might be born to them. After the first uneasy months and the break of her mother's departure, the young Duchess enjoyed four years of peace and pleasure that seemed in retrospect the happiest in her life. She danced and played cards, and regarded it her greatest sin that in response to the persuasions of elder women she allowed herself to play for money. She silenced ill-will by her disarming goodness and like the Lady of Milton's 'Comus', secure in her own virtue, passed unsullied through the licentious court.

Occasionally she made mistakes. After all, she was barely sixteen; she had no experience of life, beyond her mother's tutelage and the convent walls of Modena, and her impetuous temper had been subdued but not eradicated. She quarrelled with the Queen of England. A dispute about the use of the chapel of St. James's had occasioned the first coolness. Perhaps Queen Catherine who knew she held the people's affections through her virtue in the face of loneliness and neglect was unwilling to welcome another alien princess, who would no doubt suffer neglect and indubitably had virtue, and in addition could rival in charm and beauty the adventuresses it was so easy to despise and so hard to overthrow. But the Duchess was indiscreet. When a new star appeared in the firmament of court ladies, the wicked and irresistible Marie de Mancini, the niece of Mazarin and a kinswoman of the Duchess Laura, Mary Beatrice put family ties before morals and called upon the new-comer, only to discover the difficulty of retracing a step out of the straight. For the Queen was bitterly offended and cut her sister-in-law in full sight of the court, while the Duchess of Portsmouth had a fit of the tantrums and insisted that she also should receive a formal call. Mary Beatrice 'left cards' at her apartments but did not see her. Such small whirlpools varied the calm flow of her gay existence, but they were forgotten in the joy of her first child who was born in the New Year of 1675. She tried to make amends for past mistakes by christening her baby after the Queen. But she committed a grave error of judgment, in causing the child to be baptized privately into the Catholic Church immediately after birth. This she knew was contrary to the wishes of the King and the instructions of her husband. For James showed his customary submission to authority in agreeing that his children belonged to the State and must be brought up in the state religion. The Duchess's precipitate action showed, not only the unexpected wilfulness that underlay her charm; it indicated a tenacity of purpose in religious matters that boded ill for Protestant fortunes, should she obtain a hold over the mind of the man who would one day be King of England.

But on this occasion she had another to deal with, who, when roused, was as tenacious as herself. Charles was fond of his sister-in-law, but he would stand no nonsense. The baby Catherine Laura was carried off and baptized again into the Anglican communion. No attention whatever was paid to the mother's protests. She might declare it to be sacrilege; Charles called it common sense. But she did not take the rebuke too hardly. She was too happy, and her joy in motherhood was as genuine and as fervent as her first agony at leaving home and her subsequent delight in the pleasures that fell to a Duchess's lot.

Wrapped up in her own life with the healthy selfishness of youth, in her growing love for her husband, the supreme experience of child-bearing and the quiet joy of her religious devotions, Mary Beatrice knew little of the turmoil which her coming had stirred in the nation. To the Protestants, her marriage with the Duke had been incontrovertible proof that their Church was endangered. James had chosen a bride approved by the Pope and recommended by King Louis. Thus he had associated himself with the two bodies, most suspected by the average Englishman – the Papacy and France. Already hostility to the Dutch was fading, as business men realised that it was better to live and let live in quietude than to cut one's own throat in crushing one's trade rival. Peace was made at the beginning of 1674; the latter half of Charles II's reign witnessed the rapid growth of that antipathy between France and England, dormant for two centuries, which was to dominate the succeeding age. By his love for France, founded partly on his friendship for Louis and partly on his closer sympathy with French political practices than with the more democratic institutions of his own land, James alienated himself from his countrymen as surely as he did by his religious convictions. That he meant to abide by his principles appeared by his marriage and by the conspicuous part he played in the King's councils. When a friend advised him to placate his enemies by retiring for a while into the country, the Duke answered with the fighting instincts of a soldier that nothing should prevent him from attending upon the King 'to render him every service in his power to which duty and honour obliged him'. He refused to be beaten by the Test Act. It had only diverted his attention from administrative work to the less arduous but more dangerous paths of politics, and at the committee of foreign affairs or at informal bedchamber conclaves, his vigorous advice frequently counteracted the more moderate counsels of less decided men.

There were some who pointed out that no Test or Parliamentary measure, which might bar the Duke from this or the other office, served any real purpose while he remained heir to the throne. There was wild talk in the air. One day a stranger at a tavern in Fleet Street refused to drink the King's health, 'speaking many slighting and opprobrious words of him' and adding 'that if they would begin with the honest Duke of York's health, he would pledge it with all his heart'. It needed but a few bold spirits who would go beyond words, a regicide's stroke, or merely the natural chances of mortality, and James would be king and all good Protestants would lie at the mercy of foreign assassins. For fear and fancy played their part in these conjectures, which had none the less a solid basis in the realisation that James's change of religion meant the prospect of a Catholic king. Unless he were excluded from the succession by Act of Parliament! Why not? Was not

Parliament supreme? The words might savour of treason but they began to be spoken, at first on the impulse of the moment and then with deliberation as the revolutionary idea established itself in the minds of those who believed in facing the issues clearly.

As yet however these were a minority. Not only was James the King's brother, well-nigh unassailable in the panoply of royalty and hereditary right. He was also a man of character, respected by the majority for his past achievements as soldier and as admiral. Above all, the King's support never wavered. At times there were rumours of disagreement. On one occasion two seamen 'very honest ignorant fellows', found themselves in sore trouble for repeating 'abominable words', 'that the King and the Duke of York had a falling out and that the Duke had stabbed the King, so that he was either dead or dying, and that the Duke was fled into France, and that the whole city of London was up in arms and much more to this purpose'. The men had obtained their news from two women of Southwark who had enlivened the drab existence of prostitutes by circulating terrifying rumours.

But though Charles was undoubtedly annoyed that his brother's unfortunate conscience was giving him such inconvenience, he could not brook interference with the Duke's right to counsel and in due course to succeed him. The King was at bottom a selfish and a vicious man, yet during the next ten years he displayed true virtue in his unwavering loyalty to a brother, with whom temperamentally he had little sympathy. Into his efforts on James's behalf he put all the tactical skill, the political sense and the knowledge of human nature which the Duke lacked. For his sake, he even imperilled the ease he valued more than power or reputation.

As yet, King and Duke had the upper hand. With the contrariness of public opinion, the rampant hostility of 1673-4 dwindled into acquiescence. Two brief and querulous sessions of Parliament in 1675, during which the two

Houses did little but quarrel between themselves, and a long prorogation till the spring of 1677, gave to James two years of peace and prosperity. His affairs flourished, and his influence grew; only his final abstention from any form of Anglican service indicated the growing strength of his love for the Catholic faith. The general slackening of tension in court and country during 1675 and 1676 was partly due to the increase in material prosperity. There was an indefinable atmosphere of well-being. 'Peace and plenty abounding everywhere, Great Albion stood the envy of her neighbouring nations' wrote James in his historical memoirs, while in the spring of 1675, those who frequented the court declared that they had never known the King and Duke 'in better health or better humour'.

Yet the seeds of future tragedy were already sown. There was one whose presence at court was a perpetual thorn in the flesh to the Duke of York. He too was James, the name by which the King loved to call him, the young Duke of Monmouth, his illegitimate son. Once, the Duke of York had liked the lad and had encouraged him in his desire to be a soldier and to learn his trade thoroughly in European campaigns. At the siege of Maestricht, Monmouth had done well and had returned to his father's court no longer a child to be petted, but a man of the world, handsome, lovable and brave. Even then James was slow to envy. But while Monmouth's blatant Protestantism and the assiduous rumours of his legitimacy made him the Duke's political rival, personally the young man was the very antithesis of his uncle, making human contacts with ease and success, full of generous instincts and joy in the business of life. James would have been a saint if he had not resented his growing influence. The breach widened steadily. Monmouth was ambitious not in the Duke's dogged way but with the unbalanced zeal of youth. He did not attempt to placate his uncle. He obtained for himself the office of General of the King's Forces, which had lapsed upon Albemarle's death. James had opposed the grant for many excellent reasons which in reality cloaked his own personal pique. When in the patent of appointment, Monmouth attempted to have the word 'natural' erased from the description of himself as the King's son, James was righteously indignant and probably for the first time realised the threat to his position as heir-apparent inherent in Monmouth's power and popularity. That danger would have been still greater had the latter's character been strengthened by some moral backbone. As it was, he lacked stamina and real ability; environment had done nothing to remedy the defects of hereditary and excessive vanity and a petulant desire to have his own way vitiated a kindly nature and an open-hearted friendliness.

With his other nephew William, Prince of Orange, the Duke of York had much more in common. He respected him for what he had accomplished, as well as loving him for his mother's sake. In spite of their divergences in politics and religion, they were both men of action who liked to see things done and above all they were both Stuarts. James felt that William could be relied upon not to 'let down' the family in Europe. They wrote to each other regularly, and when William had the smallpox, the Duke was genuinely alarmed. 'I shall be in very great pain till I hear of your being quite out of danger.' There were still fourteen years to run before the Revolution.

His days of prosperity were saddened for James by frustrated hopes of a son. Catherine Laura died at the end of 1675. A second child born in August, 1676, was again a girl. The Duke did not attempt to conceal his disappointment; for the Duchess the tragedy was more personal. She had made her acquaintance with Death, and her own child had been the victim. She was growing up. Her new baby, Isabel, was as precious to her as any son, and as the child grew in apparent health her own happiness returned. She would willingly have withdrawn from the enslaving routine of the court to spend every possible moment in the nursery at St. James's or at Richmond. In

1677, she was again pregnant and thus obtained a certain amount of privacy, but as the year passed, politics began to press in upon her. Tempers were rising, old hatreds flaming anew. The quiet years were over and they were not to come again.

. . . .

While Mary Beatrice had been learning to love her England, Charles was reconstructing the edifice of sovereignty, so nearly shattered by the French intrigues, the financial expedients and the military madness of the Cabal Government. He had turned again, where safety lay, to the old Cavaliers, the Church-and-State-men who had never yet failed the Stuarts. Clifford was dead and Shaftesbury flaunted it in opposition, Buckingham continued his peripatetic course between the apartments of Nell Gwynne and the homes of the leading Dissenters; Arlington, after defending himself in Parliament with unexpected control and dignity, exchanged power for security and accepted the office of Lord Chamberlain. Lauderdale alone remained, objectionable but unique, brutalising Scotland by his ruthless persecution of the Covenanters he had previously encouraged. The new Treasurer was a man from the north, Sir Thomas Osborne, who now became the Earl of Danby, and with Lauderdale and the Duke of York was said to govern everything. Danby grafted on to the old Cavalier ideal the business methods of a hard-headed Yorkshire man and the denial of moral standards, characteristic of the Restoration court. By cash payments, as well as by the more insidious methods of opportune promotions and a monarch's gracious word, he began the systematic corruption of the House of Commons and obtained a compact majority for the King, which neither the vindictive oratory of Shaftesbury nor the moral force of Russell sufficed to undermine. Danby was not the sort of man, of whom Charles could ever grow fond; he preferred a vagabond like Buckingham or an honest man of the Coventry breed: but he was grateful to him, grateful not only for his political services but for his sound work at the Treasury. In that sphere Danby was honest as well as efficient, and aided by the prosperous state of England's trade filled the royal coffers sufficiently to enable Charles to dangle his Parliamentary opponents on the strings of successive prorogations.

James agreed well with Danby in spite of religion. While his love for his new faith was growing and deepening so that when the eventual crisis came there should be no question of surrender, the Duke did not wish to thrust it upon the public notice. To him the maintenance of the Crown's power was a matter of paramount importance. As the champion of the royal prerogative, Danby had his support and his friendship. For unlike Charles, James could never distinguish between his personal and his political relationships. It was in the same capacity as joint defenders of autocracy that he welcomed the restoration of his old friend the Duke of Ormonde to the Lieutenancy of Ireland, and worked in harmony with the Secretary, Henry Coventry, the brother of his one-time friend and servant. Henry was more politically-minded than his brother William, with a shrewder sense of humour and perhaps even less emotional drive. Both essentially moderate men, they had adopted different sides in the political duel, William Coventry associating with the opposition without surrendering his independence, Henry giving loyal service to a King and a policy of which he frequently disapproved in detail. Always balanced in judgment, tolerant in statement and controlled in his personal life, in one thing only Henry Coventry indulged to excess, in sheer hard work either in the Secretary's office or in representing the government in a fractious House of Commons. He had little thanks for his pains, for he was the target of the opposition and too little of a courtier to move easily among his friends. But good men respected him, and as the centuries have swept away the ephemera of a superficial age, there stands to his credit in the archives of his country a goodly pile of official letter-books witnessing to the labour of devoted years, and some scattered shets of private correspondence, marred by not a single line of malice or ill-will.

While these men upheld the fortunes of the Crown, others, as varied as they, thundered at Westminster against the government. The leader of the Opposition in the House of Commons was the son and heir of the Duke of Bedford, a family soaked in the traditions of the English aristocracy. Proud, independent of spirit, with a keen sense of public duty and private obligations, Lord Russell atoned in character for what he lacked in genius. He condemned alike the extravagances of the Crown and the excesses of the proletariat; he was ready to defend the balance of the constitution against the claims of the prerogative or the insidious theories of Cromwell's political heirs. Others might hear and applaud the words of Algernon Sidney, idealist and Republican; others might succumb to Shaftesbury's fiery eloquence, justifying crooked means to attain a splendid goal; Russell stood aloof, a good Christian and an honest man, armoured in his own integrity.

It was not till the crisis of a few years later that the hated name of Whig came into use; the men of the Commons, who carried on the tradition of the Presbyterians of the Restoration and had criticised alike the dictatorship of Clarendon and the double dealing of the Cabal, were proud to be known as the country party in contradistinction to the creatures of the court. Andrew Marvell was their pamphleteer, and the lyricist of happier days sacrificed his muse to satirise the vices he detested. But the majority were moderate men, who stood for clean government, sound finance and a foreign policy consonant with the trade interests of the country. It was these men who now resented Louis's aggressions on the Continent as earlier they had resented the rivalry of the Dutch; and a war to enforce peace in Europe under the leadership of

William of Orange became their platform cry. At home Charles's self-indulgence alienated their sympathy and soured their loyalty. The honest hearts and the business heads of the sober English burgesses were alike exasperated when the royal coffers, filled by the chimney tax, were rapidly emptied to please His Majesty's whores.

The opposition to the Crown was equally strong in the House of Lords. The group of noblemen, who guided its debates were bound together not merely by intermarriage but by a common background of interests and education. Not far removed from the feudatories of the Middle Ages, they resented royal interference as a personal insult, while their hostility to Catholicism was partly a heritage from their forefathers, whose estates had been enlarged by the sequestration of the monasteries. Their association with the lawyers in the previous generation, when they had together opposed Charles I's innovations, and their reliance on the support in the lower House of the business men of the towns made them jealous of the sovereignty of the law and lenient towards Protestant dissent. A fundamental tenet of their faith was the conviction that Popery and slavery went hand in hand, that absolutism would not only offend their principles but would ruin their careers and that control of the legislature was of little avail if they did not by fair means or foul control the executive as well. In many cases, personal ambition made them vulnerable to the approaches of the King or the bribes of the French Ambassador; but such surrenders were likely to be short-lived, so essentially opposed were the interests of the aristocratic clique and of a sovereign who still founded his rule on the philosophy of divine right. Meanwhile, the organising genius of Shaftesbury welded the Lords into the leaders of a new political party, while he consolidated the rank and file by the propaganda of tracts and news-sheets and by debate and good-fellowship at coffee-house and Green Ribbon Club. Had coloured shirts been the fashion, his 'Brisk boys' would have worn green: young men of enterprise joined the ranks of this informal regiment of supporters and derived much pleasure from disturbing the streets of London.

Two men stood apart from the Church and State squirearchy whom Danby guided, and the country party whom Shaftesbury was transforming into the Whigs. George Saville, Viscount Halifax, had temperamentally much in common with his uncle and mentor, William Coventry; by his social position and marriage connections he was linked with the Whig lords. But he had infinitely more intellectual brilliance than the Coventrys, more state-craft than Russell, and a firmer sense of moral values than Shaftesbury. He applied to the mysteries of religion and the maelstrom of politics the keen scrutiny of a first-class academic brain; party shibboleths left him cold, and he preferred a moderate opponent to a violent friend. A desire to apprehend the truth impelled him to enquiry and decision, and some hardier strain in him, heritage of his north country ancestors, induced him to action in emergency. The very fact that he was remote from the waves of passion that were blinding and confusing other men made that action the more impressive, and his ability to put concisely on paper the reasons for his decision enabled him to influence many of the more sober sort of citizen, who had been alienated by his colleagues' excessive emotionalism. It was not therefore till after the tragic folly of the Popish Plot when the country was ready for calmer counsels, that Halifax dominated his contemporaries; even then, an intellectual reluctance to court the possibility of error made him loth to associate himself with any body of men or principles. He preferred to apply his brilliant genius to each occasion as it arose, declaring in a typical sentence, 'Circumstances must come in, and are to be made a part of the matter of which we are to judge; positive decisions are always dangerous, more especially in politics.' A respectful agnosticism characterised his religion. 'He was a Christian in submission and he believed as much as he could, and he hoped God would not lay it to his charge if he could not digest iron as an ostrich did, nor take into his belief things that would burst him.' Personally, he was an exhilarating companion, his wit as biting as any Restoration satirist's but free from the alloy of licentiousness; conscious of the true values of life, he esteemed a high moral code and the joy of friendship as man's most precious possessions. And yet, just as in politics the progressive bent of his intellect was hampered by an instinctive desire to conserve things as they were, while his ability to decide was clogged by his academic refusal to argue from the particular to the general, so in his personal relationships, in spite of his theories of goodwill, he lacked the warmth and the faith in humanity which would have made him a good friend. At once the greatest and the most disappointing of the men of the Restoration, he towered above his fellows like a Colossus, and failed to stride the world.

And finally there was Robert Spencer, second Earl of Sunderland, who served and betrayed in turn three Kings of England. His sister had been first wife to Halifax; his mother was Dorothy Sidney, Waller's 'Saccharissa'. His father died on Newbury field, one of the finest of the young Cavaliers. Robert himself was born in Paris in 1640 and his disturbed childhood and undisciplined youth helped, in him as in so many others, to sap his manhood of its moral fibre. Precocious and gifted, he studied in turn in Southern Europe and at Oxford; he married a rich heiress, the Earl of Bristol's daughter, and served his political apprenticeship on embassies in Spain and France. Now in the prime of his life, he was obviously a coming man; handsome in bearing, efficient in his employments, a politician *par excellence* and a delightful man of the world, his success seemed assured whether among the leaders of the opposition, with whom he was connected in so many ways, or at Whitehall where his ability and his readiness to court his betters made him a welcome guest.

Something there must have been in him, beyond mere good looks and business aptitude to justify the confidence which Charles, James and William placed successively in this wretched man, whose character his formal biographer sums up in the damning words: 'He has generally been considered, and probably with justice as the craftiest, most rapacious and most unscrupulous of all the politicians of the age.' Something remains unexplained about him, some mysterious power, either of brain or personality, which made greater men than he believe against the evidence of their own senses in his virtue and goodwill. Or was it, not that they believed him virtuous, but that all alike were ready to use to their own advantage the subtle wiles of this Prince of Politicians? If so, they reaped their own reward.

. . . .

The high-water mark of Danby's successful régime was the visit of William of Orange in October, 1677. The possibility of a marriage between him and the Princess Mary had been put forward in 1675, when Lord Ossory had accompanied a political embassy to Holland in order to broach the matter. Charles had chosen Ossory because, although as Ormonde's son his loyalty and his churchmanship were beyond suspicion, he was a close personal friend of the Duke's and one of those happy men who are incapable of giving offence. But in 1675, William had not decided whether he wished to marry his English cousin; two years later he came to London with his mind made up, and characteristically had the whole matter settled within a month. He was the only person who did know his own mind when he first arrived. Charles was particularly anxious as to how James would take the matter and was apparently prepared for even more opposition than he received. Danby had urged the proposed alliance, insecure in his knowledge of unsavoury dealings with Louis XIV, with whom he had concluded certain secret agreements on the King's behalf. He was anxious to have the

Dutch marriage to his credit, in case of Parliamentary attack. Charles had objected; 'My brother will never consent.' 'Perhaps not,' answered Danby, 'unless the King took it upon him to command it.' But James, from the beginning, had steeled himself to the fact that his children were England's, not his own. He was not brow-beaten into giving his consent (he was not an easy man to bully), but agreed of his own accord in loyal submission to his brother's will. His implicit obedience was the logical corollary of his belief in royal authority, but it is none the less to his credit that throughout twenty-five difficult years, he never diverged in practice from a theory which many had professed but contradicted in action. He did not like the marriage but he had no personal objection to the Prince of Orange. On the contrary, he never forgot that he was his sister's son.

When William landed, the air was full of rumour. 'His voyage gives great alarmings everywhere,' wrote Henry Coventry to Ormonde, 'and as many several guesses at the design of his voyage . . . I believe the issue . . . will neither be so bad as they fear abroad, nor so good as we hope here, but certainly should it end in a bare visit, it would have ill consequences.' 'And,' concludes Coventry, 'this is as big a letter as Newmarket will endure, where many a man hath made an end of his treasure in fewer minutes than I have been writing this letter.' The Prince had been met by coach at Harwich, and brought thence to Newmarket. At the end of the week, after spending the night with the King and Duke at Lord Arlington's house at Euston, he returned with his royal hosts to London. He was more at ease when the time came for business than in the atmosphere of the racing town, where his serious bent of mind savoured of priggishness and it was difficult to dissemble his impatience of delay. When discussion began James showed a tendency to temporise, or at least to embark on the consideration of diplomatic problems, the terms to be imposed upon Louis in the forthcoming treaty, English trading rights and other such pitfalls for politicians. But William had decided that the next task to be accomplished in consolidating his position in Europe, was to marry the Duke of York's daughter. It was a necessary step towards defeating Louis, and Louis's downfall had become the only dream in which he allowed himself to indulge. He refused to discuss politics until the match had been negotiated. Charles was impressed. 'If I am not mistaken in the Prince,' he declared, 'he is a very honest man; he shall have his wife. Go and tell my brother so.'

On October 23rd, 1677, the marriage was announced; on November 4th, it was solemnised, and on November 19th, William and Mary left for Holland. On the 13th, Coventry again wrote to Ormonde, apropos of the most recent committee meeting, 'where you will, I hope, think we have been quicker than ordinary that a Prince should come and woo, marry, bed and carry away the Princess Mary in a month's time'. For him it was a matter of committees, though, 'what all honest men have long wished for'; for William, it was additional power to his elbow in a lifelong struggle: for Mary it was a miserable end to the hopes and dreams of girlhood. She wept when the time came to go. Queen Catherine tried to comfort her. 'I wept when I came here,' she reminded her, 'and see how happy I have been.' 'Yes, Your Majesty,' answered Mary, with the superb insularity of her breed, 'but you came to England; I am leaving it.'

A husband's solicitude would soon have weaned his bride from capricious homesickness, but Mary had no illusions about the fact that to William she was merely a pawn in the political game. A year after her marriage she was still miserable and lonely, so much so that her impulsive young stepmother crossed incognito to Holland with the Princess Anne, in the hope of cheering her. Six months later Mary was 'well in health, but in mind as sick as ever'. Abortive confinements, the sad curse of Stuart Queens, added real tragedy to girlish disillusion, and her husband followed the fashion of the time, and took as mistress, Elizabeth Villiers, her vivacious maid-in-waiting. Lady Villiers had been Mary's governess, and her daughters had shared nursery and schoolroom with the two princesses. The fatal Villiers charm pierced the armour of William's indifference, but his love affairs were temporary aberrations to which he gave little attention, and Mary was wise not to let an occasional infidelity, which signified nothing, wear her down into fretful jealousy. It was, in fact, his insensibility to female society and his partiality for good-looking young men, who possessed the social qualities he lacked, which gave rise to the contemporary opinion that he practised an unnatural vice. But his power of concentration on practical affairs, the force of his religious convictions which gave to his defence of Protestant Europe the character of a crusade, and the love and respect which Mary grew to feel for the strange man she had married, are all ponderable arguments against an unhealthy or vicious life. The inhibitions of an unnatural childhood, his ill-health and the mental strain he imposed upon himself in adult life produced in him a streak of inhumanity, but in place of deterioration his nature grew fuller and finer with the passing of years, to which development the love of his wife was a contributory cause.

For not in vain had Mary been educated as a good Christian. Her Father in God had been William Compton, the Bishop of London, who had confirmed her a year before her marriage. This son of an Earl, soldier turned priest, was never quite able to reconcile the difficult paths of man of the world and follower of Christ. But there was a robust reality about his faith that made him an excellent pastor for young folk. He had made Mary feel that her religion was an abiding joy and strength, not merely a matter of creeds and customs. Now in the hour of her need, she turned to it. Not only did it comfort and sustain her, it gave her happiness in the material as in the spiritual world. For as time passed, her unaffected goodness made her so beloved of the Dutch people, that she found in her foreign home fellowship and content. And by giving to William, not merely her body but herself, allowing neither neglect nor infidelity to sour her spirit, she was able in the end to do him great service and to win his love. Gradually she attained peace of mind, which was reflected in the weekly letters she never failed to write to her father in England, and to which he or his wife every week replied.

The Duke had seen his daughter depart the more readily in that, on November 7th, 1677, his wife had borne him a healthy male child. Their joy was marred by anxiety, for there was smallpox in the royal household. Lady Villiers, the governess, died and the Princess Anne had a mild attack. She was, however, convalescent before her stepmother had recovered from her confinement, and on December 3rd, she visited the lying-in-chamber and paid her respects to the Duchess and the new baby. Anne, barely well from the smallpox bent down and kissed her stepbrother! A few days later an eruption appeared on the child's neck, which the midwife made a fatal effort to repel. Six days after Anne's visit, he was dead.

The Duke gave more open expression to his grief than on any other occasion. He wrote to William, accepting his condolences: 'I wish you may never have the like cause of trouble, nor know what it is to lose a son.' The sorrow of the young Duchess was as intense as his, and tinged with bitterness. For in addition to the instinctive longing of a woman for a son, she was realising that by the death of her children she was in danger of losing James. The affection she had grown to feel for him had been sadly bruised by the fact of his infidelity. The tie of their common religion and of their children, had they lived, might have combined with his own sense of shame and his wife's charm to keep him straight, but after his son's death and the political gruelling of the next few years, he relapsed into his old bad habits. The young woman whose charms were to prove irresistible, was already in the Duchess's household. She was Catherine, the rather ugly daughter of Sir Charles Sedley, the famous dramatist and wit. Her father had endeavoured to marry her to young Colonel Churchill, the Duke's favourite and Arabella's brother. But Churchill was reluctant; he was, in fact, falling in love himself with a completeness that surprised him and rendered unbelievable his earlier romantic escapades. His love was the Duchess's lively maid-in-waiting, Sarah Jennings. Sarah was good-looking, but it was personality rather than looks, which had won from the Princess Anne a girl's unstinted devotion, and now enslaved the handsome Churchill's heart. Catherine Sedley was amused at her suitor's defection, as indeed she was amused at most things that happened to her in life. John and Sarah, who had no money and only their own brains and the goodwill of the Duke and Duchess to help them in the world, were married secretly in Mary Beatrice's private apartments some time early in 1678. Princess Anne was delighted at the match, so much more romantic than her sister's marriage. The Duke, too, was pleased; since Falmouth died he had never had a friend for whom he cared so much as he did for Churchill. But he was intrigued by the level-headed young woman whom John had refused to marry. He developed the acquaintance. In due time Catherine became his acknowledged mistress. 'I don't know what he sees in me,' she used to say, 'It cannot be my beauty, for he must see I have none; and it cannot be my wit, for he has not enough to know that I have any.' But more than any other woman she held and fascinated James. For Mary Beatrice it was a grief to which she could never grow reconciled. It was her one consolation, now that politics began to invade her security, that as his lawful wife she alone could share his troubles though others might participate in his triumphs.

During the greater part of 1678, Whitehall and Westminster were fey; there was an epidemic of nerves, productive of rumours and counter-rumours, disputes and reconciliations, and endless talk. 'We live in a world of words. One would think Babel were not far off.' Buckingham and Arlington were quarrelling as usual, and it was impossible to crush the former who complained of his rival, 'I gave him to the King as one who could tell that two and two made four, and two more six. But I did not think you would put him to rule kingdoms.' But Buckingham was mistaken; though the King confirmed the marriage between the Duke of Grafton, his natural son, and Arlington's lovely daughter, Lord Chamberlains do not rule kingdoms. Others held the helm. But even the Lord Treasurer Danby had ceased to be sure whether or not he ruled; his position had been particularly insecure since a disagreeable incident at one of Nell Gwynne's evening entertainments. There, the treasurer and his wife had been the subject of some ill-natured abuse, and when a friend of Danby's had remonstrated with Charles, His Majesty replied that he 'would not deny himself an hour's divertisement for the sake of any man'. The Duke of York in this case was rightly shocked with his brother's levity, but his friendship for Danby was also wearing thin. He could not forget that the Treasurer had been the prime mover of the marriage that had made his daughter miserable, and that such religious designs as he still harboured were directly contrary to Danby's policy. That James had definite religious designs at this time is improbable, but the existence of an undercurrent of Catholic activity is proved by the injudicious correspondence of Edward Coleman. The latter was the Duchess's secretary and a born meddler whom James himself had rebuked, on occasion. There was a growing presentiment in the country that all was not well with the Protestant religion. When the Archbishop of Canterbury died, it was expected that Compton would be promoted from the See of London. He was Danby's friend, the exponent in the Church of the Cavalier orthodoxy Danby sponsored in the State. Instead the choice fell on Sancroft, the Dean of St. Paul's, the son of yeoman parents who had won eminence through his learning and his piety. The Duke was blamed for the appointment; if it were his, it did him credit. But Sancroft was a student and a priest, not an ecclesiastical statesman; time alone would show if he had courage as well as virtue, should the principles of his church be attacked or endangered. Compton himself was bitterly disappointed, and a spice of personal animosity was added to his intellectual dislike of all that the Duke of York represented.

Over all the political estrangements and religious fears brooded the shadow of a war with France. The foreign policy of the Opposition was insular in the extreme and subservient to political tactics at home, while the foreign policy of the Crown was complicated by the facts of French subsidies on the one hand and the family tie with William of Orange on the other. Neither party paid any regard to consistency, or to the interests of the whole state of Europe. The Opposition had demanded war for years. At last Danby, who had a sincere respect for William of Orange, had steered the policy of the Crown in the same direction. Charles hesitated, and the war-party received an unexpected ally in the Duke of York, who recovered the thrill of youth in contemplating military adventure and saw in the prospect of a command the possibility of regaining the goodwill of the English people. He talked of going out himself to Flanders at the head of a British Expeditionary Force, and corresponded with William about details of strategy. But there were unexpected difficulties. Louis trusted to money and human frailty as well as to the force of arms, in attempting to achieve universal sovereignty. His agents were in touch with the leaders of the Parliamentary Opposition. Even the ethics of Algernon Sidney were sufficiently confused to permit of him receiving presents from King Louis. In such cases as that of Lord Russell or Holles, the old Puritan with 'the soul of a stubborn Roman in him', bribery was impossible, but subtle suggestion was likely to be effective. England was raising forces, and eventually there was a camp on Hounslow Heath of ten thousand 'well-clad and promising men'. Fear of a standing army, the natural concomitant of 'Popery and Slavery', impelled the men who had declaimed against France for years to refuse the supplies which would have made war possible.

While Louis's Huguenot agent, Ruvigny, approached the Opposition, Barillon, his official ambassador, was busy at court. Nothing was to be left to chance. It was a critical moment. Louis wanted to make peace on terms dictated by himself; William of Orange wished to continue the struggle with English help and to force France to abate her claims. But his Dutch countrymen were less bellicose than he, and Danby was his only thorough-going supporter in England. Barillon had long conclaves with the King and the Duke, and the latter repented his momentary apostasy to his friendship with Louis. A secret treaty was signed, by which Charles received the usual financial assistance and promised to stand neuter. The money was not to be paid till Parliament was prorogued and the new military forces disbanded. 'The Duke of York took the affair up with warmth, and . . . appears greatly desirous to deserve the same share of Your Majesty's good graces which he had heretofore,' wrote Barillon to Louis. Parliament was informed that peace was imminent and gladly voted money to disband the army, but before Charles had received the subsidy from Louis, the latter made one of those arrogant gestures which were the first sign of the overweening pride that was to bring its eventual nemesis. He refused to surrender the Flemish towns, demanded from him by the treaty under discussion. James was genuinely shocked and declared in council that nothing could be more evident than that 'France intended an universal monarchy, and nothing but England could hinder them'. The Commons, moved to real anger and fear, voted the King more money to continue military preparations. The army was kept on foot and Parliament prorogued before it could change its mind. Charles lost his subsidy from Louis, but for once he did not care: he had been roused out of his usual nonchalance and he acted with vigour. Forces were sent to the Continent, the Duke of Monmouth in eager attendance, under the command of the Earl of Feversham, Turenne's anglicised nephew and James's well-tried friend. 'Whether we shall please the Parliament as much as if we had done it sooner I know not,' Coventry surmised, 'but I dare aver we have angered the King of France as much.'

After all, it ended in smoke. Louis was too clever for his enemies. He made a separate treaty with the Dutch, critical of their Prince's military activities. William fought an engagement at Mons and threw away some good lives to register his discontent, but at long last the other allied powers agreed, and a general peace was signed at Nimeguen.

Charles had finished with foreign affairs. For ten years, England ceased to count in Europe. But that summer in the mutual jealousy and recrimination of King and Parliament the prologue had been played to the drama that was to end at the Revolution. Looking back afterwards on how it all began, men saw it through a haze of summer heat and weariness. The weather had been exceptionally warm all year and the series of acrimonious debates at Westminster had been physically as well as mentally exhausting. 'Hector Harry' as Marvell termed Coventry, had stood like an angel with a flaming sword, defending the government against irascible critics in the House. 'I am very weary,' he wrote. So it was with his colleagues and his opponents. Wrought nerves and tired bodies relaxed, as August the month of holiday closed the doors of Westminster and drove the willing court to the cool shades of Windsor. In the malodorous streets of London those citizens, who could not get away, continued their daily jobs with exacerbated tempers. In the cool of the evening they met at the coffee-houses and grew hot over political discussions and the idle rumours of the dog-days. At Whitehall a jaded remnant of the Privy Council dealt with the usual crop of informers. There was amongst the councillors an uneasy fear of latent treachery. 'I am confident there are intrigues laying in all three nations,' wrote Coventry, with an anxious eye directed towards Scotland. Danby was resting at Wimbledon; he was disturbed by a new story of a plot to assassinate the King. But in the quiet of the country it seemed impossible to treat it seriously. Only by degrees did it attract serious attention. 'In my poor opinion clouds of importance gather,' was Coventry's eventual pronouncement on the matter. It was a mild and characteristic method of describing the chaos, initiated by the activities of that genius among liars, the shrewd and vicious madman Titus Oates.

British Museum]

MARY OF MODENA, WIFE OF JAMES II IN CORONATION ROBES
From the portrait by Kneller

CHAPTER VII

WHIGS AND TORIES

'Thus have I seen a King at Chess
His rooks and knights withdrawn,
His Queens and Bishops in distress
Shifting about, growing less and less
With here and there a Pawn.'

Contemporary pasquinade.

I

TITUS OATES was a man with no morals, a lively imagination and a subtle brain. Such as he to-day find opportunities for self-expression in shady financial ventures or the less reputable forms of journalism. In the reign of Charles II they turned naturally to the informers' trade, so that the cynic might allege that while the fashionable few expressed their personalities by committing adultery with impunity, their counterparts in the lower classes turned their attention with effect to the ninth commandment and satisfied their vanity and greed by bearing false witness against their neighbours.

But Oates's personality was too complex to be content with the simple fabrication of falsehoods. A spice of truth in a dish of probability would, he knew, give to his inventions a verisimilitude, difficult to gainsay. Even those who felt they were being hoodwinked found it impossible to put their fingers on the exact point where he deviated into lies, and the uncomfortable feeling that there might be something in it prevented men of common sense from allaying the panic fear of less level-headed colleagues.

The life of Titus Oates had been spent in a series of expulsions, from Merchant Taylors School and Cambridge

University, and after an unsuccessful interim as schoolmaster from that most disreputable of professions, a naval chaplaincy. His father had been Anabaptist and Anglican as the times served, and Titus was a true son of his father. His ugly bull-neck, his sunken eyes and bow-legs seemed to proclaim the viciousness of a nature, devoid of any saving grace. In respectable society he was a failure, and he decided to live by his wits. In 1677 he was reconciled to the Roman Catholic Church and expressed a wish to join the Jesuit Order. He was sent to the English seminary at Valladolid, but they could not stomach him for more than six months. In November he returned to London unabashed, appealed for another trial and was sent to St. Omer by his Catholic patrons, who in their anxiety for converts had forgotten that as Jesuits they should have read character more truly. But St. Omer soon wearied of his effrontery. Again six months proved the limit to his teachers' sufferance and again he was expelled as a buffoon and bully, without spiritual grace or intellectual humility. He had not, however, been as stupid as he appeared. Both in Spain and France his ears had been attuned to the secret whisperings of those about him. On his final return to England in June 1678, he concocted 'a true and exact narrative of the Horrid Plot and Conspiracy of the Popish Party against the Life of his Sacred Majesty, the Government and the Protestant religion'. He worked in alliance with one Israel Tonge, an equally miserable specimen of humanity, a parson who denounced Rome with impartial regularity but who lacked Oates's vigour and whose acrimony verged upon the insane.

When all was ready, a dramatic disclosure was staged. Oates had pretended that as a side-line to the plot he had been commissioned to kill Tonge, and that the latter had persuaded him to turn informer. A copy of his narrative, relating the various horrid ways in which King Charles was to be assassinated, was hidden by Oates in a place where Tonge conveniently found it. It was stated that the plot had been concerted at the meeting of the Jesuits in the spring, which indubitably had taken place. Tonge read the deposition to an acquaintance, who on account of a post in the Royal Laboratory had access to the King, and the acquaintance, horror-struck, agreed to inform Charles of his danger. He intercepted the latter on August 13th as he was strolling in St. James's Park. 'Sire, your enemies have a design against your life. You may be in danger in this very walk.' 'How may that be?' asked Charles. 'By being shot at,' replied the agitated chemist. Charles promised to speak to him later, and coolly continued his walk.[1] It would take more than threat of assassination to disturb Charles when he was in good humour. He was off to Windsor and he did not mean to be detained; Danby was left to inquire into the matter. Dr. Tonge was examined but in spite of an effective air of mystery, his attempts to prove that two men were haunting St. James's Park and Windsor, with guns primed to shoot the King, remained singularly unconvincing. He was even reduced to excusing the absence of one supposed assassin on the grounds that he had a cold. Charles refused to be interested, but showed his sense of the danger latent in the position by forbidding Danby to mention the matter to anybody else, particularly the Duke. Danby remained anxious but inactive at his country house until, at the end of the month the informers took a further step. The Duke's confessor, Father Bedingfield, received a batch of letters, supposed to come from Jesuits concerned in the plot. They were obvious forgeries, and the priest at once showed them to James, who handed them over to the King. Next time the informers approached the court, they were snubbed both by Charles and Danby. But what the King feared had happened. James, aware of the supposed existence of a Catholic plot, felt that his own reputation was at stake. The informers were particularly incoherent in their statements

[1] This narrative is taken from the brilliant study of the Popish Plot, by John Pollock (London, 1903).

about the Duke. Whether he was to be assassinated with his brother, or to be made King in the latter's room, was a point upon which they contradicted themselves in a confusion of mind, natural in view of the dangerous ground upon which they were treading. But the mere fact of his Catholicism involved James in the attack upon his co-religionists, and the demand which he now made for a full inquiry in council, however impolitic, was the instinctive action of a man of honour. Charles could not do other than shrug his shoulders and agree. Oates obtained what he had desired from the beginning, an examination in council where he could bluff the councillors to his heart's content.

The King was hard to bluff and after being present on Michaelmas day at Oates's second appearance before the Council, he caught him out in various inexactitudes and declared him a very lying knave. But his councillors could scarcely be expected to share his insouciance. 'If he be a liar,' Coventry wrote, the day after Oates's examination, 'he is the greatest and adroitest I ever saw, and yet it is a stupendous thing to think what vast concerns are like to depend upon the evidence of one young man who hath twice changed his religion.' And on October 8th, he wrote again, 'We have much noise, and we of the Council much business about a plot. Would two witnesses swear but half that which one doth, there would be enough to hang a great many men.'

Folk were beginning to realise that it was to prove a hanging matter. Two events were instrumental in intensifying the atmosphere in which the case was being considered. Oates in his deposition on Michaelmas day had implicated Coleman, the Duchess's secretary. Coleman had twenty-four hours in which to make his escape, but he failed to do so. He destroyed a few papers, but he seemed to have no conception of the danger in which he stood. On Monday, the 30th, he surrendered to the Council and his study was searched. A box of papers were found, largely composed of cipher correspondence with a Catholic agent in France. The letters were undoubtedly treasonable in their general tenor if not in specific detail, and James and his friends were roused to the fact that things were seriously amiss. Coleman was committed to Newgate, and the bed-rock of truth in Oates's narrative thus unexpectedly revealed put an end to any idea of suppressing his disclosures.

The second event was yet more dramatic. Professing himself afraid of Catholic revenge, Oates had deposited a copy of his information with Sir Edmund Bury Godfrey, a well-known and respected justice of the City of London. He had taken this step early in September when the possibility of Charles refusing to take him seriously drove him to consider the alternative of raising a storm in the city. The change in the court's attitude relieved him of the necessity of further action and Godfrey remained in uneasy possession of his knowledge. He was a man of exceptional appearance, tall and spare, with a slight stoop and hooked chin. His look was frank and open and his bravery in the disastrous years of the Plague and Fire had won him the people's love and the Crown's reward. Later he had shown himself equally undaunted in upholding justice against a servant of the King's. A deep kindliness of heart made him tolerant to Dissenters and Catholics alike. He was the very man to be made wretched by his knowledge of the plot, not from any selfish anxiety for himself, but because he hated injustice and cruelty, and because as a magistrate his duty would impel him to reveal his knowledge and set loose the fears, that would wreck justice and mercy alike. His health had been bad for some time and he had not the resilience to cast aside his care. On Saturday, October 12th, he left his house at nine in the morning and did not return. Next day his clerk made unsuccessful inquiries at his mother's at Hammersmith and at his brother's in the city. For days the search continued and the air grew thick with rumours. On Thursday, 17th, he was found dead at the bottom of Primrose Hill, with a sword thrust through his body.

By common repute he had been murdered by the Catholics. It is possible his death was engineered by the informers to give colour to their tale, but it is hard to credit such unrelieved infamy. It is possible he committed suicide, his mind deranged by the events of the month, but the details of the deposition of his body render this unlikely. The probable murderers were Jesuit agents, and the motive for the crime has been ascribed to their fear that Godfrey had obtained possession of dangerous information unknown to Oates. The Jesuit gathering in London in the spring had actually been held at St. James's Palace. If Godfrey had discovered this, he must at all costs be silenced. Such a supposition, rendered possible by Godfrey's personal friendship with Secretary Coleman, adequately fits the case. But it remains supposition.

The tragedy set the town ablaze. The body lay in state in the street, and hundreds fed their rage and fear upon the sight of it. When Parliament met a few days later, the government in self-defence could not do other than put forward the facts of 'the Plot' for full enquiry. It was thus in the heated atmosphere of the two houses, that Oates continued his work, assisted by men, as vile as he, who were ready to come forward with incriminating evidence. Suspects were seized and tried in the courts which had been invaded by a dangerous zeal for politics. In turn, Secretary Coleman, and others far more innocent, were charged with treason, convicted and executed. Three men, servants of the Queen were sentenced for Godfrey's murder and died protesting their innocence. Various Catholic peers were arrested and impeached. Two years after the inception of the plot, the Earl of Stafford, an old man of eighty, paid with his life for the folly and brutality of other men. Then England began to sicken of the orgy of hatred, which party politicians had not hesitated to exploit for their own purpose. The febrile insanity ceased, but fifteen men had been judicially murdered and Titus Oates grew fat on a State pension.

The plot gave an impetus to the suspicion of James, which nearly cost him the throne. He was genuinely horrified by Oates's testimony, though he had allowed the Jesuits to meet under his ægis and had regretted the failure of the schemes of 1670. He may have indulged in a vague contemplation of plans to re-establish his faith, but he would never have condoned treason nor such a murder as Godfrey's. The tie of family, precious to every Stuart, which impelled Charles in spite of a temperamental lack of sympathy, to defend the Duke's interests to the last ditch, would have rendered it impossible for James to plot against Charles. He was still at forty-five, a sound man, morally and mentally. It was only the entanglement of the political and religious issue, subsequent to the Popish Plot, the shame of exile and the attack upon his rights which embittered James. Once in the chase a stag turned at bay upon his pursuers. 'That,' cried James, 'is how the English have made me feel.'

The fall of 1678 was a critical time for the Duke. Parliament petitioned the King to execute the Penal Laws and to banish the priests. By exempting those in the Queen's service but refusing to extend the licence to the Duchess's household, Westminster signalised its distrust of Mary Beatrice, while it expressed its hostility to James by asking the King to exclude him from all committees of council. The Duke was shocked at Parliament's interference in matters in which it had no concern; his letters to William of Orange at this time show that it was the political aspect of the situation which most affected him: 'all things look as they did in the beginning of the late rebellion and the republican party is very busy at work.' 'Things go on very ill still and I am afraid that they will every day do something to lessen the King's authority.' His reaction was that of the military man and the incorrigible 'die-hard'; to stand firm and defy their endeavours;

Charles's preference for the more subtle paths of compromise caused a temporary alienation between the brothers. Very grudgingly the Duke consented to absent himself 'from all places where any affairs of the nation were agitated'; while with less reluctance he declared in the Upper House that his religion 'should only be a private thing between God and his own soul'. The King assured the members that he would agree to any measure to safeguard the Protestant religion. The Commons replied by pushing forward a bill to exclude Catholics from both Houses of Parliament. In the Lords, a proviso was added, exempting the Duke of York. After a fiery debate, the amendment was accepted in the Commons by a majority of two votes. The King gave his assent without demur. Danby's proficiency in graft, and a relic of the old Restoration loyalty which still lingered in the House, had secured the narrow margin of victory for James, but it was not without genuine grief for his co-religionists that he saw the Catholic peers of England walk out of the House of Lords on December 1st, 1678.[1] The old wounds of five years earlier were re-opened. He determined that when he was King, justice should be done.

At this critical stage, Danby was impeached. A jealous ambassador had revealed his secret dealings with Louis on the King's behalf. Charles made a loyal attempt to save his minister by dissolving the Parliament which had served him since the Restoration. Shaftesbury and his friends were delighted. Danby was ruined, and a new House of Commons, elected in the atmosphere of the Popish Plot, would produce no awkward majorities of two in the Duke's favour at critical moments. Elections went on apace in the usual seventeenth-century fashion, by which awkward voters were liable to be kidnapped and the candidates rivalled each other in making the electorate drunk on bad beer. Yet in spite of the crudity of election methods, somehow or other the will of the people made itself felt. There

[1] Nor did they return until the repeal of the Tests in 1928.

could be no doubt about the colour of the new House nor the immediate action upon which it would embark. Charles was in a dilemma. He could not change his brother as he could change his minister. But he might convert him: surely any man with sense could see the absurdity of refusing formal compliance with the established religion of the country he would one day rule. So in January, 1679, James received a call from the pious Sancroft, Archbishop of Canterbury and the learned Morley, Bishop of Winchester. They were both his friends, and they harangued James with courtly insistence, reminding him of his father's martyrdom, extolling the merits of the Anglican Church 'a lilly among thorns'. They granted him to be 'too generous a soul to be frightened into a change by danger', but uttered the pious hope that truth would prevail.

James listened for close on half an hour without interrupting his visitors, then he ended the audience without argument, telling them briefly that 'they must not wonder, if by reason of the greater hurry of business he was forced to dismiss them without entering into any farther debate about what they had urged'. Later he wrote more fully to Sancroft, assuring him with dignity 'that . . . it was . . a full conviction in all controversial points that forced him to embrace a Religion, he well foresaw would change his condition in this world, from one of the happyest Princes in Europe to that of the most unfortunate and abandon'd man upon earth'.

A few days later he received a letter from the King, bidding him withdraw from England. 'I am truly sorry for the occasion,' Charles wrote, 'in the meantime I think it proper to give it you under my hand that I expect this complyance from you and desire it may be as soon as conveniently you can.' On February 28th, 1679, James received the letter. On March 3rd he said farewell to the court 'not without many tears shed by him at parting, though the King shed none'. A gesture of friendliness would have meant much to the Duke, but perhaps Charles dared not show it. There was some consummate acting ahead of him, if he were to deceive the men he hoped to deceive; it would not do to delay too long in assuming the role. He was also genuinely annoyed with James for the trouble his obstinacy had created. There was too thin a line between kingship and vagrancy for Charles to think kindly of his brother's religious fads. With an unusual streak of harshness he refused to allow Anne and Isabel to accompany their father. Mary Beatrice elected to go with her husband into exile, rather than to stay with Isabel whom she adored. The Duchess like the King had no room for tears. She was furious. Charles had the grace to accompany them to their boat. A fresh breeze was blowing, and the King cried instinctively, 'The wind is contrary; you cannot go on board at present.' Mary Beatrice turned to him with the withering scorn of intolerant womanhood. 'What, sir, are you grieved – you who sent us into exile? Of course we must go since you have ordain'd it.'

Two days after the Duke's departure Parliament met. The Commons at once renewed the impeachment of Danby. Not even the King's pardon could save him from committal to the Tower. Charles put the Treasury in commission, with the Earl of Essex, the moody son of a Puritan father, at its head and as its working members two young men who were to make a name for themselves in politics. Lawrence Hyde, Clarendon's younger son, lacked his father's genius, though he equalled him in orthodox conservatism and Anglican piety. No government to which he belonged could be suspected of countenancing tyranny or Popish plots. He was an eminently safe man. Sidney Godolphin, whose father had died for King Charles fighting down a village street on Dartmoor, had come up to London from the Cornish homestead beneath Godolphin Hill and had made his way at Whitehall mainly through his capacity for never obtruding himself. He was never in the way and never out of it, and his only passion was the gamble of the cards. He had a genius for figures and for organisation, and no particular principles in politics to confuse him. In the years to come when Churchill had become the Duke of Marlborough and fought and won at Blenheim and Malplaquet, his victories were to depend not only on his genius and the courage of his men, but on the tenacity of purpose, the loyalty and the quiet faith of this servant of the State, who was to husband England in Queen Anne's fruitful days. For the moment he stood for efficiency as opposed to Parliamentary fireworks, and Charles's choice of him and his associates indicated the line he meant to follow.

At the end of April he acted. His Privy Council was dismissed, and in its place was established an experiment in government which had originated in the active brain of Sir William Temple; a council of thirty was appointed, half of whom were King's men, while the other half were composed of the Parliamentary leaders. Shaftesbury himself was invited to preside. A scheme was laid before Parliament providing for the stringent limitation of the powers of a Catholic successor. Charles was stealing his opponents thunder.

To the Duke in Brussels, his brother's action seemed akin to madness. He wrote to William of Orange, as one strong man to another, bewailing the King's lack of resolution. 'In my mind all things tend to a Republicke. For you see all things tend towards the lessening of the King's authority and the new modell things are put into is the very same it was in the tyme of the Commonwealth. . . .' If Charles consented to limit or exclude the Duke, then, wrote James, 'I shall . . . look on his Majesty as lesse than a Duke of Venice, and the monarky and our family absolutely ruind and given up.' And with a desire for vigorous and straightforward action such as William alone seemed capable of in these degenerate days of intrigue and cabal, he concluded in words that sound strangely from James, nine years before the Revolution, 'But what to do . . . is very hard to say. I could wish you in England. . . .

Consider well with your self whether it be fitt for you to go or no.' William of Orange was content to bide his time.

Charles knew what he was doing. His new council could never have worked for reasons obvious to all who have suffered upon large committees. But Charles did not mean it to work. Once he exclaimed in private, 'God's fish they have put a set of men about me, but they shall know nothing!' These were his real feelings, and Shaftesbury and Russell knew it. They attended out of politeness, but they did not care a fig for Temple's experiment. The real centre of fight was at Westminster. Charles's offer of limitations had been rejected for the sound reason that his successor might not abide by it. On May 15th, the first Exclusion Bill was introduced into the Commons and passed its second reading six days later. The King's nearest ministers were uncertain what action he would take. Few had such a sure guide to their own conduct as Henry Coventry who declared 'How far his Majesty will struggle or run with this Tempest I know not. . . . I think we are nigh a great crisis. . . . For my own part, I am resolved to be honest according to my understanding. For my safety, I leave it to God's providence.' So, without hesitation, he gave his vote against the measure and spoke up for the Duke, while many of James's closer friends kept silence. From Brussels, James watched and noted Coventry's loyalty, which served to underline others' delinquency. It was his first experience of the frailty of man's friendship, and he took it hardly.

He had a better ally than he knew in his brother, who at this juncture prorogued Parliament, and in July dissolved it, summoning another to meet in October, 1679. He thus gained time though little else, but time was precious. Passions might cool, opinions have a way of changing; Charles knew his Shaftesbury; given time, he would probably go too far. Meanwhile, the triumvirate whose counsel seemed to predominate at Whitehall were Essex and Sunderland, and the distinguished newcomer Lord Halifax, whose objection to extreme measures assured his opposition to exclusion. James considered him the most dangerous man he knew, but in the immediate future he was to prove a good friend.

During these uncertain months, the Duke and Duchess had established themselves at Brussels, after an honourable and friendly reception by William and Mary and a short sojourn in Holland. A little court soon came into existence, dominated by John and Sarah Churchill, trusted friends and good companions, and enlivened by the addition of the latter's sister, de Grammont's beautiful young widow. The devoted Talbot renewed his clumsy wooing, this time with hope of success. The young Duchess, her nature mellowed by adversity, was almost happy. In April letters from 'dear England' made her laugh, with a companion sigh for the beauty of the English spring. Even the Duke accepted the inevitable, and sent across to Colonel Legge his Master of the Horsc, instructing him to send over by the Dover-Ostende route 'to be as little as they can upon the sea. . . . Dixey and Hooper with their two setts of horses, and the hunting coaches, as also two pads and fower of the somer (summer) hunters, whereof Windsor and Griffen to be two'. It was not the last adventure upon which Dixey, the coachman was to embark in James's service. He liked some of them less than this summer trip to Belgium.

To Legge James wrote regularly, pouring out as to no one else his uneasy jealousy of Monmouth, justifying his own attitude – 'till he spake to me himself at Windsor some five or six years ago, of his having a mind to be Generall, I never took anything ill of him' – and criticising that of Charles. 'There is one thinge troubles me very much and puts odd thoughts into my head, it is that all this while his Majesty has never sayd a word or gone about to make a good understanding between me and the Duke of Monmouth, for tho' it is a thing I shall never seek, yett methinks it is what his Majestie might presse. Tho' one must never despaire, I look upon my condition as very bad.'

Monmouth's triumphant return from crushing a revolt in Scotland and Halifax's insistence that James must be kept out of the way reduced the Duke's hopes to their nadir. Yet at this very moment he broke into a defence of his religion, which is perhaps the finest thing he ever wrote. 'Pray once for all never say anything to me againe of turning Protestant,' he admonished Legge. 'I never shall and if occasion were, I hope God would give me His grace to suffer death for the true Catholic religion, as well as Banishment. What I have done was not hastily, but upon mature consideration, and foreseeing all and more than has yet happened to me. . . .' Three days later he sealed up the letter, disappointed that the English post had brought him no word from the King. 'I am not used like a brother or a friend. I am so tyred with writnig I can say no more.'

This was in July. The exile was likely to be lengthy and in August, Anne and Isabel were allowed to join their parents. To William on August 21st, James wrote from Brussels, 'This place is as barren of newes as it is empty of company'. On August 22nd, Charles fell ill at Windsor.

It was the first of those seizures which a few years later were to prove fatal. On this occasion it was alarming enough to terrify the triumvirate, for if the King died Monmouth, as general of the armed forces of the kingdom, would have little difficulty in establishing himself in James's absence. While they hesitated, Charles had a relapse. Either on their own initiative, or reinforced by a hint from the King, they sent secret word to the Duke to return alone and speedily. On September 8th, James left Brussels, wearing a black perruque and a plain stuff suit without his star and garter. He rode post to Calais attended by a few companions and fretted nineteen hours away in a slow voyage across the Channel. From Dover, James set out for London with Churchill, the latter travelling as a French officer and the Duke as his servant. The

Postmaster at Dover glanced keenly at the pair; he took Churchill by the hand, but looked full in the face of the man in the black perruque. 'He was glad to see him,' he said to Churchill, 'but by God he should be much gladder to see a better man than he.' The oblique welcome cheered James. The Postmaster was an honest man and held his tongue. The riders pushed on to London, where James took hackney coach to a friend's house, and hearing from Hyde and Godolphin that his arrival was yet unknown pushed on to Windsor with such haste that he arrived at seven next morning, just as His Majesty was shaving.

For Charles had confounded his friends and his enemies by making a complete recovery. His own 'extraordinary calm temper' had counteracted the pernicious activity of the doctors. James pretended to have returned on his own initiative and Charles graciously forgave him. Halifax and Essex were in a dilemma and urged that the Duke should again leave England. The Duke argued that in that case Monmouth should be relieved of his military commission and should also leave the country. Eventually, on September 24th, Monmouth sailed for Holland, and a few days later James left for Brussels. Halifax and Essex breathed freely again. But within a few days they found that they had been tricked. The Duke of York had merely gone to collect his family, and was to take up his residence in Scotland. He was supposed to go direct by sea but the Duchess's ill-health was made an excuse for another brief sojourn in London. She was an execrable sailor, and was so wretchedly ill on the cross-Channel voyage that she vomited blood, an indication of the lung trouble that endangered her life a few years later. Her 'dear England' welcomed her with three weeks of incessant rain, but in spite of her depression she insisted on accompanying her husband when he set out for Edinburgh on October 27th. Their only comfort was the clear evidence that Charles had tired of conciliation. Again Parliament had not been allowed to meet, and Shaftesbury had been dismissed the

Council. Essex resigned from the Treasury, and Halifax, who was not above vexation of spirit when his opinion was disregarded, retired to the privacy of his country home.

The Duke and Duchess journeyed alone down the great North Road. Cheers and hisses alternated from those who watched the passing retinue of royalty fallen upon evil days. At Hatfield where they sought hospitality the Earl of Salisbury had withdrawn, leaving his house bare of food or candles. James and his friends fared as best they could, lighting fires from the faggots in the basement, and leaving coin of the realm to pay for the firewood they had taken and to witness their disdain. At York, remembering the loyal fervour of his previous visit the Duke was hurt by the lack of formal greetings which he interpreted as disrespect. But when he reached Edinburgh he had no cause to complain. The Scots welcomed him as one of themselves.

The first visit did not last more than four months. 'I live here,' he wrote, 'as courteously as I can and am very careful to give offence to none, and to have no partialities.' Mary Beatrice, in spite of first impressions of a Holyrood near to ruins and a bleak northern winter, discovered to her own surprise attractions in the new surroundings. She made the best of difficult days and Christmas was passed in dancing and dramatics. She made a real friend in the Duchess of Hamilton, and friends were rare enough for the new acquaintanceship to be precious. And under the dominating crags of Arthur's Seat, she and the Duke found a favourite walk, in which they could recover quiet of mind and the ease that comes from physical exercise. It was a blessed retreat from the rancour of politics, that was soon to envelop them again. For James's thoughts continually strayed to London. He heard that Monmouth had returned to England and refused to move, much to his father's amused exasperation. He heard that Charles in January had again postponed the assembly of Parliament, playing still for time. In February the Duke and Duchess were allowed to return to London. The spring and summer of 1680 were filled with fruitless cabals and half-suspected intrigues, with complaints by the Duchess of Portsmouth that Mary Beatrice did not pay her due respect, with an attempt of Shaftesbury's to indict James as a recusant. The Duke had learnt by now to conceal his feelings. 'His Highness smiles, dances, makes love and hunts.' The Duchess said her prayers, and wept. For in August, Isabel had an attack of convulsions. For Mary Beatrice, politics ceased to count. Even James's infatuation for that chit of a girl, Catherine Sedley, sank into momentary unimportance. It seemed inconceivable that the good God in whose service she had come to England should rob her of the one thing she loved to distraction. Isabel recovered for a last precarious winter of life. The Duchess, turning her eyes upon the outer world, found that the King's third Parliament was at last to meet and that it was essential for James to be out of England.

It was the autumn of 1680, eighteen months since the second Parliament had met, and a year since heated elections had produced this new House of Commons of whole-hearted exclusionists. The Duke's friends called their opponents Whigs after the sour-faced Scottish conventiclers of Galway. The Whigs retaliated by dubbing the loyalists, Tories, a discredited soubriquet for the wild Irish Catholics. Tempers were high and the King lacked good men to defend his interests. He relied chiefly on Lawrence Hyde, Godolphin and Sunderland. Folk called them the Chits. The satirist wrote of them:

'Clarendon had law and sense
  Clifford was fierce and brave
Bennet's grave look was a pretence
And Danby's matchless impudence
  Helped to support the knave.

'But Sunderland, Godolphin, Lory,
These will appear such chits in story
  'Twill turn all politics to jests
To be repeated like John Dory
  When fiddlers sing at feasts.'

And Sunderland ratted. He urged that the Duke should withdraw and spoke of exclusion as inevitable. The Duchess of Portsmouth had also gone over to the enemy, frightened out of her wits by Shaftesbury, who had had the effrontery to indict her as a common nuisance. Charles's loyalty to the idea of hereditary right was tested to the uttermost, for while his mistress and his first minister whispered surrender into one ear, James bombarded the other with an inopportune lecture on the various mistakes in kingcraft which Charles had made since 1660. His tirade, though it nearly broke the King's patience, showed that the Duke had a considered political philosophy, the fruit of a brain, retrogade and ultra-logical, but capable of clear and reasoned thought. James still regarded the immediate problem as political rather than religious. 'Considering how low the monarchie is now brought, it has not vigour enough left to crush those who rise in opposition against it. . . . A weak distemper'd body is sensibly affected with any light accident, which makes not the least impression upon one in perfect health.' He censured in particular the failure to settle upon the Crown in 1660 a revenue sufficient for its expenses 'and so cut the ground from under the Republicans' feet'. He also blamed Charles for his desertion of Clarendon, which had reminded the Commons 'of their impeaching privilege, and the King's councillors of the advisability of pleasing Parliament as well as the King'. Undoubtedly he had grasped the salient points.

Charles saw for himself that if Parliament met while the Duke was still in London, there would be no hope of finessing. He made his brother High Commissioner in Scotland, and on October 22nd, dispatched him and his Duchess to Edinburgh by sea. For once, the latter welcomed the purgatory of sea-sickness, accentuated by the early stages of pregnancy, as a counter-irritant to mental distress. A series of magnificent entertainments by the loyal magnates of the Lowlands, and a tremendous reception at Edinburgh, came like water on parched ground to rescue them from despair. In the capital, 'all the bells of the city continued ringing most of the night and all the streets of the city were filled with great bonfires, whither many of the citizens repaired to drink Their Majesties' and Royal Highness's health, nor was anything to be seen but an universal joy in the countenance of all here'.

It was not merely a Scotsman's partiality to a free drink that occasioned the rejoicing. For too long, the ancient Kings of Scotland had been absent among the heathen Southrons. It was good to have James home again, as his brother's formal representative; there would be time enough to carp if he misbehaved. Whatever his faults might be, he was a Stuart, and the day had not yet come when the Stuarts were unwelcome in Scotland.

II

Within a few days of the Duke's departure from London, Parliament met, and on November 2nd, another Exclusion Bill was introduced into the House of Commons. On November 15th it was brought up to the Lords. Shaftesbury and Essex spoke violently in its favour and Sunderland joined his voice to theirs. Monmouth supported the Bill, thereby displaying the bad taste which at crises marred his actions and which must as surely have been inherited from his mother as his courtly ways were inherited from Charles. The latter resented his son's breach of a gentleman's code of behaviour.

At this juncture Halifax saved the situation. Impelled by his dislike of the Whig leader, his scorn of Monmouth and his conviction that Exclusion would mean Civil War, he threw all the weight of his learning, the brilliance of his wit and the force of his character into a duel of words with Shaftesbury. The better man won. The bishops without exception voted against exclusion, refusing to safeguard their church at the expense of their conscience, and the Bill was defeated in the House of Lords by 63 votes to 30. James was saved.

Halifax, nothing if not moderate, followed up his dramatic victory by introducing a scheme of Limitations, to which the enraged Commons would not give a hearing but which alienated him completely from the Duke, to whom any interference with the rights of the Crown was anathema. In January, 1681, Charles dissolved Parliament, summoning a new body to meet in March; Sunderland lost his office, and the King secretly negotiated a treaty with Louis which would give him financial independence. The Chits had flirted with Spain in 1680 in the hope of commending themselves to the Commons, and Louis had realised the value of Charles's friendship. Secure in the French subsidy, the King ordered the new Parliament to meet at Oxford away from the invigorating Whig atmosphere of London. He played with the two Houses for some days, allowing his ministers to introduce various Regency schemes which he knew the Commons would reject. When the latter, as obdurate as ever, prepared to introduce a third Exclusion Bill, Charles unexpectedly announced the dissolution of Parliament. He was his own master and he meant to remain so. Thankfully he rode away to Windsor. The excitement had been intense but when the crisis came, the Whigs, taken by surprise with no means of resistance to hand, had no alternative to the dull conclusion of going quietly home. The swing of the pendulum had begun, and in due course the Duke would become King James II.

And yet, at this very time when apparently his troubles were assuaged, the gods, who watch and wonder at the vagaries of men, must have feared the more for James's future. For in Scotland in 1681 he was no longer the private individual who had acquitted himself creditably in 1679. As High Commissioner, the representative of the King, he made his first essay in the difficult art of ruling men, and he showed that he possessed neither clemency nor common sense. He translated the involved problems of Scottish politics and religion, in terms of his own frustrations and ambitions, failing alike in the insight and sympathy which constitute greatness in kingship and in the practical wisdom which suffice for lesser men.

Admittedly, Scotland was no easy undertaking. In effect its government had degenerated into an unending duel between the council, who normally represented the King's authority and the religious schismatics, whose strongholds were the uplands of the south-west. In Scotland as in England in 1660, Episcopacy had been restored, but while in the southern kingdom Presbyterianism had been a new habit donned largely for political reasons, in Scotland it was bred in the bone. There, contrary to events in England, the Reformation had come from below, the stern theology of Calvin had appealed irresistibly to a dour and earnest race, and Knox's genius had welded into a national whole the religious experiences of many. But in Mary of Scotland, in the pedantic James VI and his obstinate son, Scotland had been fated to endure three sovereigns who differed from their people and, in the current political philosophy, believed that the ruler had the right to impose his beliefs on those he ruled. Two of those three had lost their heads in consequence.[1] It could not be expected that Charles II's restoration of Episcopacy would be received with equanimity. For seven years while Clarendon was supreme in England the Commissioner Rothes assisted by Archbishop Sharp, the least Christian of churchmen, endeavoured to break the ranks of Presbyterianism. But consistent persecution only evoked a dour heroism in the Covenanting ranks, against which the might of man was powerless. In hidden places on mountain and moor they held their secret worship. Twice there was open revolt, tragically crushed. Lauderdale had added to their wretchedness, not sorry that an

[1] See Hume-Brown *History of Scotland* for a good general sketch of the history of the time.

obdurate minority should give him the excuse for raising troops, which might on occasion be of use in upholding the King's prerogative in Scotland or in England. The troops were quartered on the malcontents in an attempt to bully them into compliance. A quality of desperation entered into the resistance of those who stood firm. Their ranks were dwindling. Sharp had been murdered; Lauderdale was growing less vigorous in old age; periodic lapses into leniency had produced sporadic Indulgences. On each occasion some succumbed to the temptation, that may have been true wisdom, of quiet lives and friendly relations with their fellow-men. The remnant reviled them, and one can give to men like Richard Cameron the admiration and honour due to a man ready to die in a desperate cause. But by the time James arrived in Scotland, the conventiclers who still withstood authority admitted that their hands were against the State, and in attempting to subdue them, James was merely fulfilling his duty as preserver of the peace. This was the attitude of his chief lieutenant in the south-west, John Graham of Claverhouse, whose ruthlessness to those he considered intractable was tempered by his readiness to leave in peace those who benefited by the lesson and hastened to conform. Claverhouse was a man after James's own heart, obedient to his King and his immediate superiors with the staunch loyalty of the Highlander and the soldier. He modelled himself on his beloved relative Montrose, whom he resembled in personal bravery and an uncompromising code of honour. But he had not escaped the blight of the age. Though he remained simple and true of heart, uncontaminated by the more obvious vices of the Restoration, the sexual licence of the south or the drunkenness of the northern capital, some strain of harshness or uncharitableness made his name accursed among generations of Covenanters and betokened in him a spiritual lack, which was shared by all but a very few of the men of the Restoration. Yet he remains in many ways among the finest of their number.

Unfortunately James did not stop at crushing illegal revolt. Throughout his rule in Scotland, which remained under his direction after his return to London in 1682, he continued a series of petty persecutions, justified neither by his own religious opinions nor the exigencies of the situation. The time had arrived for generosity and moderation. But James withdrew the Indulgence, which had been passed at Monmouth's instigation, and endeavoured to enforce church-attendance. This stirring up of the muddy waters of ill-will partly resulted from his desire to show that although a Catholic he had no wish to attack the Episcopal system; a tragi-comedy, enacted for the benefit of his enemies in London. He meant his behavious in Edinburgh to convince the world that 'he was not so blindly zealous in his Religion as that . . . he would force those who would not go to Mass, to go to Smithfield.' Moreover, if challenged, he would have argued that he was not a free agent but his brother's representative who must carry out the Crown's traditional policy. No one could be more meticulous than he in keeping within his formal powers.

But undoubtedly his severity to any who were suspect of covenanting fervour was mainly due to his conviction that Presbyterianism meant pernicious politics. To two wretched women about to be executed, he offered pardon if they would say 'God bless the King'. In the face of death the prisoners refused, one of them asserting that she was sure God would not bless the King and therefore that she would not take His name in vain. This was the spirit with which James had to deal. He had come to Scotland determined to uphold autocracy and to allow no eruption of the disease which to his mind had contaminated southern Britain. And like most enthusiasts, he was unbalanced. When the Scottish Parliament met in 1681, he agreed to the passing of a Test Act which would enable him to crush in embryo any attempt at insubordination. It could be imposed at will upon persons in any position of trust and exacted an oath of fealty to the true Protestant religion, to which was appended a declaration of loyalty and non-resistance to the Crown. It was a piece of muddled thinking, emanating from a servile council, which James accepted for political purposes. For the Duke of 1681 was bruised and embittered in mind and spirit. He used the Test to serve his own ends and lost the sympathy of the best of the Scots whom he was endeavouring to bully into subservience. His chief victim was Argyll, the red-headed Campbell whose reservation that he took the Test 'in so far as it was consistent with itself' was made an excuse for a charge of treasonable misrepresentation of the Laws. The Bench was divided as to his guilt and it was said that an old deaf judge, who had slept during the evidence and gone home early to bed, was brought back to the court to give the casting-vote which convicted Argyll. When the news came to London, Halifax exclaimed 'I know nothing of Scotch law, but I know that we should not hang a dog here on the grounds on which my lord Argyll has been sentenced!'

The Campbell escaped from Edinburgh Castle through the pluck and ingenuity of his stepdaughter Lady Sophia Lindsay. Her page exchanged clothes with Argyll when she visited him in prison, whence she emerged weeping seemly tears at bidding adieu to the captive. But when the sentinel looked too closely at her awkward page, she twitched her train from the latter's hand and dashed it across his face, with the angry cry, 'Varlet, take that for knowing no better how to carry your lady's garment.' In his embarrassment at such behaviour, the soldier let them pass. Argyll slipped away down an Edinburgh wynd to fend for himself. He came at length to London, but when a busybody endeavoured to inform the King, Charles would not listen. 'Pooh! Pooh! hunt a weary partridge?' he exclaimed. Eventually, Argyll fled to Holland, to watch events in England and take his opportunity.

It was his personal animosity against such men as Argyll,

and the absence of any sign of emotion, when Covenanters were executed or tortured for information, that gave rise to the legends of James's cruelty. It was said that when the 'Boot' was applied to a prisoner and the heavy wood was screwed into the naked flesh, others, more squeamish than he, would find some excuse to absent themselves from council, but that the Duke would remain, watching his victim with sadistic satisfaction. There is no serious ground for the tradition. Torture could only be legally inflicted by the Council and it was customary for a councillor to be present to prevent abuse. James's attendance, though it showed lack of feeling, was in the interests of justice and there is no record of any particular brutality to justify the charge of sadism, while specific examples of leniency do exist. He was by nature a severe man and there is a hint of cruelty in his face, counteracted though it is by an air of sadness, as if he felt himself apart from other folks. Yet after 1688, Claverhouse wrote that James could not 'alter the clement temper that has ever been found in the family and has eminently appeared in his person.' Possibly his harshness on occasion emanated from severity of judgment rather than brutality, from lack of understanding rather than absence of decent feeling. He was supercilious rather than bestial. Yet if one regards the year in Scotland as the prologue to his reign, it is significant that James did not shrink from the barbarous customs of the north. It may have been that he was plunged into this land of strange contrasts, of coarseness and learning, of heroism and brutality, of unequalled loyalty and savage revolt at a time when he was unstrung by the attacks of his enemies in London. He was not a man who stood hate well; rigid and self-centred, he repaid it with hatred. A grave change took place in him some time between the last Dutch War when he fought against odds with English courage and won his seamen's love and the years of his reign when he failed so disastrously to rise to the stature of an absolute monarch. Some of the causes of that change have been indicated, the loss of his post, the looseness of his life, the shock of the Popish Plot and the bitterness of the Exclusion struggle. The work of killing men in Scotland undoubtedly accelerated the process, while it gave him an intoxicating experience of autocratic power. Yet apart from politics he performed his task well. He was assiduous in the routine of government, recovering something of the satisfaction he had known in Admiralty days. He gave his brother a lengthy report on the administration of Scotland which showed not only a grasp of the main problems of organisation and government, but contained sound suggestions for improvements in the future. It was the work of a man of industry and ability. If only a kindly fate had made him a civil servant, James would have been a happy man.

For Mary Beatrice the days passed in lazy monotony. While James found relaxations in playing golf, his wife drank tea, and wrote or failed to write letters to her friends. She was still, at twenty-two, an impetuous and warm-hearted young woman. 'Pray when ever you write to me, don't do it with any forme or ceremony,' she begs of the Duchess of Hamilton, 'for i can't indure it from a friend, i look upon you as mine, and i assure you i am without any compliment, truly yours, Mary.' And to another correspondent she excuses herself. 'But whenever I don't write to you, it is want of time, or at most a little laziness, and now, of late, after having been so long, I grew so ashamed of myself, that I did not know which way to go about it, and so put it off without considering that I did still worse and worse.'

She was a brave soul. For March of 1681 had proved a terrible month. In March, Charles met his last Parliament at Oxford. The exiles in Scotland could not appreciate the sure signs of a turning of the tide which nerved the King to take drastic action: they distrusted the influence Halifax had regained and knew that he would put forward schemes for curbing the powers of a Catholic successor. At that moment, their political future looked more hopeless than ever. But there were griefs that came closer than exclusion from the throne. On March 2nd, Isabel died at St. James's. Her parents' grief was embittered by their enforced absence from their 'loveley' child in her last illness. She was just four, and old enough to be frightened; Mary Beatrice was tortured with thoughts of her crying for the mother who did not come. She had been very ill herself, for the child she had carried in her womb that dreary winter was born dead in this same month of March. It was little wonder that when the cold winds of spring ravaged Edinburgh, Duke and Duchess pleaded to come home.

But Charles refused their appeal. He knew how tender a plant is the growth of good-feeling, where before there has been rancour; less than ever, he felt it to be a time for those methods of dictatorship his brother would have employed. Also he was worried. He might baffle his friends by his easy words or trick his opponents by unexpected action, but he was as much at a loss as less clever men. He could not be certain that the Whigs would play into his hands by over-reaching themselves and indulging in treason. He could only be sure that his ease had vanished, and that James was the cause of it. His better self was disgusted by the Duchess of Portsmouth's apostasy and Monmouth's friendship with his father's enemies. But these were the people he loved, and he could find it in him to hate the man who had caused their backslidings.

Yet his people longed for quiet as earnestly as he. If James would appease their fears, by a few formal attendances at the public services of the Established Church, they would be thankful to cease fretting and accept him as their future king. In August, Lawrence Hyde appeared in Edinburgh with a message from Charles. If the Duke would agree to go to church occasionally, he could return to England, and no further attempt would be made to interfere with his private theological beliefs. If he refused this occasional conformity, the King could no longer support him; 'all men would desert his cause,' said Hyde, 'as they would a towne that can no longer be defended.' But the Duke's guiding principle of life, which neither the shocks of fortune nor the numbing effect of years could undermine, was loyalty to his friends and to his faith. He refused. Better exile than apostasy. Hyde 'left him with the comfortless view of being abandon'd by all the world.' Halifax, the cultured infidel, might shrug his shoulders in amaze; Sunderland, a renegade by instinct, might scorn an obstinacy he could not emulate, honest Anglicans like Hyde might admire and yet despair; even John Churchill and George Legge, the closest friends he had, might regret the Duke's decision but the fact of its courage remains unshaken, to cancel much in his conduct that was inclement or unwise.

And so the Duke and Duchess stayed in Scotland. Life had its compensations. Quiet nights and pleasant days softened the memory of earlier crises and alarms. Soon after Hyde's departure, Anne visited her parents. There were picnics and excursions to amuse the Princess. Eight coaches, full of laughing ladies, squired by four score gentlemen on horseback, were driven out into the country, for the court to 'see the gardens' and partake of wine and fruit. The hills were flushed with heather, and the air heavy with the scent of briar-rose. It was as good then as now to slake one's thirst in the heat of an August afternoon and to let the body relax, regardless of the pressure of worldly things. The joy of the country-folk, stirred by the unwonted sight of so many of 'the royal family' solaced the Duchess with the benediction of goodwill.

In the following spring, the Duke was summoned to London on a matter of business. His wife was again pregnant, and she had not yet learnt to bear that state with equanimity. She was left behind in Scotland, but she was miserable, and as she confessed later: 'I wrote at last to tell him so.' In May, the Duke returned by sea to bring her home. He set out from Margate on the sailing vessel *Gloucester,* with some two hundred souls on board, dogs and priests and musicians in addition to his own gentlemen and numerous Scottish lords. *The Happy Return* and some smaller yachts were in attendance. As the ship bore northwards along the East Anglian coast, James urged the pilot to stand further out to sea: he knew too well the shoals and sand-banks of that dangerous shore. But Captain Ayres was a surly fellow (witness his politics: he was a Republican). He was also a good sailor and the Duke trusted him, but on this occasion his contrariness exceeded his skill. Probably because he was pressed, he refused to stand out to sea. The *Gloucester* struck in Yarmouth Road, upon the sand-bank known as 'The Lemon and Oar', and James was awakened by knocks upon his cabin door and urgent persuasions to save himself in the ship's long-boat. It would have been better had he complied immediately, for there would then have been time to advise the other yachts, who could have lowered boats to rescue the *Gloucester*'s crew. But at such crises men do not act by reason; and James's instinct was not to desert his ship. She was filling steadily with water but he refused to budge, urging the willing crew to redouble their efforts to get her off the sand-bank. She was too heavily laden for success, and when there was six feet of water in the hold, necessity prevailed. James took to the boat, calling his gentlemen to follow him. Churchill was among those who came; as the shallop filled rapidly with men, some felt that greater risk was incurred by taking refuge on that perilous craft than by staying behind. Afterwards, the survivors told the usual ghastly stories of officers, with their swords, keeping back the wretches, who would have swamped the boat in a last frenzied struggle for their lives; they remembered that the Duke wasted precious moments in his anxiety for the safety of a black box of papers, those records and memoranda which, accompanying him to France, were eventually to perish in the French Revolution. Scandal-mongers spread the tale that in the hour of peril he had thought only of his priests and his dogs. Even Churchill coolly criticised his master's initial delay and subsequent conduct, regardless of the fact that he himself had been the first man James called to safety. But gratitude was not a strong point with the future Duke of Marlborough. It is not very difficult to distinguish the grain from the chaff in the conflicting tales. James ought, no doubt, to have left the ship earlier, but at least it was a brave fault. He ought not to have balanced his papers against the lives of men. Apart from that, it is hard to see how he could have acted differently. In the confusion, it was not possible to make a cool selection of the men to fill the shallop; James's first instinctive call to his friends should not be used to prove him unfeeling. Priests may have been among the survivors, but they recived no differential treatment. The Duchess's own almoner had to find safety, clinging to a raft. In the boat James showed himself humane. It was overladen and in imminent danger of capsize. But the Duke leant over the side, and dragged in the Duke of Montrose. Another pair of desperate hands grasped the gunwale. The sailor in charge tried to beat them off with his oars: one too many would mean the death of all. 'He is but a poor fiddler,' cried the Duke, recognising the anguished figure in the water, 'let us try and save him,' and he pulled him in. But the man called himself a musician, and was offended at James's tone. Afterwards he helped to spread the lying tales! As the boat rowed away, the men who were left behind gave a resounding cheer in honour of the Duke. United in the fellowship of that cheer, as others in a later century were united in the fellowship of a hymn, over a hundred and sixty men went down to death. Before the boats of the nearest ship in sight could reach the tragic spot, the *Gloucester* was no more.

The Duchess of York was not told of the disaster. By

James's instructions, the news was kept from her till he arrived in person. His presence comforted her. 'I feared nothing,' she wrote later. 'I saw the King [James] and I seemed to have power to confront every peril. He was the most intrepid of men, and looked on danger with perfect coolness.' Her strength was put to the test immediately. The two returned, as the Duke had come, by sea. How much she suffered on the voyage in physical and mental wretchedness, the Duchess never said. She forgot her fears in the joy of home-coming, and her presence restored light and gaiety to darkened rooms. Dryden, the court poet, greeted her return:

> 'For her, the weeping Heavens become serene,
> For her, the ground is clad in cheerful green,
> For her, the nightingales are taught to sing,
> And nature has for her delay'd the spring.'

But the autumn brought her fresh sorrow. Her child, born in August, died in convulsive fits, on October 6th. The strain and excitement of the spring had been the worst prelude to maternity. Mary Beatrice surrendered the lingering hope that she would ever bear a child that lived. She comforted herself with her religion and with the superficial activities of a public personage, while she watched her husband resume his old position at court and his illicit relations with Catherine Sedley. And in her oratory, before her crucifix, she found an outlet for the romance that is in every woman, by dreaming of the day when she would be Queen, and serve her God by re-converting England.

By duplicity abroad and caution at home, Charles had been steadily improving his position since 1681. The Whigs had resented the Duke's return. On April 20th, 1682, the Artillery Company of the City of London had arranged a dinner in his honour. His political opponents immediately organised a rival gathering which was to be a thanksgiving festival for the protection that 'God had granted the King, the Protestant religion and the liberties of England against the Hellish attacks of their enemies'. But the Council forbade the demonstration, and the Duke rode into London, attended by many Scottish gentlemen, once more master of the situation. Shaftesbury was committed to the Tower, where his impatient spirit had languished and broken under durance. Acquitted by a London jury, loyal to the leader they had loved, he urged his friends to resistance and instigated Monmouth to make a semi-royal progress in Cheshire, where the latter secured himself in the hearts of the people, by winning a horse-race and touching for the King's evil. The turbulent citizens of London celebrated Gunpowder Plot amid cries of 'No Popery, No York,' and the echo of 'A Monmouth'. But Charles had had enough of his son's insubordination. Monmouth was arrested as he paraded the streets of Chester, with seven hundred adherents cheering in his wake; he was only released on the promise of good behaviour. Shaftesbury, sensing with a politician's instinct that the tide was going against him and alarmed by Charles's successful attack upon municipal independence urged a general insurrection. Even the meticulous Russell joined in considered debate on the possibility of attacking Whitehall. But the tide had turned; the Whig plans had no coherence, and in November 1682, Shaftesbury fled to Holland and died in the following January.

He had been a great politician, who had realised the full danger of James's autocratic spirit. There was in him, besides the Puritan instinct of resistance to dictatorship, a remarkable power of organisation and leadership and a strain of idealism, that in other circumstance would have produced the poet or martyr. But the denial of absolute standards in conduct, which characterised his age, had produced the crooked means and the political dishonesties which eventually discredited him; and he failed because in his final advocacy of illegal measures he was denying the rule of law and ordered liberty which was the very essence of his creed.

Unfortunately in 1683, his colleagues tampered with sedition. One Robert Ferguson who had been with Shaftesbury at his death returned to England as leader of a group of desperadoes to whom plots were the very breath of life. They had conceived the scheme of assassinating King and Duke on their way from Newmarket in the spring.[1] One of the conspirators worked as malster at the Rye House on the road, and here the royal party were to be attacked. A fire in Newmarket accelerated the return of the court and the plot came to nothing; but knowledge of it reached the government. There followed the usual crop of arrests and executions, and the miserable examination of men, lying to save their own skins. There were many that deserved their fate. There were others, the victims of more subtle men, who were whirled into this maelstrom of assassination and sudden death, ordinary folk who knew nothing of political philosophy, but who had their principles and were lured by the thrill of risk and adventure and gain. They paid for it by their lives. There is something very pitiable about the list of humble names. 'The butcher Harris, Smith a tailor . . . Joseph How, a distiller in Whitecross Street, Cole a brewer, James Wood a weaver in Spitalfields, and John Adderton a glazier . . .' May they rest in peace!

The King was not interested in them. But he seized his opportunity of ruining the Whig leaders. They had no share in plots to murder, but they had not discountenanced the unruly element in their midst, and had continued to debate resistance. On June 26th, Lord Russell and Algernon Sidney were arrested and sent to the Tower. Three days later, rewards were offered for the capture of Monmouth: he was not to be found; perhaps nobody searched for him very carefully. Hampden, the

[1] The scheme had been planned originally in the previous autumn and was revived in the spring of 1683.

grandson of the hero of the Civil Wars, Lord Howard and Lord Essex were seized in turn. In the crisis, Howard lost his nerve and told all he knew: of secret meetings and lengthy discussion, in which sedition had played its part, though Russell and his friends had disapproved. But they had continued to associate with the men who did approve. It was sufficient for the King, who had now all the cards in his hand. On July 13th, 1683, Russell was sentenced to death. He spent his last days in cheerful fortitude. It rained the night before his execution. 'Such a rain to-morrow would spoil a great show, which is a dull thing in a rainy day,' he said. He was not afraid. There were worse ways of ending one's life than a violent death. 'It was only the being exposed to be a little gazed at, and to suffer the pain for one minute, which he was confident was not equal to the pain of drawing a tooth.' Tillotson, a gentle bishop, was with him much, but he was disappointed that he felt none of the religious transports that others had enjoyed in like circumstance. Excess even in devotion was not in his nature. But 'he had a full calm in his mind, no palpitation at heart'. He took the Sacrament the day before his execution, said farewell to his young children, and parted from his wife in silence. She loved him well enough to know she could help him most by being calm, and she was not betrayed into tears. 'The bitterness of death is past,' he said, and retired to his chamber. Next day he went quietly to the scaffold, singing psalms upon the way, with a smile and an apology, 'he would sing better very soon'. The integrity of his life and the gentle courage of his ending gave to his death the seal of martyrdom. His aged father, the Earl of Bedford offered his huge fortune as a ransom for his son. The King had refused, it was rumoured at James's instigation. The Earl did not forget.

In December, Sidney followed Russell to the block, convicted with difficulty on the strength of his own published writings by a brilliant bully of the name of Jeffreys. Russell had died like a Christian; Sidney met his end like a Stoic. 'He died very resolutely,' commented the Duke of York, 'and like a true Rebel and Republican.' Sidney would have wished no other epitaph. Lord Essex, irresolute and in despair, remembering years of loyal service to Charles in Ireland and at Whitehall, looked out of his narrow prison in the Tower and broke his heart. They found him dead, his throat cut with a razor, which he had obtained to pare his nails.

Monmouth was eclipsed. Afraid to stand out longer, in November 1683 he saw the King, confessed his sins, and spoke freely of his association with the Whigs, seconding much that Howard had already reported. He was granted a pardon and appeared at court. Even the Duke greeted him amicably. But the report in the *Gazette* made it appear that Monmouth had betrayed his friends. Perhaps the Duke was partly responsible for the impression that got abroad. Monmouth tried to recover the letter of confession which he had written to Charles, feeling that his honour was impugned. Charles lost his temper. He bade Halifax 'restore him the paper and send him to Hell'. Monmouth compromised by going to Holland.

The Tories were triumphant, and but for the selfish wrangles of his own friends, the King would have been free to enjoy the quiet he had so skilfully won. But the atmosphere of Whitehall, which robbed men of all the power and virtue that was in them, was not conducive to peace of mind. Halifax, the Lord Privy Seal, had been Charles's henchman in the years of cautious advance, but in the triumphs of 1683 he had given ground before Hyde, now Earl of Rochester, and Sunderland, the politician on the make, who had worked his way once more into favour. Rochester was James's brother-in-law, and the latter never disregarded family ties. When the rivalry between Rochester and Halifax became acute, the Duke was glad of an excuse to break the superficial friendship he had been forced to conclude with the latter on his return from Scotland. He had never forgiven Halifax's advocacy of Limitations; moreover, the two men were poles apart in character and mentality. Nor did the satiric philosopher, whose wit attracted Charles, find anything congenial in Rochester's formality. The latter was hemmed in by all the taboos of an English gentleman; Halifax was intellectually a free-lance, though his fastidious taste restrained exuberance. Eventually, with unworthy satisfaction, he charged Rochester with maladministration at the Treasury, and saw him kicked upstairs into the dignified sinecure of the Presidency of the Council.

James, though prominent at court and council, had returned to his first love, naval administration. Disregarding the Test, he began to control the Admiralty again, though he missed Samuel Pepys who had lost his office in the Popish Terror. He vowed he would have him back again as soon as he was King. The rhymsters were busy, and down the very streets in which twelve months ago the rioters had cried 'A Monmouth', and battered the inn sign at 'The Duke's Head', they whistled the verses: 'The glory of the British Line, Old Jimmy's come again.'

In July 1683, plain dumpling Princess Anne had married George of Denmark, a dull and worthy prince who had been suggested as a suitor by King Louis of France. Pedestrian though the match might seem, the young couple were satisfied, and a loyal affection to each other that endured domestic tragedy and the merciless glare of the throne acquired by its very unpretentiousness a dignity more lasting than the transient brilliance of romance. The young couple remained in England, and there was a burst of merriment at court, reminiscent of the first jocund days of the Restoration. Nowadays cards were preferred to dancing, and lords and ladies tired themselves out in the service of pleasure by playing long for high stakes. The silent Godolphin who succeeded Rochester at the head of the Treasury could always be found at the tables, doing business with half an eye on his cards when a clerk sought him out to ask instructions or urge the need of some decision. Mary Beatrice was used to cards now; she had learnt to compromise on more matters than gambling. But she preferred the days in the open air at Windsor or Newmarket or Winchester, where the King was building himself a new house in the loveliest city in England. She loved riding, and in spite of one or two bad falls in Scotland, excelled on horseback. The court spent some weeks at Winchester in the autumn of 1683, idyllic days when work was in abeyance and the only jarring note was uttered by Thomas Ken, the Dean, who refused to provide lodging for Nell Gwynne, the King's mistress. Charles respected his courage and knew a saint when he met one. Ken became Bishop of Bath and Wells, the next See that became vacant. James rode out every day to hunt, returning twenty miles after a kill as the swift September twilight dimmed the ripened corn. He took his wife to visit Portsmouth and Southampton, and showed her the docks with pride. And the King's palace grew in pomp and majesty under the shadow of the great cathedral that called him to the contemplation of eternity.

Perhaps he answered the call, conscious of failing health. As the next year drew to a close, beneath the mask of merry-making, those who loved him best could detect a forced gaiety in Charles. He was worried about his son. Gently, Halifax pushed his advantage. In November 1684, Monmouth came secretly to England and visited his father. He returned to Holland with the promise of a speedy recall. The air was full of rumours, and men waited upon the event.

It came like a burst of thunder on a sultry day. 'It was on the 2nd of February (1685) that the King was seized with a violent fit of an apoplexy just as he came out of his closet where he had been for some time before he was dress'd.' Before the Duke could be summoned, a doctor had let blood and there were signs of a complete recovery. On February 6th, Charles took a turn for the worse.

There only remained the weary business of dying; even at the end a King could not be left in peace. Two bishops were introduced into his presence. One of them was Ken. Very simply he asked if Charles were sorry for his sins, and when the King had answered yes, he gave him absolution. But the proffered Sacrament was refused with the last polite evasion of a King who had excelled therein. The Duke standing by his brother's side saw his opportunity. Motioning away the company who were crowding round the bed, enjoying an orgy of emotion and satisfying their curiosity, he asked the King if he should send for a priest. 'For God's sake, Brother, do, and please to lose no time,' was Charles's rejoinder. Father Huddleston the Benedictine monk who had aided Charles in the first mad flight from Worcester was at hand in the Palace to help him in a yet more difficult escape. By the back-stairs and a private closet he was brought to the royal bedside. In the hour of his extremity, Charles acknowledged himself a Catholic, and received the succour the Church of Rome offered to faithful believers. Then in his own inimitable way he said farewell to his friends and his brother and commended his mistresses to the care of the nation. Just before midday he died. The bells of Westminster tolled the news and the city churches echoed the sad peal; by the coaches and the post-boys the word spread over England with the rapidity of evil tidings. And the heralds proclaimed his brother, the Duke of York, as James II, ruler of England, Scotland and Ireland. 'The King is dead! Long live the King!'

PART IV

POWER

CHAPTER VIII

MONMOUTH

'He failed and perished.'

John Evelyn.

'I SHALL make it my endeavour to preserve the government in Church and State as it is by Law established. I know the principles of the Church of England are for Monarchy, and that the members of it have shewn themselves good and Loyall subjects, and therefore I shall always take care to defend and support it. I know likewise that the Laws of England are sufficient to make the King as great a monarch as I can wish, and therefore as I will never depart from the just rights and prerogatives of the Crown, so I never will invade any man's property. I have often ventured my life in defence of the Nation, and will go as far as any man in preserving it in its just rights and privileges.'

With these words, King James II greeted his Privy Council on the day after his accession to the throne of England. By these words he must be judged. Were they spoken in sincerity? Was the tragedy of the dawning years inevitable because to James his 'just prerogatives' included powers incompatible with a limited monarchy, while his ideal of liberty of conscience was so alien to the principles of the Church of England that by its obscurantism it forfeited his support. Or was his pretence of conciliation merely a ruse to obtain himself a Parliamentary income, his reign a consistent whole that aimed at the overthrow of the English Church and English liberties? Or was he neither a scoundrel nor a just man misunderstood, but a ruler, honest in his convictions but ignorant of the heart of his people, swayed by passions and fears, and urged to suicidal haste by the unwise counsels of those whom he trusted and the inexorable pressure of time, reminding him that he was growing old. These are the questions his reign must answer, and disclose therein a story of human suffering and mistaken heroism, of turpitude and sacrifice seldom crowded into four short years.

. . . .

They shouted for James, when the heralds pronounced him King, and heads ached in Cheapside with the clamour of the bells. His speech to his council was printed and preached upon, and folk thanked God for the prospect of quietude. 'We have now the word of a King, and a word never yet broken.' They crowned him on St. George's Day with all the pomp and ceremony in which the Englishman delights, expressing thereby the love of colour and shape and harmony which reserve forbids him to display in the life of every day. The regalia of former Queen-Consorts had not survived the civil wars, and Mary of Modena appeared in radiant but quiet beauty, her dress bright with a hundred jewels, with diamonds sewn upon every seam. Children scattered April flowers before her feet and as in dignified devotion she joined in the Anglican responses, her seemly behaviour touched the hearts of the beholders. The King kept silence with that curious twist to his full lips, which turned a smile so quickly to a sneer. But it was a coronation of exceptional beauty and ostentation. Nothing was omitted of past tradition or present custom, save the Sacrament. That omission gave food for anxious thought, but there are times when the wise will not think too deeply. From ten in the morning till seven at night, the wearisome ceremonial continued, till those about the Queen feared lest her strength should give way. For she was only just convalescent from an attack of pneumonia that had proved her lungs to be permanently weakened by the fogs and rains of English Februaries. The unaffected rejoicings of her new subjects was tonic sufficient to uphold her though she seemed subdued in spirit, in part because of two occurrences that might well be reckoned of evil import. When the Archbishop placed the crown on her husband's head, it tottered; his thin high forehead was of different shape from Charles's broader brow. There was one at hand to steady the diadem with a witty word. 'This is not the first time, your Majesty that my family has supported the Crown.' It was unfortunate it should be Henry Sidney, a man whom James hated because once long ago he had made love to Anne Hyde, a man whose brother had died a convinced Republican and who was himself William of Orange's friend.

It was a small accident and James and his Queen had deeper cause to be disturbed by omens: that day a child of his had died. The child's mother was Catherine Sedley, who, with her wit as acid as her thin features and her arrogant assumption of superiority, had recently been only less prominent at Whitehall than Charles's own women. On his accession, James had resolved that she should leave the Palace and had made fresh resolutions to lead a moral life. Catherine, who had hoped to ape the Duchess of Portsmouth, had submitted with no good grace and already he knew it was not going to be easy. But to do him justice, he had no intention of shirking his task as king, whatever self-denying ordinances it might be necessary to impose upon himself. He tackled the work of sovereignty in a thorough if doctrinaire manner. Some of the results were admirable. Drunkenness and duelling were suppressed with rigour, it was made clear that adultery was to be conducted in a seemly manner if it were to remain respectable, and by frugal finance and the dismissal of unnecessary staff, he succeeded in bringing his court alike into 'method and magnificence'. He acted with similar authority and ability in the affairs of the nation. Samuel Pepys was restored to a responsible position in the Admiralty, and under James's direction set about a whole-hearted reformation of the Navy. The

King's legal position might be doubtful in continuing to collect the customs that had been granted to his brother but not as yet to himself, but the merchants saw that it was an assumption of authority that prevented dislocation and delay. They appreciated the many small ways in which he showed, not merely that he had the interest of trade at heart, but that he had a sensible man's appreciation of what those interests were. Had he kept his hands off religion, he could have stretched his prerogative very far without offending the Whig business men of London and the ports, whose lodestar in matters political was generally to be found in their pockets.

As for the Tories, the promotion of Rochester to the office of Lord Treasurer on February 12th sufficed as a guarantee that nothing could go radically wrong. The issue of writs for a Parliament to be held in May completed the sense of well-being. Barillon, Louis's agent, was disturbed; James in spite of protestations of friendship was showing an independent spirit. He excused his Parliament as a necessary gesture: 'I know the English, you must not shew any fear in the beginning.' In that temper, he faced the large and loyal Tory majority with which the elections had provided him. 'The best way to engage me to meet you often is always to use me well,' he told them plainly, in asking for a revenue for life. They responded to the treatment and granted him large supplies, to which they added supplementary subsidies on news of a rising in Scotland.

It was the cloud no bigger than a man's hand that foretold the coming storm. Argyll's abortive effort to rouse the clans failed not merely because it was ill-timed, preceding by some weeks the insurrection in the south with which it should have coincided, but also because he himself lacked loyalty in the past and leadership in the present. He was captured with the shedding of little blood, and in Edinburgh, on the strength of the sentence passed against him three years before, he was executed for high treason, glorifying a disparate life by the manner of its ending. His last sleep garnered immortality: 'he prayed often . . . and went to the scaffold with great serenity.'

To those who could not stifle thought the callous use of the three-year-old conviction aroused misgivings. Argyll deserved to die, in that his enterprise constituted treason, but a new trial would have been more seemly; there was no need to flaunt an ancient insult.[1] There was a blatant stupidity about it, a flinging away of popularity won so dearly and so hard to regain, which also characterised other trials that spring. On the 8th of May, Titus Oates was dragged from the King's Bench prison, where he had been confined since the previous year, and was condemned as a seditious libeller. He was sentenced as was customary to a fine and the pillory, and also to be whipped from Aldgate to Newgate and forty-eight hours later from Newgate to Tyburn. That he survived for the ensuing 'imprisonment for life' was proof that his body was as tough as his conscience. But as he underwent the cruel flogging some bade the executioner desist with shouts of 'Enough! Enough!' Oates, a *poseur* still, replied, 'Not enough, good people, for the truth, not enough!' The crowds forgot that innocent men had died through his testimony and remembered the grain of truth among the chaff. He became a martyr to many who witnessed his agony as the executioner's whip drew blood from his heaving shoulders. James did not watch; his feelings in the matter were simple and direct. 'Now the Popish Plot is dead,' he commented, and approved a courtier's addendum, 'long since dead and now it would be buried.'

But while Oates had stood pilloried in Palace yard, another prisoner was at the bar before the Lord Chief Justice. He was Richard Baxter, an old man of seventy, imprisoned in the previous year as a dissenter. He too was charged with libel, not in slanderous word or unjust accusation but in a reflection on episcopacy contained in his 'Paraphrase

[1] The King considered that a new trial would cast an aspersion on the legality of the previous sentence.

of the New Testament'. He asked for further time to instruct his counsel, for he had been a fighter all his days. The Lord Chief Justice fumed. 'Not a minute! Not to save his life,' he cried. 'I can deal with saints as well as sinners. There stands Oates on one side of the pillory; and if Baxter stood on the other, the two greatest rogues in the kingdom would stand together.' They were light words to the bullying in which the Judge indulged as the trial proceeded. 'Richard, thou art an old fellow, an old knave, thou hast written books enough to load a cart, every one is as full of sedition as an egg is full of meat; hadst thou been whipped out of thy writing trade forty years ago it had been happy.' The prisoner, one of the greatest divines and the most lovable men of his age, listened quietly to the tirade and when sentence had been passed returned uncomplaining to his captivity.

The name of the Justice who had so little sense of decorum was Jeffreys. He was a self-made Welshman, still under forty years of age, who had studied law with the thoroughness of a man who has no fortune but intends to get on in the world. He had other assets: undoubted ability, good looks and abundant energy. He was a *bon viveur* and a 'good mixer', and his atrocious lack of manners was so blatant as to be amusing. At the bar or on the bench the joy he took in bullying his victims was not resented in an age when politics rather than justice coloured the atmosphere of the courts. He had married young and romantically, made his way in the city, toadied to Bab Chiffinch and at the age of twenty-nine became Solicitor-General to the Duke of York. Now as Lord Chief Justice he had his eye on the supreme office which Lord Chancellor North's failing health brought within tantalising reach. All that was necessary to secure his life's ambition – the Woolsack before the age of forty – was the opportunity to do the Crown a signal service. It had needed no skill to convict Oates or Baxter; something more spectacular was required.

Monmouth's tragedy was Jeffreys's opportunity. In the early hours of the morning of Saturday, June 13th, two jaded horsemen reached London with the news that Monmouth had landed at Lyme Regis and was raising the country against the King. They had left Honiton on Friday at midnight, and rode through Sherborne and Shaftesbury, over the downs about Basingstoke, under Windsor Castle and across the river at Staines. They had ridden a hundred and fifty miles, as dawn grew to daylight, through the midday heat and the waning afternoon, through dusk and darkness and the white light of a second dawn, until at four in the morning they reached the house of Sir Winston Churchill, the member for Lyme Regis. Within an hour the King had been aroused; later in the morning the messengers from the west told their story to the House of Commons. It was the beginning of three weeks of suspense and anxiety; crowns had fallen under less likely shocks than this. The rapid raising of forces, the recall of troops serving with the Dutch in Flanders, the passing of an Act of Attainder against Monmouth could have availed nothing if the loyalty of the country as a whole and London in particular had not stood firm. Remembering the events of the exclusion struggle, James could scarcely expect undeviating loyalty; that he found it was due to the good impression he had made in the first months of his reign, and to the average Londoner's sense of fair play which prevented the capital from surrendering to Monmouth's glamour. But the King was frightened and angry, and determined for his people's security and his own, that when he gained the upper hand he would make such an example of the rebels that insurrection should never raise its head again.

The story of Monmouth's expedition is so fraught with romance and tragedy that it is difficult to regard it clearly as a military adventure. Still to-day they will show you in Somerset rusty weapons that the thatchers have found, thrust into the roofs where King Monmouth's men had hidden them, in a trembling agony of fear when the gamble had been lost. To the children and the children's children of the men who died at Sedgemoor, Monmouth's rising was no sterile incident of politics but an epic of the West Country.

There had been a Prologue, five years before, when the Duke of Monmouth, at Shaftesbury's instigation, rode through Somerset and Devon as a Prince of the Blood Royal. Charming and debonair, a good sportsman and happy of heart, he pleased the simple folk who had no need to ask if wisdom and integrity made sure foundation to his facile nature. Once he touched for the King's evil; and at Exeter, a thousand 'stout young men' shouted their adherence to the darling of the countryside. West-Country folk are tenacious in memory. On June 11th, 1685, three foreign vessels, showing no colours, were seen off Lyme Regis. From one of the ships two men had landed and rode inland. The curious citizens of Lyme looked out from the Cobb and wondered. At evening Monmouth landed with about eighty companions. The chief among them was Lord Grey, sole representative of the Whig aristocracy on whose support the success of the rising must ultimately depend. There was a professional soldier from Germany called Buise and two Scotsmen, worst and best of their type: Ferguson, Monmouth's evil genius and Fletcher of Saltoun, steadfast in his patriotism, forceful and brilliant but as irritable as only a disillusioned idealist can be. Ferguson, had drawn up the manifesto which now was read in the market-square of Lyme to the crowds who thronged to listen. They did not listen very deeply; enthusiasm was too intoxicating for critical thought. All that mattered was that Monmouth had come again.

Yet that manifesto damned the invaders' cause. It showed that neither statecraft nor honesty was to be found in him or his advisers. In denouncing James as a usurper, it declared him to be guilty of crimes too hideous to be absurd, too obviously false to carry conviction. Not only had he fired the City of London in 1666, he had poisoned his brother, the late King. He must be deposed, and a successor, 'elected in free parliament'. James's response to this tirade was not unnatural, a price of £5,000 was placed on Monmouth's head.

The insurgents remained at Lyme throughout Friday and Saturday, June 12th and 13th, unloading arms and ammunitions from the ships and enrolling volunteers, who poured in from the neighbouring villages. Their numbers left nothing to be desired, but their quality was disappointing; it had been better for Monmouth's spirits, and so for his cause, if he had known nothing of soldiering. He had arms and to spare, but how could he trust them to the uneasy hands of shepherds and ploughmen; how in a few brief weeks train shopkeepers and artisans to form a prince's cavalry? There were good men among them: men of substance and intelligence, the leading dissenters of the small towns who were to prove themselves as brave in body as they had been in mind. But everything depended upon the gentry, Tories as well as Whigs, who might be attracted by their hatred of Catholicism. Monmouth waited and his gay looks darkened, but the gentry remained at home.

On Saturday, came the first foreboding of tragedy. Fletcher of Saltoun, the best soldier in the rebel army, was eagerly preparing for an attack on Bridport where the Somerset militia was stationed. He found a fine horse in camp that had been given to 'old Dare', a rough Dorset man much respected by his neighbours, who had come across with the little band from Holland. Fletcher took the horse, and Dare resented the Scot's high-handed act. He told him plainly what he thought of him, provoked not only by the appropriation of his property, but by all the repressed irritation of the lengthy voyage and the companionship of republican extremists. Dare's harangue ended with a switch upraised, as if to strike. Fletcher's dangerous patience broke suddenly; civilisation forgotten, he was a clansman in a rage; he whipped out a pistol and shot dead the Dorset man. There was an uproar. Monmouth had no choice of action. Fletcher was shipped aboard the frigate that was about to sail, on the understanding that he was to be landed at Bristol for trial In fact he sailed for Spain, and so to fresh adventures in war against the Turks till Scotland needed him in 1689. Thus Monmouth lost the one man in his ranks who had brains as well as courage, experience of war and an unselfish loyalty. Even he by his faults had betrayed his unhappy leader.

The attack on Bridport took place on the Sunday. Had Grey been less infirm of purpose, the effective enthusiasm of Monmouth's volunteers might have given the rebels a real success. As it was the militia retained the centre of the town, and Monmouth moved across the county towards Taunton, occupying Axminster but avoiding the Devon regiments who were advancing to combine with the Somerset men. Monmouth should have attacked boldly before regular forces had arrived from London, for the militia men were ready to desert on the slightest pretext, and while their morale was still good his own men might have worked marvels. Unfortunately, his military experience and his real skill as a soldier made him so conscious of his army's defects that he wasted precious days in vain effort to discipline and train his men instead of risking all in a bold enterprise that could alone succeed.

At Taunton, his recruits were of a better class, and his army reached 7,000 men. The joy his coming had aroused transformed the prosperous little town into a place of festival. The pupils of Miss Musgrave's school presented their hero with a banner, worked by them in happy haste. The 'maids of Taunton' knew little of politics, but Sarah Blake, 'captain of the virgins' who led the bright procession, and her elder sister, who spoke her lines without a tremor, had never had such a wonderful day in the whole of their short lives. The Duke came out from his lodgings to greet them and receive their gifts, the banner and a small Bible, whose truths he vowed he would defend and 'seal it with his blood if there should be occasion for it'. Cheers and laughter followed him and the happy cries of children as he rode into the town. At Taunton on Saturday, the 20th of June, he allowed his followers to proclaim him King. It was a last attempt to attract the gentry; it merely alienated the moderates. And meanwhile forces were approaching from London, and Monmouth was doing very little about it.

The next sixteen days are a record of futility. On June 21st he left Taunton, and marched a week too late upon Bristol. He found that the garrison had been heartened by reinforcements from London, and he withdrew without attack, a chance conflagration among the ships in the river occasioning the rumour that the town had been fired by the defence. He approached Bath, and sent forward a trumpeter to demand its surrender. The trumpeter was shot as a traitor by the King's troops in possession of the town. Disheartened and afraid, the rebels retraced their course, rallying in a sharp and successful engagement at Philip's Norton on June 27th and re-entering Bridgewater on July 3rd.

The alternative to retreat into Somerset had been a bold attempt to cut through to Shropshire and Cheshire where the name of Monmouth was still potent to rouse men to daring ventures. But Monmouth himself was no longer the man of bold action he had thought himself to be. Throughout the purposeless days, the fear of assassination preyed upon his mind. A price was on his head; a well-aimed bullet from his own ranks was a greater danger than enemy fire. Once he was shot at, he knew not by whom; he went in mortal terror of another shot. In secret conclave, he and the few who had come with him from Holland debated whether flight were possible, regardless of the betrayal of their followers. But they had no ship: they must go on. It rained incessantly, dull deadening summer rain, and Colonel Churchill, most able and vigorous of the

King's officers, harassed their outposts and made each march a dangerous and uncertain passage. Nerves were frayed and anxious questionings replaced the first enthusiasm among the wearied ranks. But the wish to strike a blow in the open was uttermost in the honest minds of the men who had risked all for Monmouth. At long last they had their opportunity. The King's army was encamped on Sedgemoor, a few miles outside Bridgewater. Monmouth was on the point of leaving the town, in another vaccillating move towards the north, when he encountered a resident named Godfrey, who told him that he had visited the royal army and found it ill-disciplined and off its guard. Monmouth determined to attack, and Godfrey offered to lead him across the rhines, or ditches, which made the marshes of Sedgemoor impassable without a guide.

It was decided to make a midnight march and endeavour to surprise the enemy on the flank. Monmouth chose 'Soho' as his battle-cry, a word of good omen, the name of his London home. At eleven o'clock on Sunday, the 5th of July, the rebel forces set out on a circuitous journey of six miles' duration. Each man was ordered to pistol his neighbour, should he make a sound. But it needed no such exhortation to impose upon the marching men a silence, pregnant with hope of victory and fear of death. A thick mist had fallen after the rain, which gave a ghostly unreality to the adventure. The men and horses struggled safely across two of the rhines, guided in nervous eagerness by Godfrey. At one o'clock, the dazed, excited army lined itself up, within a mile of the enemy camp. Lord Grey and the cavalry rode ahead to surprise and if possible destroy. All was still and eyes strained through the mist for the first flare of light that would tell he had succeeded. Instead there came the sound of a single pistol shot. The venture had failed. The camp had been aroused.

When the alarm was given the King's Commander-in-Chief was sleeping peaceably in a cottage in the village. He had a good digestion and an easy conscience, and saw no reason why he should not sleep. His affable inefficiency was the despair of Churchill, his second-in-command, who happened to be a genius and resented the fact that Lord Feversham was put over him in command. Louis Duras, Earl of Feversham, was certainly not a genius, though nephew to the great Turenne. He was a fat easygoing harmless creature and a good Protestant, but he was a Frenchman and for that reason alone a shrewder man than James would not have put him in command of his army. Yet he was a good friend and the King trusted him, and in days to come he was to teach more brilliant men a needed lesson in loyalty.

Feversham was awakened and lazily got out of bed. Later they told in the Somerset villages how he 'set his cravat string at a little paltry looking-glass' and went out to see what was happening. He found his men lining up for battle, while 'old Patch' the warlike Bishop of Winchester, who had accompanied the Wiltshire militia, was doing yeoman service in hauling up the guns.

Meanwhile Monmouth's men advanced to fight and die. They found another ditch impeding their progress, one of which, by misunderstanding or mischance, they had not known. On the sides of this rhine, the battle began, in the thick darkness that precedes the dawn. 'Who are you for?' sounded the challenge as Grey's men tried to cross. 'The King,' came the reply. 'What king?' 'Monmouth and God be with us.' 'Take this with you then,' shouted the Royalist troops and a volley of shot was poured into the cavalry ranks that caused the horses to stampede and chaos to reign in Grey's squadron.[1] His precipitate flight spelt disaster for Monmouth's cause. In his justification it must be said that his so-called cavalry was in fact untrained horses, ridden by inexperienced men. Their failure was inevitable, though a less easy acceptance of that fact on the part of their leader would have made the

[1] I must acknowledge among secondary sources the chapter on Sedgemoor in Judge Parry's *The Bloody Assize.*

collapse less inglorious. The infantry fought, and fought well. All the passions of the last few weeks were poured out in a last defiant struggle with destiny. Scythe and billhook, no less than sword and pistol, did their deadly work in the strange mêlée. While darkness enwrapped the combatants, it was possible still to hope. But as relentless daybreak pushed aside the dawn, Monmouth for one saw that his cause was lost. Petted in childhood, courted in his youth, beloved by the King and flattered by the King's enemies, he had never thought of anyone but himself. Now in the supreme moment of trial, a selfish desire for life smothered finer instincts and his soldierly abilities. He turned and fled, leaving to men who had no mercy, the people he had wronged.

Joining Grey and the German officer Buise, Monmouth rode with a remnant of the horse towards the Bristol Channel. Could he have reached Wales, some loyal souls might have aided him to safety. But his spirit was broken. Still infirm of purpose he turned south with Grey and Buise, found refuge for one night in a good friend's house near Shepton Mallet, and plunged into the New Forest. Their horses' strength failed on Cranbourne Chase. They turned them adrift, disguised themselves as best they could as countrymen and went each on his own way, knowing the game was lost. The troops were closing in about the forest; the promise of the large reward spurred the soldiers to unwearying search. From shelter of haystack or hedge or covert, the starving, aching fugitives looked out on to the implacable forms of sentries keeping guard. At seven in the morning of the 8th of July, they found Monmouth, last of the three to be discovered, sleeping under a hedge in the shadow of an ash tree. His straggling beard prematurely grey, his trembling hands, his haggard wandering look disguised him more effectively than any peasant's cloak. They could not recognise him, but they knew him by the 'George', which they found in his pocket among some dried peapods.

The prisoners were taken up to London. Grey played the poltroon no longer. He had recovered his poise and maintained a pretence of calm. But Monmouth was a broken man. In a last frantic effort to save his life, he wrote to James pleading to see him, vowing that 'by one word' he could explain everything. 'I have that to say to you, Sir, that I hope may give you a long and happy reign.' To Rochester, in similar strain he wrote, 'I am confident, if I may be so happy to speak to him . . . I can give him such infallible proofs of my truth to him, that though I would alter, it would not be in my power to alter.'

Whether these were but the frenzied outpourings of a terrified man, or whether in fact Monmouth had some knowledge of significance to give to the King, nobody ever knew. At least, the wording of the letters justified James in seeing his wretched nephew. He was accompanied by Lord Sunderland, his Secretary-of-State, an indication that the interview was merely political. It may have been Sunderland's presence that sealed the prisoner's lips, since the one saving word he would have spoken was possibly of that statesman's treachery. Whatever he knew of the plotting and counter-plotting of which The Hague had been the centre during the last few years, Monmouth told the King nothing. He simply grovelled at his feet and asked for mercy; he vowed that he had not meant anything by the charges in his manifesto. 'Ferguson drew it and made me sign it before ever I read it,' he declared. James was rightly enraged. 'This is trifling. Would you or any-one sign a paper of such consequence and not read it.' He put an end to the painful interview. Monmouth must die.

Yet Grey he pardoned, who was only less guilty than the Duke. For Grey behaved like a man, and neither trembled nor excused himself. Pity and generosity came hardly to James. A friend of Monmouth's who saw him pass to the King's presence declared in after years, 'I could never get him out of my mind, I so loved him personally.' In

James's heart there was no love; and untempered justice signified death. He could not be expected to pardon Monmouth, who deserved to die if ever rebel did. But all that was best in the King was wrapped up in the soldierly virtues of bravery, honour and resolution. To this side of his nature Monmouth made no appeal; Grey, who did, was spared.

When the King turned away, impregnable in his hatred of cowardice and his fear of usurpation, Monmouth's courage returned. He was a soldier and had faced death before. He could face it again. It was the uncertainty, the agony of self-distrust which had made the last weeks unbearable. On Monday, 13th July, he was informed that he must die on the following Wednesday, barely five weeks since his landing on the Dorset coast. He accepted his fate with a fortitude which seemed to him, conscious of his earlier surrender to despair, to be a direct response to prayer. It was well for him that he had this assurance, for his last days on earth were not made easy for him. He was invited to see his wife, the Scottish heiress united to him in childhood, for whom he had no feeling save the knowledge that he had wronged her. The interview took place with a mutual cold forbearance that at least was honest. His thoughts were full of another woman, who had lived with him in his exile, pawned her jewels that he might not lack money in his venture, blessed his departing with her tears and by her love weaned him from the easy life of promiscuous gallantry in which at his father's court he had indulged. Lady Henrietta Wentworth was his wife in the sight of God. The Bishops did not agree. Turner of Ely and Ken of Bath and Wells, who were sent to offer him consolation, could not undermine his conviction of the essential rightness of a connection immoral in the opinion of the world. Nor could they persuade him to give lip-service to the doctrine of absolute obedience to the Crown, of non-resistance in matters political, which theologians during the last decade had placed in dangerous proximity to the doctrines of the Anglican Church. In these circumstances they felt compelled to refuse him the Sacrament. At Monmouth's request Tenison was summoned, the Vicar of St. Martin-in-the-Fields then as now the centre of progressive churchmanship, and though he could not feel deeply about non-resistance except to deplore its prominence, Tenison agreed with the bishops that the prisoner's refusal to acknowledge his sins debarred him from receiving the Communion.

It may be that Christ would have thought differently; it may be that the Church had failed to keep itself unspotted from the world, that theology and politics had intermingled to the detriment of spirit and of truth. But Thomas Ken was a man of charity; his action may have been mistaken but it was done in all honesty and with a grieving heart. He and his colleagues conceived of the Sacrament, not as a piece of formal ritual, but as an act of worship demanding from those who sought the divine sustenance true and earnest repentance and the desire to follow the commandments of God. However they might feel as individuals, as officers of the Church they could not offer it to one living in unrepentant adultery.

It meant less to Monmouth than he had expected. He was wrapped in a strange serenity as if Christ had found His own way of comforting the wretched man whom circumstance and his own frailties had broken. He came on to the scaffold at Tower Hill at ten o'clock on Wednesday, the 15th of July, and neither the approaching agony nor the continued exhortations of the divines who accompanied him could make him doubt that he was at peace with God. Ken withdrew himself from persuasions that approached too near to baiting. 'God accept your repentance . . . your very imperfect repentance,' was his repeated prayer. At Monmouth's first appearance upon the crowded scene, 'a murmur of sighs and groans went round the whole assembly which by degrees sunk into an almost breathless silence, as if every syllable he had to utter was sacred and not to be profan'd with the unhallowed intermixture of any vulgar sound'. But the victim would not make the speech required of him. Nothing would have pleased James more than a public repudiation of rebellion. The King was afraid; he might kill Monmouth's body but he could not kill the people's love for him which had returned in full force in the hour of his distress. But Monmouth would not speak. He said something of his love for Henrietta: the only thing on which he wished to dwell. 'Are you married to her?' interrupted the sheriff with brutal directness. He affirmed again his belief in the sanctity of their union and gave his toothpick as a last token of love, for someone to give to her. Then he indicated a paper he had written, briefly admitting his illegitimacy. That was all. 'I shall say very little. I come to die,' he declared. 'I am very sorry it ever happened . . . I will not make a speech. I come to die.'

Jack Ketch the headsman prepared to strike. Two years before he had executed Russell and made a bad job of it; Monmouth urged him to be more careful, promising a good reward if he struck straight and true. But Ketch was a man underneath his mask, keyed up like everyone else at that dreadful scene, conscious of the vibrations of the crowd hating him, hating the King, hating Authority. He tried to strike, and the axe barely wounded the prisoner who looked up reproachfully but said not a word. The headsman struck thrice and still the body writhed in agony. He threw down the axe, declaring that he could do no more, and the mob broke loose in pandemonium. Somebody spoke firmly; Ketch took up the axe and finished. He used a knife at the end. And the crowd surged forward to bathe their handkerchiefs in the blood of their murdered hero.

For hero he remained in the imaginations of men. Those who loved him urged that his very faults had risen from excess of virtue; that he had shown too much forbearance and kindliness to men less worthy than himself, that he had been too ready to concede the opinions of others. As Fox wrote, 'the sagacity of Shaftesbury, the honour of Russell, the genius of Sidney, might in the opinion of a modest man, be safe and eligible guides'. But not even Fox can justify his reliance on a scoundrel like Ferguson or his betrayal of his men. At bottom, beneath a lovely exterior and a lovable and generous temper he lacked the wisdom and probity that are the requisites of those who would command.

. . . .

The rebellion was over; there remained retribution. It fell with unbelievable severity not only upon those who had escaped death at Sedgemoor, but on many who had done nothing worse than handle Monmouth's manifesto or express their joy in his coming. The summary executions, committed immediately after the battle by the troops just home from Tangiers, were probably no worse than the excesses that disgraced many a Continental battlefield. But they were contrary to the temper of British warfare, and the lascivious enjoyment with which wretches were hung and quartered and their entrails burnt in boiling pitch dismayed and disgusted those who had been loyal to James no less than those in danger of like punishment. The debased and cynical Colonel Kirke, who had grafted the vices of the East upon the brutal thoroughness of the Nordic race, commanded the men in charge of the proceedings, a regiment raised in honour of Catherine of Braganza and wearing her emblem of the Paschal Lamb. The name of *Kirke's Lambs* spread terror through the countryside. It was said that sometimes Kirke called for music that his victims, quivering from the gibbets, could dance their way to death. They told how a girl had pleaded for her father's life, and how Kirke had promised his pardon if the suppliant would give herself to him. How the girl consented, and awakened in the morning to see through the open window, the one for whom she had betrayed herself, hanging from the gallows tree. These may have been only legends, as exaggerated as most tales of atrocities in time of war, but they bore sure witness to a people's hatred of Kirke and of the power behind him, which was the power of the King. Yet for these excesses James was not to blame. When news came to London of the dire example that was being made of rebels in the West, he had a sufficient sense of justice to object. The thing must be done, not in the hot blood of battle, but legally and of set purpose. Kirke was rebuked and a commission of gaol-delivery was appointed with the Lord Chief Justice at its head, to try and punish all who had been seized on suspicion of complicity in Monmouth's rising. Four other judges accompanied Jeffreys, as a check on his ferocious temper and an earnest of the King's desire to abide by the letter of the law. Their personalities were entirely swamped by that of their sadistic chief.

Jeffreys opened his assize at Winchester on August 25th, when the judges listened in state to a sermon at the Cathedral. On August 27th in the Great Hall of that ancient town, Dame Alice Lisle was tried and sentenced for sheltering a rebel fugitive. She was a widow of over seventy, devoted to good works; her husband had been a friend of Cromwell's and a judge of Charles I; but she was too old to meddle in politics and too kindly to be unfriendly to any of her neighbours. Jeffreys had decided that as the most prominent Whig in that part of the country, she must if possible be convicted and executed. It was said that he had extracted a promise from James not to pardon her, if he should succeed. Her death therefore was part of a considered policy, of a ruthlessness that was to make the repetition of revolt unthinkable.

Lady Lisle, as she was called in courtesy, had given shelter on July 28th, to a Nonconformist clergyman called James Hickes. If it could be proved that Hickes had fought at Sedgemoor and that Lady Lisle knew him to be a rebel fugitive, she could legally be convicted of treason. But as the trial progressed through the heat of the summer day, it proved unexpectedly hard to establish either of the two points. The prisoner declared that she only knew Hickes as a minister, 'that used to preach and not to fight'. The old lady was very deaf and dozed through most of the trial, while daylight waned and candles were brought in to send their flickering light about the arches of the great roof and the painted face of King Arthur's Round Table suspended on the wall. Jeffrey bullied and browbeat the wretched man who had introduced Hickes to Lady Lisle, till he cried in despair, 'My Lord, I am so balked I do not know what I say myself; tell me what you would have me to say, for I am cluttered out of my senses.' But he would not swear that he had told Lady Lisle that Hickes was a fugitive from Sedgemoor. And every plain man in the court was impressed by the prisoner's simple statement that she had never harboured a good wish for the rebels, and that her own son had fought on James's side. 'It was I that bred him up to fight for the King.' With those words in their ears, the jury returned a doubtful verdict. Jeffreys sent them back to think it over. He meant to have a conviction and in face of his implacability, the jury gave in. 'If I had been among you and she had been my own mother, I should have found her guilty,' declared the Lord Chief Justice, as he commended their verdict. A few days later Alice Lisle was executed, with words of charity on her lips: 'I forgive all persons that have done me wrong, and I desire that God will do so likewise.'

Her death was but the first of some two to three hundred executions. From Dorchester, where over seventy died, to Exeter and Taunton, where five hundred were awaiting gaol delivery, Jeffreys and his train of clerks and lawyers and fellow-judges swept like a devastating fire. At Wells, Bishop Ken visited the sick and comforted the captives, doing all that was in his power to strengthen and to calm the hundreds who awaited the inevitable punishment. The countryside, beautiful in the calm fulfilment of the month of harvest, was desecrated with gibbets and cauldrons of boiling pitch. The youth and promise of many of the victims, young men on the threshold of life who had answered Monmouth's call as a summons to adventure, wrung the hearts of all who witnessed the savage justice wreaked upon them by conquerors who knew no mercy. The trials themselves were conducted in an atmosphere of cruelty too subtle to be described as bestial. Jeffreys himself was suffering agonies from the disease of the stone, and it seemed as if his consciousness of physical pain, which was making his triumph a drear futility, impelled him to revenge himself by torturing his victims. At these moments, as his brutal words battered the bewildered mind of a wretched prisoner, his face changed. He was normally good-looking, except for the indelible marks of heavy drinking and gluttony. Now the thin lips twisted into an inhuman sneer; in some indefinable way, evil contorted his features and the devil himself looked out of the piercing eyes. Those who had seen him thus never forgot; those who knew him only as a successful man-about-town had no conception of this other Jeffreys. One of the maids of Taunton, a child of eight, brought into court and examined by the Lord Chief Justice, hid her face in her hood and was led away weeping, to die soon afterwards of suspense and shock. Young Sarah Blake who had worked Monmouth's banner died in prison of the smallpox: the other children eventually were pardoned, after an experience that would shadow their whole lives.

In the horror of the Assize and Jeffreys's personality, the fact has been sometimes disregarded that the men who followed Monmouth *had* been guilty of treason; they had fought against the King, or welcomed the usurper in their midst, with their eyes wide open to what they were doing and in nominal agreement with the most foul charges against James. It must in fairness to him be admitted that many of the best of the young men who died in Somerset were correctly sentenced and had technically forfeited their lives. The large numbers who were sentenced to fines, flagellation or transportation were suffering the customary punishments of the day, replaced in later centuries by solitary confinement, a less brutal method of dealing with crime but not necessarily one that imposes less permanent injury. Those transported to the plantations would after a certain number of years regain their freedom, and the fact that there was no effort to recall any large number after the Revolution would seem to indicate that there were not many obviously unjust convictions.

It would not have been in keeping with James's character to go outside the letter of the law. But it would have been more in keeping with the character of a Christian king to have let love of his people cast out fear. Leniency would have been at once the wisest and most virtuous course, but James had never believed in compromise with rebellion. He considered that his father had lost his life through tampering with concession and that true mercy lay in establishing peace through firmness. He must be regarded as ultimately responsible for the severities in the West. It is impossible to plead that he was ignorant of Jeffreys's activities when he wrote to Barillon on September 24th: 'As for news there is little stirring, but that Lord Chief Justice has almost done his campaigne; he has already condemned several hundreds, some of which are already executed, more are to be and the others sent to the plantations.' For the results of the Bloody Assize, if not for Kirke's Lambs, the King must take responsibility. For the brutality of Jeffreys's methods and for the unspeakable horror of the scene in the West, he was less to blame. For in an age when news travelled slowly, when transport was difficult and each section of the community, both geographical and social, was a self-contained unit knowing little of its neighbours, the people in London had no real knowledge of how things were happening in Winchester and Taunton. No news came from the West to offend the most respectable citizens; John Evelyn, always impeccably correct, dined with Judge Jeffreys after his return from the Assize without any feeling of contamination. Such trials as took place in the capital were conducted with scrupulous fairness. Lord Delamere was acquitted, although no one had any real doubts about his guilt, because nothing but circumstantial evidence could be proffered against him; others were pardoned after conviction. It is difficult to say what share of blame accrued to the King for the shady financial dealings whereby the less reputable of the courtiers procured pardons for the despairing rebels. The parents of the maids of Taunton paid heavy fines before their children were restored to them and the money was allotted to the Queen's maids-of-honour. Greed and corruption there certainly was, about which Sunderland probably knew more than his master. It is hard to judge on a matter in which contemporary standards and practices were so far removed from those of a later age. The majority at Whitehall were unthinking rather than vicious. And just as many a gentlewoman of to-day will sweep into a West End store past a hawker on the kerb or sit over her fire in ignorance of the squalor of the mines, without experiencing any sense of guilt, so the Queen and her ladies said their prayers and played their cards in sincerity and without heartache because imagination seldom pierces the veil of ignorance, and few at Whitehall knew that in the West Country men and women, who had been through Hell, were waiting in silence for deliverance.

James's policy of ruthlessness so far as it was based on the determination to obtain security, had at least a foundation in policy. But it was in part actuated by the desire for revenge. The twisted mind of the man who was King was still warped by the memory of the treatment meted out to him by the Whigs and their predecessors. He had never been able to express his distaste for all they represented in politics and religion. All the more deeply, that hatred had possessed his soul. It was this lust after revenge which drove him to a last frenzy of legalised brutality. In this final episode, Jeffreys was not concerned. In October, 1685, an attack was made on the Whig dissenters of the City of London, the very people whose loyalty had made it easy for James to subdue Monmouth. Alderman Cornish, who had been prominent in the days of the Popish Plot, was convicted of treason on grounds as slender as those by which five years before his own party had murdered the aged Earl of Stafford. Cornish himself was in such agony of mind on the scaffold, denouncing the unfair methods used against him, that some said he died in a fit of fury. Others less prominent than he suffered upon ill-proved charges of consorting with rebels. Among them was Mrs. Elizabeth Gaunt, who was said to have sheltered a proscribed man at the time of the Rye House plot. Burton, the individual in question, had escaped and returned with Monmouth, had fought at Sedgemoor and was captured in London. He then saved himself by informing not only on the man who had sheltered him after Sedgemoor but on Elizabeth Gaunt, who had protected him in 1683. The prisoner was a woman of quiet ways, an Anabaptist, who went about doing good. It was her business to help people, whatever their politics; that she should sympathise with the folk of her own class and religion was natural. She may have committed the crime with which she was charged, but her only sin was too wide a charity. Nor was there any attempt to give her a fair trial. She was found guilty and sentenced to be burnt, as was appointed in the case of women convicted of treason. 'I do not understand the law,' was her bewildered cry. She was sustained, at the end, by the fortitude that is the crown of martyrdom: as she arranged the straw about her feet that her death might be as speedy as possible, she did not deny what she had done, but declared that she suffered for a religion that was all love, and that in succouring those in distress she had been helping Him in whom she would have her reward. Those who watched her did not shout as they had done when Monmouth died in a frenzy of anger and dismay; they went away reverently, with tears in their eyes as from a holy place. But in their hearts was the unquiet whisper, the terror-laden thought: the fires of Smithfield had been lit again!

CHAPTER IX

SUNDERLAND

A Proteus ever acting in disguise
A finished statesman: intricately wise;
'A second Macchiavel who soars above
The little ties of gratitude and love.'

– *Contemporary Satire on Sunderland.*

IN the autumn of 1685, James II was at the height of his power. Good luck and a discernment, with which his brother would never have credited him, had supplied him with a despot's main requirements, a regular income and a standing army. Monmouth's rising had given him an excuse to levy troops, which he did not disband when the crisis was averted. A camp was established on Hounslow Heath, in dangerous proximity to London, and the King took an increasing interest in his army, making it his hobby as once the ships had been, and entrusting its command to personal friends or dependable subordinates, many of whom happened to be of the Roman Catholic Faith.

The first outburst of Tory enthusiasm had borne such practical fruit that financially James was in a better position than any of his Stuart predecessors. In the first weeks of the reign, before Parliament assembled, he and Rochester on his behalf had not scrupled to maintain a close association with Barillon in the hope of the continuance of French subsidies. But whatever their words, their actions showed an independence which made Louis withhold payments till he was more certain of the benefits he would receive in return. James's summons of Parliament and his vigorous administration soon made it obvious that he was not fitted for the role of pensioner of France. To his credit, the payments ceased, and throughout his reign as in the final catastrophe he refused aid from Louis. Yet two statements that were made during the negotiations were significant. James reiterated to Barillon his unceasing devotion to Louis. 'I was brought up in France, I have eat of your master's bread and my heart is France.' And Rochester affirmed as fact that James and Louis must stand together in self-defence against the interests opposed to them, represented by Austria, William of Orange and the English Parliament. What hope could there be for English unity and progress, when the King in all sincerity felt himself more closely bound to a foreign sovereign than to his own people? And felt truly, for undoubtedly as autocrats and Catholic potentates as well as cousins and friends, the Kings of France and England lived in the same world and breathed the same rarefied atmosphere. But James had little in common with his people; it was his ambition to make himself 'still more master of his country' and he 'hated all popular things as below the dignity of a king'. He distrusted the proletariat as potential rebels instead of regarding them with that paternal affection, which, breeding mutual goodwill, alone could justify rule by divine right.

James was a formalist; he might be a Shylock who demanded his pound of flesh, but he resented the charge of tyranny and would not willingly be unjust. He pardoned the arch-plotter Ferguson, who had accused him of the blackest crimes imaginable, with the words '. . . and no longer say your King is inexorable. . . .' He was too hidebound by convention and conscientiousness to emulate a dictator or organise a *coup d'état*, but he did believe himself justified in exercising the prerogatives which accrued to the Crown. If a prince were not to be trusted with any powers capable of abuse, his sovereignty was a farce. 'Lawyers, physicians, servants, tradesmen,' all had power to hurt as well as to aid those who depended upon them. So the King argued, and in stressing the truth that all government and indeed all civilisation is one gigantic confidence trick, forgot to observe the rules of caution and common sense.

Monmouth perished and James, triumphant, had the opportunity to put his political theories into practice. He was in a quandary. His theories were Tory but his aims were Whig. 'Trade he had much at heart,' noted the Scot, Ailesbury, 'and his topic was liberty of conscience and many hands at work in trade.' The noise of the shipbuilding yards was living testimony to the things he meant to do, and when King Louis revoked the Edict of Nantes and Huguenots took refuge in England, as is the habit of Europeans in trouble, James authorised a house-to-house collection in their aid and encouraged them to teach their industries and impart their skill to the English villagers among whom they settled. His difficulties arose in regard to liberty of conscience. The inconsistencies of James's reign seem best to be explained by the assumption that after the failure of the schemes initiated at Dover, he had tried, as he himself stated, to regard his religion as a personal affair. As Duke of York, his political friendships had been with Anglican Tories, and he had resented the insubordination of his brother's Parliaments as part of the same vicious temper that had overthrown his father. He was blinded therefore to the fact that the ideal of religious liberty was more in consonance with Whig principles than with the exclusive attitude of his Tory supporters, and only when his political power was firmly established after Monmouth's collapse and he set himself to the furtherance of his religious schemes, did he realise how incompatible they were with the Tory alliance.

There was still a possibility of success. While maintaining the Tory ministry, he could have concentrated upon the arduous but not impossible task of educating his people to the idea of toleration. He had a staunch ally in William Penn, the Quaker, whom he had befriended in youth and who had returned from his 'Holy Experiment' in Pennsylvania, to frequent the King's court and pour into James's ear counsels of amity. The King's own child, Jane, who had been born in Paris of an unknown mother, had joined the Society of Friends; a strange, forceful honest woman, she cast away her rank in 1688 and lived the life of a villager in Wisbech. James himself had attended Quaker meetings and one of his first acts as King was to release many who suffered for conscience' sake. He had less sympathy with the other sects but during 1686 large numbers were set free. Could he convince them of his sincerity, they were bound to welcome his offer of security. John Locke, who had once been Shaftesbury's friend, had preached toleration as a practical proposition among the very people most inclined to oppose James politically, while even the Tories might have been helped by theories of non-resistance to bridge the gap between disapprobation and consent. Had he allayed his people's fears by just and mild governance, kept within the letter of the law and restricted his activities to establishing freedom of worship, he might in time have succeeded. But James neglected the significance of time. That which he might have accomplished in a lifetime, he endeavoured to crowd into some four and twenty months. He could not forget that his daughters and his son-in-law were his heirs and staunchly Protestant. He was conscious of the years, pressing in upon him. He was exceedingly energetic during the earlier part of his reign; he hunted whenever he could, in wet weather as in fine, returning with his exhausted followers more 'like drowned rats' than 'appendices to royalty'. He was over fifty, and there may have been a physiological explanation for the restlessness which manifested itself not only in his bodily activities, but in a last outburst of sexual indulgence, his unflagging industry and the intemperate haste with which he pressed on his religious schemes. Whatever the cause, it was fatal.

He made two other irremediable mistakes. He stretched his prerogative beyond its limits, and by breaking the laws alienated the very section of the community best able to appreciate his ideal of religious liberty. And secondly, he did not rest content with fostering toleration; he set his heart upon the repeal of the Tests and by the repeated advancement of Catholics to military and civil posts of importance, stirred the fears of the ordinary Englishman to whom the political ascendancy of the Papists was tantamount to persecution if not to massacre. When a century and a half afterwards, a belated public opinion achieved what he had failed to accomplish and in 1828 the Tests were repealed, a grateful people struck a medal to celebrate the triumph of righteousness and engraved upon it the words, 'Truth, Freedom, Peace and Charity.' But in 1686 'repeal' spelled disaster and the danger of civil war, and while one can argue that James had been tutored by adversity to a more Christian attitude than that of many of his contemporaries, it must be admitted that the methods by which he tried to force opinion, and the individual Catholics he promoted, justified the common fear that toleration and equality were only meant to pave the way for Catholic ascendancy and autocratic rule.

These errors of judgment, his unconstitutional methods, his precipitancy and his preoccupation with repeal, were gradually made apparent during 1686 and 1687. They were probably due to two fresh factors in the situation, the dominance of Sunderland, and the deepening of James's own religious life. While Sunderland through malice or audacity proffered rash counsels to the ready ear of the King, the latter burnt with the zeal of a fanatic, to save his people from damnation and avenge the wrongs of his co-religionists.

The Tory alliance did not long survive the extirpation of revolt. In October, 1685, Halifax was dismissed from the office of Privy Seal, the first indication that the policy of moderation had ceased to charm. Parliament assembled for its second session in November amid prognostications of disturbances ahead. The failure to disband the troops, raised in the summer, and the appointment of Roman Catholic officers in defiance of the Test united the apostles of non-resistance with the Whigs in their mutual distrust of the Pope and a standing army. Nor did James attempt to excuse what he had done. He made it clear by his speech that his actions had been no emergency measures, but part of a studied policy. In reference to the recent rebellion he declared, 'I hope everybody will be convinced that the militia, which has hitherto been so much depended on, is not sufficient for such occasions, and that there is nothing but a good force of well-disciplined troops in constant pay, that can defend us from such as either at home or abroad are disposed to disturb us.' His audience had scarcely adjusted themselves to a point of view contrary to all their preconceived opinions when they were shocked by a brief statement that the Catholic officers were known personally to the King and that he trusted their loyalty. 'Let no man take exception . . . I think them now fit to be employed under me.' The tone of his words approximated dangerously near to those placed in his mouth years before by the satirist, Andrew Marvell:

> 'I'll have those villains in our notions rest
> And I do say it: therefore it's the best.'

He concluded by stating that he had no expectation of conflict, for the good understanding maintained between himself and his Parliament since his accession had augmented the prestige of England abroad and increased her internal prosperity. In which, he undoubtedly spoke the truth.

But of course there was trouble. The Commons, instead of thanking the King for his speech, made an address to the Crown pointing out with dangerous courtesy that the Test Act had been broken. The King replied curtly that he would be 'steady in all his promises' but that he had not expected such behaviour. 'I hope we are all Englishmen and not to be frighted out of our duty with a few hard words,' cried a certain Mr. Cook. He was sent to the Tower 'for his undecent speech' and ten days later Parliament was prorogued. It did not meet again.

The ensuing months witnessed the true crisis of the reign, none the less real because undercurrents of personal jealousy and intrigue complicated and confused the issues. The year 1686 passed quietly on the surface. There were signs and portents to offend anxious minds, the erection of Catholic chapels in London, the manœuvres at Hounslow, the repeated suspension of the Test Act in particular cases. But the easy-going or the optimistic could disregard the omens; there was no obvious discomfort, no alarms and excursions, while at the head of the kingdom stood a sovereign who at least was industrious and a Queen who was dignity incarnate.

But below the surface things were happening which caused the Revolution two years later. Rochester, the Tory Treasurer, was fighting a losing battle with Sunderland, the Secretary-of-State. Sunderland and Rochester hated each other. They had nothing in common, beyond a childhood spent in exile and a fortuitous connection as the Chits. Sunderland was a member of the ruling class, a man of property, linked by impalpable threads with the hierarchy of noblemen and landed gentry, who throughout the years had in turn served and fought their King and whose families were to rule England through the ensuing century. His wife, Anne Digby, the richest heiress in England, was her husband's political confident and Henry Sidney's lover. Sunderland, charming and inscrutable, was an aristocrat to the finger-tips, never discountenanced by Whig lords or Tory courtiers because he belonged to their social set. His love of gambling and his affected drawl, his gardens and his works of art at Althorpe were all part and parcel of the role of man of the world. But Rochester was just not one of them. Without being actually middle class, he could claim no ancient lineage nor influential connections. Clarendon's disgrace while his younger son was still at the University had resulted in Lawrence Hyde having to fend for himself in a way that had coarsened his fibre while it sharpened his brain. Even his vices made this apparent. He did not seduce women but he drank too much beer; he was able to control himself over the cards but when he lost his temper he swore like a trooper. He had been an unassuming youth, but his modesty had suffered eclipse during his rapid advance in power and place. As a politician, he was an opportunist, and the difficult job of keeping the Treasury solvent had left him not unversed in the art and craft of intrigue and corruption. His public as his private behaviour might at times run contrary to the formal piety of his religious observances, for like most of his contemporaries, Rochester was using the mental concepts and the devotional language of the Age of Faith while acting according to the moral standards of the Age of Reason.

Yet at bottom he was a simple soul. He had lost a married daughter, who was very dear to him, shortly before King Charles II's death. Upon the anniversary of his bereavement, he wrote down certain reflections which bring him very close to us. Reminding himself of his isolation in early manhood and his subsequent success, he wrote, 'I seemed like a tree planted by the water-side whose leaf did not wither'; office and the perquisites of office, influence and the friendship of kings had fallen to his lot, and, he reflected, 'through all this glittering pomp and vain shows, I had not given glory to the Divine Majesty above.' His daughter's death, after surviving without difficulty 'the two greatest dangers to young women in their lives, the smallpox and the first child,' shocked him into recognition of the emptiness of earthly triumphs. He pondered on the tragic ignorance in which he had continued the usual avocations of life, while his beloved lay dead, unknown to him. 'I had wrote from hence to her, after the time she was dead,' he recollected, and had predicted a quick recovery and a meeting in the near future. This loss and, so a cynic would have added, the searching criticism of his colleagues had brought him to the brink of retirement when King Charles died. Rochester then found himself unexpectedly first minister of the Crown. He had spent the days 'in perpetual hurries of public business,' and latterly in 'fears and jealousies and misapprehensions on all sides'. There had been relaxations, some that would not bear recording. Unfortunately they were recorded by the Tory diarist Sir John Reresby, who noted in February, 1686, 'a great debauch of wine' at an Alderman's house, where the Lords Chancellor and Treasurer of England (Jeffreys and Rochester) 'drank to that height as 'twas whispered that they stripped into their shirts, and had not an accident prevented, would have got upon a signpost to drink the King's health, which gave occasion of derision, not to say more of the matter.' Was it an uneasy memory of this scene which impelled Rochester to end his reflections with the naïve but heartfelt prayer, 'Teach me to number the days of this world's greatness of which I have so great a share, and teach me to look upon them as vanity and vexation of spirit: and be Thou pleased to forget some of them and forgive them all'?

Throughout the year 1686, Sunderland and Rochester fought for the King's confidence. In Charles's day it would not have been necessary or possible: he believed in a multitude of counsellors and, himself an apt practitioner of kingcraft, would have agreed with his cousin Louis, who had exclaimed, 'God's fish, when rogues fall out, the master is like then to know the truth.' But James beneath his bluff was diffident. Like his father and James I before him, he needed the heartening assurance of one man's counsel and support. In Admiralty matters he had been guided by Pepys and had chosen well; now when the whole kingdom was in his power Sunderland won his affections and consequently controlled his judgment. The King's reliance upon him was of an intellectual character and had nothing in common with the physical attraction of James I to his young men, or Charles's emotional dependence upon Buckingham. Lord Dover, who used to be Harry Jermyn, was still the King's best friend. With him, James indulged his hobby of soldiering, to Sunderland's annoyance. But when it came to politics, Sunderland was supreme, encouraging James to discuss politics with him and a small group of Catholic advisers in Chiffinch's apartments. Not merely the Privy Council, but the inner ring of the Cabinet, were frequently left in ignorance of decisions of policy or foreign news. Thus Sunderland gained his ends by 'the art in which he surpassed all men . . . the art of whispering.'

In the last resort it was not James, but the Queen, who decided the battle in the Secretary's favour, and it was an unworthy move of Rochester's that brought his ruin upon him. The King had met Catherine Sedley again. That pert young woman did not consider that a pension and a house in St. James's Square were adequate compensation for her brusque dismissal from Whitehall; by accident or design, and where Catherine was concerned it was probably design, she encountered the King one September evening in 1685 at Bab Chiffinch's notorious apartments. The old enchantment still held; there were further meetings, and soon the world was whispering that once again the King was Catherine's lover. Charles used to say that his brother's mistresses were as ugly as sin. But perhaps Charles disliked Catherine, as one of the few women he had not been able to subdue; plain though she might be, she was her father's daughter, a wit and a woman of brains, and it was small wonder if her company proved exhilarating and irresistible to a man of hot blood and dull mentality such as James. His wife was partly to blame. The good resolutions with which he had begun his reign had not been merely a pose; if he drifted apart from his Queen it was partly because she herself was different. Even to the casual observer her 'outward affability' was 'much changed to stateliness'; she spent an increasing amount of time among her priests and at her devotions, and the decorum of the court was such that Sedley himself satirised it in his most recent play, apologising in a Shavian preface lest it should be too lascivious for the new fashion of the times. 'This sudden change of theirs made me call to mind our English weather, where in the same day a man shall sweat in Crape, and wish for a campaign coat three hours after.' Though her prayers came first, Mary Beatrice did not neglect business nor the regulation of her household. Her secretaries filled letter-books with her formal correspondence, written on various occasions to European potentates. But she spent as much time as possible at Windsor, endeavouring to recover her health. For during the first eighteen months of her husband's reign, she was very ill, so much so that names of possible successors were freely canvassed on more than one occasion. Continuous ill-health wore down her nerves and lessened her effectiveness both as woman and Queen. She was not in a fit state to think of politics, for she was facing a crisis in her own personal life, in spiritual loneliness and in the consciousness of her husband's infidelities. For there were others it was rumoured besides Catherine Sedley, and she was bitterly offended by the recall to England of the King's two sons by Arabella Churchill, to whom contrary to an early promise, he gave the appellation of Fitz-James.

Mary Beatrice had not forgotten the missionary glow which had nerved her to come to England. She had come to save a country from damnation. Ten years had passed, and she had accomplished nothing; she had known gaiety and friendliness, the hatred of the multitude and the silent grief of a woman bereft of her children, but England remained stubbornly Protestant. Now, beyond all expectation, they were King and Queen with power to achieve. For her, sovereignty was a solemn trust; its sole end the fulfilment of the task the head of Christendom had given her to do. She chafed at the leading-strings of Tory domination; English liberties were empty syllables to her, an Italian nurtured in autocracy. She chafed at her own ill-health which kept her depressed and impotent, and at twenty-six in a woman's first panic realisation of the certitude of middle age, began to use the rouge she had hitherto disfavoured. And she chafed at her husband's waywardness, longing in bitter loneliness for the children who had died, for the vanishing hope of a new child who would bind James to her and give to England the prospect of a race of Catholic kings.

Then Sunderland began his whisperings. Rochester, he hinted, was Sedley's advocate. As Arlington waxed prosperous behind de Querouaille's petticoats, so would the Tory clique control the King through Catherine. The Protestant mistress should out-face the Catholic Queen. Rochester's intrigue came near to success. On January 21st, 1686, James created Catherine Countess of Dorchester, giving her a pension and appointments such as the Duchess of Portsmouth had enjoyed. Her ambition was fulfilled, for three days! She had miscalculated the force of a virtuous woman's anger. Mary Beatrice had never disguised her feelings: 'Give her my dower, make her Queen of England, but never let me see her more,' she had cried in a burst of her old tempestuous wrath. Now she refused to speak or eat, and the days passed in discomfort so acute that the King was soon as miserable as she. At last she sent for him. The King came into her apartments to find her surrounded by her priests. She told him, with a restraint more effective than temper, that either he must give up his mistress or she would withdraw to a convent. Kneeling before him, her priests declared that his sin invalidated their prayers, that the cause of Catholicism in England could never prosper while he indulged in vice. The King was conscience-stricken; he mumbled excuses and withdrew, to spend hours of wretchedness before his crucifix and to scourge himself in punishment of his sin.

The Countess of Dorchester was ordered to leave London. Flanders was suggested as a suitable place of residence, but Her Grace replied that the multitude of convents would offend her Protestant sentiments. Eventually she went to Ireland, to return after six months' absence and occasionally to meet the King, but never to essay again the rank and respectability of a *maîtresse en titre*. She was not dissatisfied. She lived in semi-retirement, and in due course received a pension from William III, whose court she attended, to the annoyance of his Queen. But the latter's cold looks only amused Catherine, who reminded Mary of Orange that if her distaste was on her father's account, she hoped she would remember that as she (Catherine) had broken one commandment with him, Mary had made no scruple of breaking another; therefore she thought they were very even upon his score. There was an element of truth upon the sinner's side.

James's submission to the exhortations of the Queen and her priests was the outward sign of the increase in his religious zeal. Hitherto his confessor had been a Franciscan, Father Mansuet, like most of his order a humble man of God. In the turn of the year a new influence appeared, and the Franciscans were replaced by Jesuits, those strange and vital brethren. Sunderland had a protégé, a certain Father Petre, on whom the populace were pleased to fasten innumerable villainies but who was little more than a weak and amiable creature, beset by the sins of vanity and a desire to serve both God and mammon. 'He hoisted up his mainsail but lost his ship for want of ballast.' He obtained a remarkable hold over James, who was attracted by his specious talk and was naïvely delighted when Sunderland, whom he considered a good judge of character, seconded him in thinking well of the Jesuit. Father Petre was housed in the apartments at Whitehall which the King had occupied as Duke of York; he was encouraged by Sunderland to take an interest in politics and used to attend the coterie in Chiffinch's rooms.

Meanwhile James immersed himself more deeply in his devotions. At times, as many as ten hours a day were spent in public worship or private prayer. Coming from his oratory to the junto's deliberations he fell an easy victim to Sunderland's guile and Petre's facile phrases. Political strategy and administrative skill were alike subordinated to the burning desire to convert his people and advance his religion. For any who opposed him, whether Bishop or Don or Tory nobleman, he had no further use.

The main events of this time of transition can be briefly chronicled. In December, 1685, Bishop Compton was excluded from the Council, a blunder so colossal that it might well make King Charles turn in his grave. For Compton, aristocrat and Whig potentate, had not lost his fighting spirit when he exchanged the sword for the mitre, and if others more lowly of heart than he might find a higher place in the Kingdom of Heaven, in the troubled passages of the political arena, good Anglicans knew that those who attacked the Protestant Church would at the very beginning have to fight the bishop.

In April, 1686, James attempted to legalise his use of the dispensing power by engineering the trial of a convert to Catholicism who was an officer in his army. Sir Edward Hale's coachman charged him with breaking the Test Act and in the court of King's Bench the judges, with only one dissentient, found for the defendant. Although the trial was collusive, it was a genuine attempt on the part of the King to have legal authority for his actions. The right to suspend laws in emergency did rest with the Crown. But there could not be continuous emergency. The terms were self-contradictory, and it was obvious after Hale's case that James had no intention of using his prerogative only on rare occasions. In May, an Anglican clergyman converted to Catholicism was allowed to retain his office; in July four Catholics were admitted to the Privy Council. Among them was James's loyal but foolish friend Harry Jermyn, now Lord Dover and unexpectedly devout. In July also, the King appointed a Court of High Commission to try cases connected with ecclesiastical affairs, on the ground that they should be removed from the direct control of a Catholic sovereign. But to the Protestant majority the court was an insidious attempt to curb the Church's freedom and the dangerous prelude of greater illegalities to come. Sancroft, the aged and timid archbishop who could always screw his courage to the sticking-point when he saw clearly what he ought to do, refused to officiate, and the Commission consisted of three subservient bishops, together with Jeffreys, Lord Chief Justice Herbert, Sunderland and an unhappy and confused Rochester. In September the Commission justified its ill-repute by suspending the Bishop of London, for refusing to punish a clergyman for unwise words in the pulpit. At Christmas in 1686, a new Catholic chapel was opened at Whitehall for public worship, a magnificent work of art, replete with marble statuary, with coloured frescoes and a glorious throne, where bishops and priests in rich copes made 'divers cringes . . . with a world of mysterious ceremony'. 'I would not have believed I should ever have seen such things in the King of England's palace,' was the observation of that mild man, Evelyn.

In January, 1687, Rochester went. His tenacious adherence to the Anglican Faith was urged by Sunderland as a reason for dismissal. The Treasurer had no desire to own himself beaten and he agreed to a conversation with the King's confessor with a view to being converted. But when he was faced by the priests, love of office and money and the perquisites of royal favour faded into nothingness before the training of youth and the honest conviction of years. He broke off the conference, declaring his loyalty to the Church, to which he and his fathers had belonged. A few days later he surrendered the white staff. He was beaten. But in his defeat he had shewn himself the better man.

Soon after Rochester's defeat, his elder brother, the Earl of

Clarendon was replaced by Tyrconnel as Lord-Lieutenant in Ireland. The Tories were eclipsed. Sunderland was flirting with the Whigs. In April, 1687, James's first Declaration of Indulgence suspended the execution of the Penal Laws against Catholic and Protestant dissenters. Political equality between men of all religion was to be accompanied by freedom of worship. Unfortunately, James, though he had accomplished much, had only been able to do so by stretching his prerogative to the utmost. The legality of his piecemeal preferments and dispensations was at best questionable. He set his heart on the Parliamentary repeal of the Test and the Penal Laws which should give substance to what he had achieved in skeleton form. His prorogued Tory Parliament was useless to him for this purpose and he dissolved it in July. By a series of closetings at court, and the imposition of a questionnaire upon the electors in the counties, he tried to sound public opinion, while in the manipulation of Lord-Lieutenancies and municipal elections he attempted to copy his brother's policy of muzzling the opposition. But when Tory gentry and Whig business men proved equally unwilling to fall into line, the effect of muzzling was merely sullen silence.

In the City elections that year, 'all the jolly genteel citizens were turned out' and 'sneaking fanatics' were put in their places. Thus James secured the election of a Whig dissenter as Lord Mayor, but to his surprise not only did the new officials take the Test but they ordered November 5th, gunpowder-treason day, to be celebrated 'in the usual fashion'. And disregarding a suggestion that he might modify the service in the Guildhall if he wished, 'the mayor though he went sometimes to the meetings of the dissenters, yet he came often to church, and behaved himself more decently than was expected of him'.

There was no possibility as yet of a Parliament willing to give favourable consideration to repeal, and reluctantly the issue of writs was postponed. James had no desire to be a tyrant; he wished intensely to give his religious policy a legal standing, but he failed to realise that one cannot force public opinion and instead of holding his hand before the last shred of popularity had vanished, he plunged into fresh activities calculated to alienate the most moderate among his subjects. 'As for the consequences, I shall leave them to Providence,' he said.

In July at Windsor he gave a solemn audience to the Papal Nuncio. Somerset, the Lord-in-waiting, hesitated to introduce the Pope's representative. James remonstrated: 'I am above the law.' 'But I am not,' replied Somerset. He was removed, and the Duke of Grafton, James's nephew, performed the unpleasant duty. The nation was even more horrified by the formal inclusion of Father Petre in the Privy Council in November; even the Queen 'beg'd of the King not to do it, that it would give great scandal not only to Protestants but to thinking Catholics . . . notwithstanding which the King was so bewitched (to use His Majesty's own words) by My Lord Sunderland and Father Petre, as to let himself be prevail'd upon to doe so indiscreet a thing'.[1] Indiscreet was a mild term for a piece of criminal folly, to be balanced by an equally foolish attack on the Universities, the stronghold of Church and State Toryism. Cambridge was antagonised by the deposition of the Vice-Chancellor, who had refused to admit a monk to a degree, and at Oxford the Fellows of Magdalen were expelled by the King in December, 1687, after an unseemly wrangle over the appointment of a President, in which James showed himself irritable and obtuse.

But no mere relation of a few impolitic measures can express the general feeling of strained nerves and unhappy expectancy. Fears and cogitations, far more potent than bare facts, stirred the minds of men to suspicion and their hearts to revolt. In the King's new army, they had

[1] Clarke, *Life of James II*, Vol. II., p. 77.

something visible upon which anxious distrust could concentrate. His whole-hearted enjoyment of the fighting machine he had created, paying for it out of his own income since there was no hope of a Parliamentary grant, was beyond the comprehension of a people who thought it the supreme manifestation of the King's disregard of their interests and liberties. James loved the pomp and ceremony of military display; he sent out his men along the Great West Road to welcome the Queen from Windsor and escort her to the camp; he was delighted with the summer manœuvres and the steady improvement in the men's skill and morale. But his people believed that he must have a deeper purpose and that the army would be used to impose his religious beliefs upon the country. Their views were admirably expressed in the jingle of the rhyming journalist:

'He'll teach his Men in warlike sport
How to defend, or storm a Fort;
And in heroick Interlude
Will act the dreadful scene of Bude;[1]
Here Lorraine storms, the Vizier dies,
And Brandenburgh routs the supplies;
Bavaria there blows up their train
And all the Turks are took, or slain.

All this performed, with no more harm
Than loss of simple gunners arm:
And surely 'tis a greater good
To teach men war, than shed their blood.

Now pause, and view the Army Royal
Compos'd of valiant souls and loyal
Not rais'd (as ill men say) to hurt ye,
But to defend, or to convert ye:
Time was, the Word was powerful
But now 'tis thought remiss and dull,
Has not that Energy and Force
Which is in well-arm'd Foot and Horse.'

[1] The seige of Budapest, by the Turks.

There was no real danger of dragonnades from Hounslow, but the propinquity of the camp disturbed the citizens, just as the multitude of Catholics about the court irritated the Protestant noblemen, who remained as far as possible on their own estates. Lampoons were affixed in conspicuous places.

> ''Tis thus our sovereign keeps his word
> And makes the Nation great,
> To Irishmen he trusts the sword
> To Jesuits the State.'

or on the gate of a Catholic chapel:

> 'Then pray for the soul of Gabriel John
> Or if you please you may let it alone,
> 'Tis all one.'

The more sober citizen kept silence, 'so puzzled with new and daily surmise, that we speak but little and cannot tell what to think'.

The Catholics themselves were in a like state of uncertainty, distrusting the King's haste and suspicious of the influence of the Jesuits. Even the Queen was dubious. Lady Sunderland had ingratiated herself in her favour, but Mary Beatrice still distrusted the minister. She refused to recommend the King to make him Treasurer after Rochester's resignation, and Sunderland was denied his chief ambition, for James, who saw clearly as soon as the matter was purely one of administration, believed that greater efficiency could be obtained through a commission. The Queen was relieved but she still lacked confidence. By degrees one thought dominated all others. If she had another child, the need for the haste that frightened her would no longer exist. Secure in the possession of an heir, the bogey of old age would no longer scare James to unseemly action. And she herself would be happy not only in the joy of the child but in a new bond of union between herself and the husband, from whom she had drifted apart. In the summer of 1687 she suffered a severe loss in the death of her mother the Duchess Laura, whose strong personality had subdued distance, and had never let go the child whom she had left reluctantly in England. Every week they had written to each other, and Mary Beatrice had continued to interest herself in the affairs of Modena and had even imperilled her husband's good relations with the Pope in her eagerness to help her uncle to attain his Cardinal's hat. Her mother's death aggravated her loneliness, and her unhappiness was intensified by the insolence and ill-disguised hostility which had replaced the placid affection with which the Princess Anne had once regarded her. One of her few friends at court was to her own surprise the silent Sidney Godolphin, who had fallen in love with his royal mistress, and only surrendered his secret passion when it clashed with his principles and his prosperity.

But in spite of her doubts and loneliness the Queen was better in health than she had been for many years. Recently she had spent much of her time at Windsor or at Richmond, coming up to Whitehall for a brief season of festivity in October, in which month both her own birthday and the King's happened to fall. But as soon as she could escape from the bassett tables and the music-parties, as soon as New Year and Shrove-tide revels were over, she would hasten to the homely red-brick pile at Richmond, where the tranquil beauty of the Thames lay below her windows. The quiet country life did her good and the fresh air checked the disease that had threatened her lungs. So with the return of better health she recovered something of her old initiative. In September, 1687, she visited Bath, to take a course of the famous waters, which were supposed to be excellent aids to conception. And, possibly with greater effect, she greeted James who visited her on a progress in the West with something of her old allure and sweetness. James made no secret of their desire for a child. Going on his way northward, he visited the shrine at Holywell and prayed for God's blessing on their love. In October, King and Queen were together at Whitehall, and as early as mid-November a rumour arose that the Queen was pregnant. At the end of the month she told the good news to her stepdaughter, Mary of Orange. But Princess Anne also wrote to Mary, scornful letters, coloured with a sneer. She herself had known trouble that spring, and had not only miscarried but had lost two of her infant daughters. The curse of physical pain and mental anguish which the years held for her, the most unhappy of royal ladies, had already shadowed her life. So her own bitter disappointment was twisted into angry jealousy when just before Christmas her young stepmother's pregnancy was publicly announced. During the next few months the ladies of the court made plans and preparations with the happy Queen. 'It really is enough to turn one's stomach,' wrote Anne to Mary, 'to hear what things are said to her of that kind and to see how mightily she is satisfied with it.'

Mary was a good woman, but her husband and her church were the two passions of her life. The court at The Hague was thronged with malcontents from England, who hinted that only the fact that she would be the next ruler prevented them from organising revolt. If a son were born to James, she would no longer be the heir; her husband, who was living for the day when the men and resources of England would be his to use in a final onslaught upon Louis, would find himself checked and thwarted. What would he do? What would the English refugees do? What should she do if she had to choose between her father and her husband? The inconvenience, nay the danger, of a son and heir in England was so manifest to Mary, that like her sister Anne she refused to believe it. It was so many years since Mary Beatrice had borne a child that lived. She was delicate: folk had talked freely of the possibility of her death. It was absurd!

So everyone was saying, up and down the streets of London and wherever men congregated to smoke and drink and talk. They began to compose ribald rhymes about it, mocking the King's pilgrimage to Holywell. There was a jingle that began:

> 'In Lombard-Land, great Modena's Duchess
> Was snatched from her Empire by Death's cruel clutches
> When to Heaven she came for thither she went,
> Each angel received her with joy and content.
> On her knees she fell down
> Before the bright throne,
> And begg'd that God's mother would grant her one boon
> Give England a son (at this critical point)
> To put little Orange's nose out of joint.'

The coarse gibes and the sly insinuations came inevitably to the Queen's knowledge, but she was too happy to care about them and laughed at them among her ladies. At Easter, a false rumour of her brother's death reached her. The shock upset her and for some days she was very ill. There was more talk over the tankards and the coffee cups. Those who had previously denied her pregnancy now declared that she had miscarried, and continued to reiterate both statements with commendable impartiality.

It might have been wiser when such rumours were abroad if Mary Beatrice had not withdrawn into her own world of expectancy. Policy dictated an approach to her stepdaughter. Anne would have been convinced if she had seen the Queen at her toilet. So she said, later. But though the fashions of the time knew nothing of reticence, Mary Beatrice was full of natural delicacy and reserve, and she hated the necessity her royal position imposed upon her of offering herself to public gaze; the most that she could bring herself to do was to allow Lady Sunderland to assist her to disrobe. After the alarm at Easter, Anne of her own accord used to absent herself from the presence-chamber as if she dreaded confirmation of the fact she wished to deny.

For the Princess of Denmark was in a thoroughly uncomfortable positon. Her religion lacked the intensity of her sister's faith which had approximated through the years to William's Calvinism, but she was a sincere Protestant, honestly disturbed by her father's public actions and in constant expectation of an attempt on his behalf to force her into Romanism. To his honour, James never made the attempt; except for a long and rather pathetic letter one Christmas to his elder daughter, describing her mother's conversion, he never approached his children concerning their religion. But Anne could not help a feeling of isolation, among the fervent converts of the court or those who paraded their Protestantism in ostentation. For she was a plain woman, in mentality and character as well as in looks, and perhaps all the better for it in an over-subtle age. In her own words, 'one sees so many saints meer devils that, if one be a good Christian, the less show one makes it is the better in my opinion!' She hated shams. Lady Sunderland, cheating at cards and flirting with her gallants, and then hurrying off to church at the popular St. Martin's 'morning and afternoon (because there are not people enough to see her at Whitehall Chapel)' disgusted Anne. 'She runs from church to church after the famousest preachers and keeps such a clatter with her devotion that it really turns one's stomach.' That was a favourite phrase of the Princess of Denmark's and described fairly accurately her chronic state of mental dyspepsia. The Churchills stood by her. She loved Sarah Churchill's forthright ways, and let the Colonel manage her affairs. Inevitably, he had drifted away from his master, to whom he had spoken frankly on the matter of religion, but their mutual interest in the army was still a binding-link.

Anne had grown to dislike her stepmother. She thought her haughty, believed her to be susceptible to the flattery she decried, and doubted the sincerity of the affection offered to herself. It was partly a young woman's ineradicable resentment towards a stepmother. When her physician suggested a visit to Bath, she arranged to go, regardless of the fact that she was probably robbing herself of the opportunity of attending her stepmothers' confinement and settling her own doubts. She left London at the end of May with the parting words to the Queen, 'Madam, I think you will be brought to bed before I return,' and by her departure did her father the greatest disservice it was in her power to render.

Early in June, the Queen began to fret to be away from Whitehall. She had not found happiness there. Her child should see the light in the old Palace across the Park, which had been Mary Beatrice's home when first she came to England. On June 2nd, she expressed her wish to go there quietly and 'await the good hour'. But the workmen were in; her rooms would not be ready for some days. The hot Italian temper that English winters had subdued flared out again. 'I mean to be in St. James's to-night if I lie on the boards,' she declared on the 8th. But next day she was still at Whitehall. That night they played cards as usual. The Queen was tired. But good manners forbade that she should rise till the 'rubber' was finished. It was eleven o'clock before the tables broke up. Late as it was, she still meant to go to St. James's. The King gave in to her whim, and they carried her across the Park, beside the quiet waters wrapped in the warm darkness of June.

The Queen slept undisturbed that night with James beside her. The King rose early next morning. It was Trinity Sunday, and he was anxious to go to his devotions. But he had scarcely left her, when Mary Beatrice called him back and bade him summon her women. Her time had come. A good dame called Dawson hurrying into the room found her sitting on the bottom of the big bed, shivering with nervous excitement. The small pallet couch intended for her confinement was still unmade, and Mrs. Dawson urged her to return to the large bed she had left. She requested a warming-pan as naturally as a woman to-day would ask for a hot-water bottle. Yet afterwards, a suppositious child was supposed to have been smuggled thus, between the blankets.

Most of the Protestant ladies-in-waiting were at eight o'clock communion at Whitehall; as Lady Sunderland knelt at the altar an urgent message was whispered in her ear. The news soon spread, and bishops and soldiers, privy councillors and ladies of the court, crowded into the bedroom to testify to the Queen's delivery. She loathed their prying eyes. There were sixty-seven people present but not the Princess Anne who would have been worth them all. She was still at Bath. Mary Beatrice in the midst of her labour looked up and saw Judge Jeffreys in the crowd. She begged her husband to bend lower over her bed, that his perruque might hide from her the sight of the Chancellor's handsome, fiendish face. At ten o'clock the baby was born. The Queen listening for the sound that meant life, exclaimed anxiously, 'I don't hear the child cry.' Lady Sunderland had agreed with the King to pass her hand across her forehead if it were a son. James saw her hand rise, and could not believe. 'Is it a boy?' he cried. When they answered yes, he bade the doctor kneel by the bedside, and knighted him on the spot. Lord Feversham, radiating good-humour, lifted the baby into his arms and bore him into the inner chamber with the shout 'Room for the Prince.' The excited chattering crowd dispersed, and Mary Beatrice lay relaxed, ready to welcome the sleep that follows labour. In the small hours of the next morning she awoke, restless and thirsty, and called for a drink. There was no reply; no lady-in-waiting watched by her bedside. Alarmed, she called again and a young serving-girl came in and carelessly told her news that brought her near to collapse. The baby prince was ill and Lady Sunderland had been called away to help; the King was praying in the Oratory for his son's life. The anxious doctors, who gave nature as little chance as possible, had already given him physic and in error had dosed him twice. The attack passed, and miraculously the baby lived.

In London, dismay and incredulity greeted the news of the birth. For the Protestants, it meant the perpetuation of the present unhappy state of affairs. The prospect of a Catholic heir made Revolution no longer a mere academic possibility, but an immediate and tragic necessity. And since few wanted Revolution, the crowds gave easy credence to the rumours that were soon rampant of the suppositious child. Others less innocent were not sorry to have so excellent a battle-cry as a sham Prince of Wales. There were many variants of the myth, jumbled together with an entire disregard of consistency; a child had been brought in with the warming-pan, the baby had died at birth, or in its first illness, and another had been put in its place; gradually as more subtle brains got to work, the stories were concocted into a credible whole. There was some criminal libel and much honest doubt. People in a mass are very gullible, and the most cruel slander in history was believed without investigation by a greater part of the country. Even Mary of Orange cancelled the prayers of thanksgiving she had ordered in the Dutch churches, and professed herself convinced of the fraud, after sending Anne a list of eighteen categorical questions, which the Princess answered, not dishonestly but without impartiality. Her own absence in Bath had made the fraud possible and when in October the King held a public inquiry she excused herself from attending. James was more hurt by her attitude, by the reflection on his honesty and by the fact that his relatives and his subjects could believe him guilty of such an outrageous sham, than by anything that had hitherto befallen him. It was the first of the shocks, that were to break him physically and mentally before the year was out.

The Queen probably worried less than he, the child's precarious health causing her too much anxiety for extraneous thoughts. The physicians of the day, strong in possession of the little knowledge that is dangerous, had decided that the Queen's children did not thrive on milk. They enacted that the prince should be reared by hand on barley water and sugar, enriched by a few currants! The child did not appreciate the experimental diet, and through the heat of summer, languished and revived and again relapsed, so that Anne reported triumphantly to Mary: 'I believe it will not be long before he is an angel in heaven.' Mary Beatrice had strict ideas about her children's upbringing, and believed that while she was at Whitehall it behoved her to maintain the dignity of a Queen, pursuing her accustomed routine of prayers, meals, amusements. As in the case of her former children, she had instructed the nurse not to bring the baby to her when she was in company. In August, the royal nursery moved to Richmond. There the child had another violent attack of colic. The King and Queen were summoned from Whitehall, with the warning that the child might die before their arrival, in which case a courier would be sent to meet them. They rode west by Knightsbridge through Hammersmith and past Sion House, anguish overwhelming them each time a horseman came in sight. But every horseman passed on, and they came to Richmond Bridge, unaccosted by the messenger of death. The child was barely alive. The doctors were preparing a new medicine of particular stringency; it turned to fire within one and would burn away the colic! Lady Powys, the prince's governess, was a woman of common sense. She rebelled. What the child needed, she declared, was not medicine but good mother's milk. Defying the doctors, she sent out a servant to find a woman in Richmond who could suckle the royal infant. There was a tile-maker living on the Green, whose wife had borne a child. They took her just as she was, in waistcoat and cloth petticoat, without stockings and in old wooden shoes, and pressed golden guineas into her hand as they brought her into the Palace. 'She says she knows not what to do with them.' But when they put the child into her arms, she knew what to do with him. He felt for her breast and was satisfied.

The woman was rigged by degrees in suitable attire,

and attached to the prince's suite. In due course she came to Whitehall, and her uncouth and simple ways delighted the ladies of the court. But young James continued to flourish, and on October 15th, four days before his cousin sailed from Holland to turn his father off the throne, the Prince of Wales was christened. His godfather was the Papal Nuncio! The crowds who watched the ceremony turned anxiously away to note the direction of the wind, which alone delayed William of Orange. For since the spring much had happened. The King, hurling himself against impregnable forces, had quarrelled with his bishops, while the Dissenters, to whom he had offered the hand of friendship, had remembered the Bloody Assize and turned away. The birth of an heir had shocked Whig and Tory alike out of the usual English belief that somehow things would come right without the necessity of intervention. The Revolution had begun. But the thoughts of James and his Queen were concentrated not on the religious mission for which they had risked their throne, not even on the maintenance of their own authority, but on the safety and well-being of the infant whom once they had desired for reasons of politics, but who in his coming had made them afraid to challenge fortune.

CHAPTER X

SEVEN BISHOPS

'A good sword and a trusty hand,
  A merry heart and true!
King James's men shall understand
  What Cornishmen can do.

'And have they fixed the where and when
  . . . And shall Trelawney die?
Then twenty thousand Cornishmen
  Will know the reason why!'

The Song of the Western Men.

THE prologue to the Revolution was enacted during the spring that preceded the prince's birth. The refusal of Dissent to accept liberty, that had no legal basis, rendered inevitable the King's ultimate failure. Looking back on that refusal and the sacrifices it entailed, the Whigs of the eighteenth century gave to the events of 1688 the appellation of 'glorious', to which the neo-Tories of to-day are inclined to demur, denying the existence of any grandeur of design or achievement. The Revolution is depicted as the result of a political intrigue, engineered by a group of land-owners who were jealous of the power of the crown and were supported by the trading-classes, for their part eager to assist William in destroying Louis's domination of the best markets of Europe and the East. One must, however, find in it more than this, must discover signs of spiritual fervour and of a nation moved to deep emotion if one is to justify the use of the word, glorious. One must, if it is possible, get behind politics to the mind of the average man, dismissed glibly as Tory or as Whig. Why did he dislike so intensely the policy of the Crown? Something of good there was and something therefore that was permanent in the system that James wished to impose upon his people. When those who had expelled him strove to conserve in legal phrase and Parliamentary enactment the instincts and principles which had roused them to opposition, they found that the idea which had been the foundation-stone of James's policy was sound and not to be cast aside. The liberty of conscience for which he lost his throne became in 1689 the birthright of all Englishmen. Why then did James II fail so lamentably to achieve his ideal?

The dislike of the ordinary Tory squire and citizen was rooted in resentment. They revolted from the shows of Rome, the candles and incense and statuory in the new Catholic chapels, the pomp of the Papal Nuncio and the fulsome piety of the converts. They were further offended by the King's attempts to invade the privacy of their thoughts and opinions, before admitting them to the town council or the bench of Justices. Without panic but without hesitation, the Tories felt that such things must stop; they were not seemly. They had no wish for bloodshed; had James resisted and invoked the aid of his people, there might have been much searching of heart and conflict of loyalties. Many felt that it must be wrong, whatever the circumstances, to depose one's lawful sovereign. Yet, when James had abdicated and matters had been peaceably settled, the average Tory turned with regret but with devout thankfulness to the quiet pursuit of the day's work and the religious observances, which the King's innovations had seemed to endanger. The Revolution is one of the most typically English things chronicled in English history, both in the casual way in which it happened and in the majority's acceptance of the accomplished fact. Metaphorically as well as actually, nobody lost their heads, in itself a marvellous achievement.

But not glorious? No. And yet, there was something fine in the quiet insistence of the rank and file that their church should not be disturbed. That church, which had returned triumphant and un-Christlike in 1660, had grown into a deeper spiritual life. The stress on theology and politics at the expense of ethics was still a deterrent to a true Christian church, but such leaders of thought as Tillotson and Stillingfleet, borrowing from the Cambridge Platonists, paved the way for a school of Anglicanism, more in touch with the humanities than the old theology, more tolerant of dissent and with a stronger insistence on the essentials of the primitive church. Stillingfleet, intellectually brilliant, charming and personable, who in his youth had been dubbed 'the beauty of holiness', Tillotson, who beneath his wealth of learning maintained a simple spirit and who made it his first object in life 'not to be angry with anybody upon any occasion'; Gilbert Burnet, a bustling bishop, cantankerous but shrewd, already advising Mary of Orange, for her own good and her husband's at The Hague: these were the prelates in whose care the Church would be in the brief period of vitality after the Revolution, before formalism and prosperity opened the door to decay. But there were others, less progressive in thought but holy men of God, Sancroft, who put himself as archbishop at the head of the resistance to James, and Thomas Ken, 'the good little black man', who refused to persecute dissenters and lived the life of a saint. These and others remonstrated with James in the days of his power but when he had fled, surrendered their bishoprics, rather than gainsay, in swearing allegiance to William, the doctrine of hereditary succession which they had preached. They died in penury. In upholding non-resistance they had been feeling their puzzled way towards a solution of one of the most difficult problems that confront churchmen of every age: the right attitude of Christians towards politics. Their ideal of obedience to the powers-that-be, of bringing about good in the world by the example of saintly lives and the mediation of kindly hearts, rather than by interference in the struggles of the political arena, was a reaction from the fighting parsons of Cromwell's army and the worldly prelates of the Restoration. It was far more than an academic absurdity.

These were the leaders. Among those who followed, there were many who fell short. But there were signs of genuine spiritual growth in the latter years of Charles II's reign, more particularly in the numerous 'Religious Societies' founded for young men in 1678 and afterwards. Like the Oxford groups of to-day, these young enthusiasts were concerned with devotional technique rather than with theology. Appreciating the need of complete surrender to God's guidance, they bound themselves to withdraw seven times a day from the turmoil of ordinary life for a quiet time in prayer; their standard was absolute love and their main obligation to speak evil of no man. They vowed 'to keep close to the Church of England'. To men such as these, as well as to the prelates, the reign of James was a challenge, his attempts at toleration a cloak to bring in Popery, and their religion sufficiently precious for their secular politics to go by the board. Men like Danby, who welcomed William of Orange, knew that by so doing they were putting the control of England into the hands of their political opponents. Thus even the politicians testified to the reality of the religious force that drove them to agree to Revolution.

Trade, finance, national expansion overseas were to dominate the policy of the succeeding century; Louis XIV's aggressions made no pretence at religious motives, and the Pope as an Italian Prince was Louis's enemy and therefore less than friend to James. But in spite of a changing world and the deadening effect of moral decay, which made the spirit of 1688 less fervent and admittedly less glorious than that of 1642, it was still matters of faith and conscience that sundered the tie between the King and his Tory subjects and revealed again that the Anglican compromise had grown in its century of existence into a living witness of worship and of truth.

But when all is said the Revolution of 1688 was in essence

a triumph of the Whigs, the closing act of the drama which had begun with the victories of the Ironsides. The Cromwellians had been extremists, but it had not been the radicals who ultimately triumphed. Algernon Sidney had perished on the scaffold, his Republican theories discredited by men such as Ferguson and Rumbold whose daily bread was plot and counter-plot. The landed proprietors, who controlled the movement, were moderate men, the disciples of John Locke, whose philosophy of the social contract they had adopted as their own. It was the ideals, embodied in Locke's teaching, which were the glory of the Revolution and were reflected in the spirit in which it was carried out. Those ideals, essentially English, had been challenged by James, and were defended by the Whigs, loyal to their belief in ordered liberty, freedom of thought and the sovereignty of the law. Locke had ascribed to every individual certain natural and inviolable dues such as the right to personal liberty and the possession of property. But since neither his goods nor his person would be safe from attack from others if man continued to live in that state of nature, which another philosopher had described as 'nasty, brutish and short', a 'social contract' had been made, whereby sovereignty had been established and every individual agreed to abide by the law, surrendering his untrammelled freedom in return for protection and security. Only, if the ruler invaded his people's inviolable rights by any attacks on their liberty or their property, did he break the contract and thereby invalidate his claim upon their obedience. In such extremity, the subject had the power to rebel and if successful to dispossess the King. Thus, on the premise of an original contract, less historical in itself than the idea of a patriarchal King, Locke had built up a common-sense philosophy, true in its essential teaching that unlicensed liberty for either King or subject is impossible in an ordered State, where the good of the whole demands from each individual the surrender of the right to do exactly as he pleases.

While the men of property approved Locke's stress on the sanctity of ownership, the trading classes appreciated the idea of contract. In the dawn of modern commerce, there was romance and enthusiasm as well as the desire for gain spurring young men to effort and experiment, and their whole lives were coloured by the idea of mutual trust and credit. Locke's philosophy linked up their daily job of building up a system of international trade and finance with the wider issues of social and political life.

In addition to the landed proprietors and the business men, the Whig cause drew its strength from the legal classes. The lawyers at the end of the seventeenth century had a great tradition behind them of independence and pugnacity. The great battles in the Commons over matters of privilege, the responsibility of ministers, the people's control of taxation, had been waged by the lawyers. Magna Charta had been rescued from oblivion and enshrined as the great charter of the people. The passing of the Habeas Corpus Act, which James most unwisely wished to repeal, had reduced to the minimum the royal prerogative of imprisonment in emergency without showing cause. On the whole, it was a record of which to be proud, and the lawyers were proud of it and felt it a sacred trust to maintain the integrity and independence of their calling. To them Locke's belief in the supremacy of the law made as great an appeal as his idea of contract made to the business men, and his reverence for property to the Whig landowners.

There remained the dissenters; the shopkeepers of London, the men of the West Country, and the numerous small communities who had withstood persecution up and down England. For them Locke preached the doctrine of religious toleration. In an age which had not yet freed itself from Luther's erastianism, from the theory that a State's religion should be that of the prince who ruled it, he urged that toleration was not only philosophically desirable but politically practicable. Those who had not the detached mind of the philosopher doubted and wondered, yet the idea was gaining ground when the plots and rumour of plots that formed the framework of the Exclusion struggle seemed to give the lie to Locke's assurance. The dissenters reconciled themselves to continued persecution. It was an unpleasant prospect. For over twenty years, hole and corner conventicles had been their only means of public worship. In some cases, the leniency of the authorities had lessened the hardship, in others, a vindictive justice of the peace would play with his victims as a cat with mice, commandeering the cattle and the goods of the poorer folk to pay their frequent fines. There could be no certainty of quiet.

Then unexpectedly came James's friendly overtures. The first declaration of Indulgence was issued in the spring of 1687. It offered to dissenters freedom and security in worship, as the King's avowed policy of repealing the Tests offered them the prospect of serving the State once more. There were many in their ranks particularly well fitted for public duties. The Puritan tradition was one of social and political service and the vigour and intelligence of their minds had been strengthened by the years of persecution. The weaklings had dropped out, the hypocrites had faded away, and the sense of fellowship, engendered by perils and discomforts shared, had enriched and balanced natures originally too prone to 'perverse antipathies'. It was a great opportunity; quiet in their homes, recognition in their religion, useful employment in the State; to the strong who were conscious of their own abilities as well as to the weak, weary of jaded years of malicious interference, the King's offer made an irresistible appeal. And yet it was refused.

At first the issue was doubtful. James had the satisfaction of receiving addresses of thanks from different communities. The Friends, inspired by Penn's own zeal, were enthusiastic; and certain Anabaptists from the West followed suit. But the Presbyterians kept silence. They thought it 'a great indignity put upon them to be linked with Quakers and Romanists'. Nor was this merely the exclusiveness of the sects; the largest body of Protestant dissent still looked with regret towards the mother-church from which they had gone forth in sorrow, still hoped for a change in that church's policy and constitution which might enable them to return, fellow-members of a broad and comprehensive State-religion. As a corollary they were uncertain about toleration, which by accepting the sects rendered permanent the divisions in the Protestant Church.

The Independents on the other hand believed wholeheartedly in toleration; but even they disliked the alliance with Rome which was thrust upon them, feeling it to be in essence a denial of the spirit of their religion. Halifax, stemming the tide of the addresses by his 'Letter to a Dissenter', put their doubts into words. 'This alliance between liberty and infallibility is bringing together the two most contrary things that are in the world. . . . You are . . . to be hugged now, only that you may be better squeezed at another time. . . .' But not only personal anxiety as to their future and a deep-rooted suspicion of Catholicism impelled the Dissenters to refusal. There was a question of principle involved. The King's excessive use of his dispensing power endangered the sovereignty of the law upon which their political faith depended. As Halifax urged, there was little advantage in rescuing themselves 'from the severity of one law' by giving a blow to all the laws by which their religion and liberty were protected. In the face of a common danger all Protestants should be united. 'Let us be still, quiet and undivided, firm at the same time to our religion, our loyalty and our laws.'

Like Halifax, the aged Baxter the 'Bishop of Nonconformity' saw clearly. He had been released in 1686 on the first sign of a change in the King's policy. But he would have nothing to do with the court or with the Indulgence. In the prime of his life he had resisted a greater temptation, when at the Restoration he had refused a bishopric, but now as then he acted according to his ingrained conviction that good cannot be reached by crooked paths. Others, less clear-sighted, might have been won, had James acted with circumspection during the rest of 1687, but while his advancement of Catholics, without any corresponding favour to Dissenters, alienated the few self-seekers, his reception of the Papal Nuncio and his use of the ecclesiastical commission were contrary to the spirit of compromise, while his attempts to pack Parliament disgusted the men whose fathers had died for civil liberty on the fields of Newbury and Edgehill.

For at bottom, it was the King's moral shortcomings that caused his ruin. He failed not because his aims were at fault or his methods stupid, but because he was not honest. He denied his best characteristic by aping a subtlety he did not possess, and by manifesting the same crooked streak that had ruined his father and was the curse of every Stuart. Intrigues with Louis XIV, suspected and therefore exaggerated by the rest of the world, but existent to the extent of a new secret understanding in the spring of '88, alienated William of Orange; as James's denial of that friendship at The Hague infuriated Louis, when his help might have meant salvation. His treatment of Compton and Rochester disinclined the Anglicans to believe his promise to maintain the Church. His desire for 'liberty of conscience' was vitiated by his attacks on freedom of thought in his questionnaire to electors. Above all between his coming to the throne and his peace-offering to the Dissenters stretched the black gulf of the Bloody Assize. Evil done could not be undone, and lack of charity to Cornish and Titus Oates and lack of mercy to Monmouth's wretched adherents brought its certain nemesis in '88. James failed because he denied himself: a Christian, he had been vindictive; an honest soldier, he had schemed with politicians; a patriarchal ruler, he had lost his people's trust.

And so in its hour of need the Protestant dissenters stood by the Church of England, who had treated them with little charity in her own hour of triumph. It was a worthy close to the stormy chapter of Nonconformity. In refusing to accept ease and royal favour, because it allied them with courses they could not approve and had been granted at the expense of the supremacy of the law, they made a real sacrifice, which more than anything else in the Revolution justifies the epithet of glorious.

The King's Declaration of Indulgence was reissued in May 1688, and the Council ordered it to be read in every church and chapel in the city on the last two Sundays of the month, and throughout the kingdom on the 3rd and 10th of June. Attached to the new Indulgence was an explanation of the policy behind it, and an appeal for the return of such members in the forthcoming elections as should enable the King to establish toleration on a legal basis. Upon the country's response to this gesture depended the success or failure of the King's design.

In the middle of May, Bishop Ken was working quietly in his diocese when he received the following letter:

'My Lord,

'This is only in my own name, and in the name of some of our brethren now hear upon the place, earnestly to desire you, immediately upon the receipt of this letter, to come hither with what convenient speed you can, not taking notice to any that you are sent for. Wishing you a prosperous journey, and us all a happy meeting, I remain,

'Your very loving brother,

'William Cantuar.'[1]

Travelling with Trelawney, the popular Bishop of Bristol, the Bishop of Bath and Wells reached Lambeth on Thursday the 17th of May. Next day, a meeting was held at the Archbishop's Palace to discuss the response to the

[1] Quoted from A Layman's *Life of Thomas Ken* whose account of the subsequent trial is very vivid.

order to read the Indulgence on the following Sunday. The prayer for divine guidance which began the morning's work was no barren formality; all were conscious that upon their action might hang weighty results both for their church and their nation. Throughout the long day they considered and debated, and unanimously decided to petition the King. At ten o'clock at night six bishops crossed the river and came to Whitehall. Compton, who had been present at their Councils, stayed behind in view of his suspension, nor did the Archbishop accompany them on this occasion though the petition was in his handwriting, with his name attached. Lloyd of St. Asaph who took the lead was a friend to Compton and Burnet and later whole-heartedly supported the Revolution; Ken, who seconded him, belonged to an entirely different school of thought. But all were united in the conviction that the Indulgence was illegal, that the liberty of the people was thus assailed, and that liberty had an inherent value and was not to be cast aside for any temporary advantage. The King had retired on their arrival, but he saw them in his bedchamber, apparently in no great anxiety as to the reason of their coming. A fortnight had passed since the issue of the Order in Council and in the absence of protest he had ceased to expect opposition. As he read the words of the petition, he was astounded; with a quiet assurance that was more infuriating than empty rhetoric, the bishops stated that they were averse to distributing and publishing the Indulgence, 'not from any want of duty or obedience to His Majesty . . . nor yet from any want of due tenderness to Dissenters . . . but because that Declaration was founded upon such a dispensing power, as had been oft declar'd illegal in Parliament'. They considered it a matter of so great consequence that they could not 'in honor or conscience make themselves parties to it'. James had never learnt to bear contradiction. 'This is a great surprise,' he exclaimed angrily. 'I did not expect this from you. This is a standard of rebellion. . . . I will be obeyed in publishing my

Declaration.' 'God's will be done,' was Ken's non-committal answer.

The reading of the declaration on the Sunday following came as an anti-climax. The rumour of the Bishop's Petition had been noised abroad and the Council's order was ignored in the majority of churches, 'the consequences of which,' commented Evelyn, 'a little time will show'. 'The anxiety and annoyance of the King may be imagined,' wrote a foreign observer. '. . . Things are daily advancing towards a catastrophe.' James's own foolhardiness provoked the cataclysm. On May 27th, the seven bishops (Sancroft and his six associates) were ordered to appear before the Council on the grounds that their petition comprised a 'seditious libel' against the King. James at this unhappy moment seems to have been impelled by the determination not to make his father's mistake of yielding under pressure; curiously in view of its happy issue, he accredited his brother's policy with the like fault of 'frequent goings back from such councells as had been prudently resolved upon', and he was determined to make an example of the bishops much in the same obstinate and irritated temper in which he had determined to make an example of the rebels in 1685. It was this unfortunate admixture of personal animus against his opponents which robbed the King's firmness of the quiet dignity that might have made it kingly.

James spent the first week in June in anxiety about his wife's approaching confinement; the bishops spent it in making sure that they did not do their cause less than justice through their ignorance of legal procedure. Lord Clarendon, the doyen of the High Anglican aristocracy, lent them Parliamentary journals, advised them as to counsel, and reminded them to be certain what to do if they were asked to offer bail. So when on Friday the 8th, they appeared before the Council, and were commanded 'to enter into recognisances of 500*l.* a man to answer to an information against them in the King's Bench the next term', the bishops refused to comply in view of their privileges as Peers of the realm. They added boldly that they 'were equally bound by their callings to oppose all innovations, both in government and religion'. In view of their refusal to give bail, the Council reluctantly committed them to the Tower. The bishops had used their brains to some purpose; they had put their opponents in a nasty dilemma. The latter chose the worst way out. Any withdrawal, however feeble it might have seemed at the moment, would have been better than this gratuitous making of martyrs. To the people of London it was no dryasdust matter of indictments and recognisances; the excited crowds were waiting in the streets, for the bishops had become the champions of liberty. When it was known that they were going to the Tower, the tumult grew near to a riot. The prisoners went from Westminster by water, and the citizens jostled each other by the river-side. 'The concern of the people for them was wonderful, infinite crowds on their knees begging their blessing, and praying for them, as they passed out of the barge along the Tower wharf.' A chill fell across the general enthusiasm as together the seven bishops entered the gloomy prison.

It was a marvellous week-end for the Londoner, then as now a glutton for sensation. On Friday, the bishops went to prison; on Sunday, the Queen's baby was born. It was a wonderful opportunity for James, to grant an amnesty in the general rejoicings and extricate himself from an impossible position and the bishops from the Tower. But to do the King justice, he was never deflected from a course by its difficulty or danger; having decided that it was right to prosecute the bishops, he left it at that, even though strange immigrants from the West had come up to town, singing in their soft, unintelligible voices:

> 'And shall Trelawney die?
> Then twenty thousand Cornishmen
> Will know the reason why.'

The bishops were treated well in the Tower, for the excited mob had no real conception of the situation, and their heroes' danger and the King's villainy were alike imaginary. James had no wish to play the tyrant and he was scrupulously fair in his methods of prosecution. On June 15th the prisoners having pleaded not guilty before the King's Bench, were remanded until the 29th in order to prepare their evidence. They were released on their own recognisances and when the Archbishop reached Lambeth that night, through crowds of people kneeling as he passed, the soldiers on guard, posted by the King's order, 'received him with military honours . . . and fell on their knees to ask his blessing'.

James should have been perturbed, if he heard of this; like an angry bull he was running with needless force against the prejudices and principles of his people; if the army shared those prejudices, wherein would lie his strength? But James throughout the summer was strangely oblivious to the risks he was running. It may have been an early symptom of the physical collapse which overwhelmed him in November, it may have been a repercussion of the joy in his living child that made it impossible to envisage disaster, it may have been the careless pride of *hubris* awaiting its nemesis. 'Those whom the gods wish to destroy, they first make mad.' But neither Louis's warnings, his daughter's growing coldness, the anxiety of his Catholic friends, nor the rising passion of the mob could make him more than mildly apprehensive.

The bishops came for trial in Westminster Hall on June 25th. The King had made no effort to pack the jury. It is an amazing commentary on the essentially law-abiding nature of the English, that the last act of this drama was played in the law-courts in an ordinary trial. It lasted from nine in the morning till after six at night; an eager audience followed with appreciation the attacks and counter-attacks of the learned counsel and applauded the young Whig Somers, who declared that the Petition was 'neither false, nor malicious nor seditious nor a libel'. Outside the Hall, those who had not gained admittance thronged the Palace yard and the surrounding streets, that have been the assembly-place of so many nervous concourses of anxious people. At Whitehall, the atmosphere was strained; they wished now that 'the thing had never been begun'. The court rose just before seven, and through the night, the jury considered its verdict. The twelve good men and true upon whom the lot had fallen were locked up in a small room without 'fire or candle, bread, drink, tobacco or any other refreshment', an inducement to haste which unfortunately had no effect upon one Arnold, a Brewer, who thought the bishops guilty. The other eleven were for acquittal, but their recalcitrant colleague objected on principle to giving in. About midnight, and again about three in the morning, those who waited without heard sounds of heated discussion, but at four o'clock when towels and some basins of water were sent in to revive the perspiring twelve, matters were still at a deadlock. If he could have lit his pipe, Arnold would have held out still longer but the request for a light was refused. At six he gave in, and between nine and ten the court reassembled to hear the verdict. As the foreman announced 'Not Guilty' the cheers of the multitude drowned the second word; 'one would have thought the Hall had cracked'. The news spread through the streets and away to the City. 'It looked like a little rebellion in noise, though not in fact.'

The King had ridden out to Hounslow Heath, the one place where he felt certain of content in the minds of others, as of himself. As he sat down to lunch in Lord Feversham's tent, the sound of cheering clamoured upon his ears. He asked for an explanation. The Commander-in-Chief reported that it was nothing: the soldiers were shouting on the news of the bishops' acquittal. For a moment the veil was lifted from the King's eyes. 'Nothing,' he echoed. 'Do you call that nothing?'

. . . .

On that very day, Saturday, June 30th, seven men wrote to William of Orange. Three of them were Tories: Danby, once Lord Treasurer of England, was still the most influential magnate north of the Trent: Lord Lumley had the distinction of having turned Protestant in 1687, the only year of the century in which that religion was unfashionable; Bishop Compton, though a fighter, had never yet been a rebel. Of the four Whigs, Lord Shrewsbury had been described by Halifax in the previous year as 'without any competition, the most considerable man of quality that is growing up amongst us'; the Earl of Devonshire, vigorous and dissolute, had run the gamut of Popish Plot and Exclusion but made his peace with the court after the collapse at Oxford; Henry Sidney and Edward Russell bore names sacred in the memory of all true Whigs, though the first lacked his brother's genius and the latter his kinsman's integrity. These were the men who invited William to come to England to maintain the laws and liberties of the country. In the spring, Russell had come over from The Hague, where he had been living since the Rye House tragedy, and had expressed William's readiness to intervene on the receipt of a written invitation. Halifax, in some ways the most influential man in England, still advised the malcontents to wait upon the event, but the birth of the Prince of Wales and the treatment of the bishops nerved the seven to write, in the conviction that they could no longer look to time to right the wrong, nor hope for reason from a King enthralled by the urgency of his religious desires. In their letter, they stressed the general dissatisfaction of the people, and more pertinently of the Army. 'Amongst the seamen,' they wrote, 'it is almost certain there is not one in ten who would do [the Government] any service in such a war.'

But their calculations did not err on the side of understatement. They averred, respecting the birth of the Prince, that 'not one in a thousand' believed him to be the Queen's child. Finally if he made the attempt, they urged

William to 'take care to bring some engineers' with him. In fact it was a most cold-blooded document on which to build a 'glorious Revolution'. There was nothing here of liberty or the rights of man, nothing but a bare statement of the chances by a group of hard-headed politicians to a prince, who had had his eye on England for years.

For William knew how to wait. English kings and English Parliaments had failed signally to think internationally. Insularity was the besetting sin of members of the House of Commons, selfishness the sin of all the Stuarts. But William could wait. In 1688 a new crisis was developing in Europe. For some time Louis had been dangerously quiet. Regarding him across the frontier, like wild beasts waiting for a tiger to spring, Spain and the Emperor were determined not to be caught. Innocent XI, most practical of holy men, felt Louis's ambition to be the greatest existing danger to Christendom, before which insidious evil the Turks hammering at Budapest could well be disregarded. To the north, William of Orange nerved by an implacable hate, weak in body but unquenchable in the vigour of his faith, organised, and engineered – and waited. The League of Augsburg, the first of the great European coalitions before which Louis's bid for world rule was to dash itself to pieces, was about to come into being. Only England was uncertain, the despair of the Chancelleries of Europe. James liked Louis and loved France, and he believed that the failures of Charles V and Philip II of Spain would deter any man from attempting world domination. Like most soldiers he was a peace-loving man, and his main interest in Europe was the relief of Budapest, whither in 1686 he sent his son the young Duke of Berwick to learn the art of war. And if a European conflagration proved unavoidable, the true role for England was that of neutrality and the strenuous pursuit of the trade the Dutch would be forced to neglect. It was a tenable opinion and, had James acted upon it consistently and sincerely, his fellow countrymen would have respected its independence and have condoned its selfishness. Unfortunately, James's love of designs and the habit of years inclined him to continued intrigues with the French Ambassador, Barillon, that master of shady diplomacy. The English troops withdrawn from the Dutch service were placed secretly in French pay, and Louis regarded James as a staunch friend in principle though unreliable in overt act. In the summer of 1688, he warned him of William of Orange's intentions and offered him the assistance of 30,000 Frenchmen. But James refused the proffered aid. His contemporaries believed that Sunderland urged the King to refusal, with the deliberate intention of ruining his master. But James yielded readily to the persuasions. Pride in the army he had created and his essential Englishry forbade him to turn to France for help. And when Louis in the hope of frightening William ordered his representative at The Hague to declare openly the close friendship which existed between himself and James, the latter in a stubborn humour denied the connection. Without any appreciation of his danger, but at least with a flash of pride, he alienated the only man in Europe who could help him, and thereby sealed his own fate. Louis had no use for a stupid friend. He turned his back on James and threw his energies into a dispute upon his eastern frontier. Let William go to England: at least he would be out of the way. Louis would take the opportunity of making a thrust towards the Rhine.

Meanwhile William calmed his friends. He was careful to disclaim any intention of deposing the King of England. When by his help, English statesmen had mended matters, he would return to the Netherlands. The Emperor accepted him at his word: he was not very interested in England, but English money would be invaluable in the forthcoming struggle. The Pope admired and respected William, and he had been irritated for some time by the English Queen's insistence on a cardinal's hat

Tate Gallery]

JAMES II RECEIVING NEWS OF LANDING OF PRINCE OF ORANGE. 1688.

From the painting by E. M. Ward

for her uncle, by the unfortunate embassy of Lord Castlemaine to Rome which had depressed even the weather (it rained continually) and by James's ill-timed importunities that Petre might be removed from the Jesuit order to make him less obnoxious to the English. There would be advantages in William straightening out the obvious incompetence of James's rule and securing the English alliance, which alone could ensure Louis's ultimate downfall. So by a supreme piece of irony, the Pope blessed the expedition of William of Orange.

During the early autumn, William was busy at The Hague, making his arrangements and extracting money and supplies from the Dutch burghers. In the final scenes before departure, the placid citizens were moved to tears of deep emotion. William alone kept calm, and cryptic. What were his intentions, nobody knew. His wife in hours of quiet misery had faced the fact that she must choose between her father and husband. Her heart would not give her leave to betray William. Her sister's cantankerous epistles helped her to screw her courage to the sticking-point, though each week the usual letter from her father or one of Mary Beatrice's characteristic little notes renewed the ache of her desertion. But for years she had lived, so far as her English associates were concerned, among an entourage of Whigs and rebels, who gave her no chance of comprehending her father's point of view. Her husband had no real conception of the depth of her affection. But Bishop Burnet, with the quick appreciation of a mind trained to observe character, grasped the truth of Mary's loyalty. He begged her to open her heart to William: to tell him plainly that if her father were deposed, she would not accept the Crown alone, but would insist on sharing it with her husband. With this self-denying ordinance ready for emergency, William set out to maintain English liberties, with a quiet confidence that there was only one practical solution ahead.

. . . .

In England, through the summer, life went on as usual. There was a great review of the Fleet at Portsmouth; at Hounslow, all regular officers were called up for service. But these assurances of adequate defence were the only indication of possible uneasiness. On August 23rd, the King and Queen were entertained with great magnificence by the Chancellor, Lord Jeffreys. The world had dealt well with him; he had blustered his way to fortune. But even he was beginning to wonder what the end would be. A Parliament had been summoned for November. In September, there were the first signs of panic, in a sudden change of policy. Roman Catholics were declared ineligible for election to the House of Commons; Compton was restored to his See and the Fellows of Magdalen to their college. At The Hague there was a new denial of the French alliance. But such measures at this stage could not be efficacious; all they signified was either cowardice or bluff.

At the end of September, the Parliamentary writs were recalled in view of national emergency, and Louis, asked for the loan of the ships which he had offered, replied coldly that they would not be ready till the following year. William, sure at last of Louis's abstention, issued a Declaration, referring the problems of England to a Parliament' and only awaited a change of wind before he should set sail.

James and his Queen could not even yet credit the possibility of an invasion. For them, it was more than a matter of politics. William was a Stuart, the son of James's favourite sister: he had married James's daughter. It was unthinkable that he should come. 'I confess it was very long before I could believe that my nephew and son-in-law could be capable of so very ill an undertaking,' wrote the King in his memoirs, while Mary Beatrice, in her impetuous way, upbraided her stepdaughter, 'I don't believe you could have such a thought against the worst of fathers, much less perform it against the best, that has always been kind to you and I believe has loved you better than all the rest of his children.' In October the court came as usual to Whitehall. On October 5th, the Queen's birthday, the accustomed festivities were rather pitifully and feverishly maintained. But that week for the first time, James did not receive a letter from his daughter. The Queen wrote to her, 'I don't well know what to say.' Nine days later came the King's birthday. In the Churches, public prayers were said against invasion. But it was a sorrowful day. No royal salute of guns sounded from the Tower; the sun was eclipsed at rising as if to portend disaster; the treacherous wind veered from west to east.[1] London had been restored its charter, and the Court of Ecclesiastical Commission abolished. Eventually on the 24th of October, Sunderland was dismissed. But nothing now could stem the relentless course of events. Troops were rushed over from Ireland and brought down from Scotland. Over 40,000 men were concentrated upon Hounslow Heath, while the English Navy stood to, in the mouth of the Thames. James, hurt though he was by his daughter's defection, had still heart in him. There was no question of not resisting William. His expedition was about to sail, its proud standard bearing the motto 'Je maintiendrai', its declared aim, the protection of the Protestant Religion and the Liberties of England. But the English fleet under Lord Dartmouth would in all probability succeed in engaging William. Then in spite of assertions to the contrary, whatever their religion or their politics, the English seamen faced by a Dutch enemy would undoubtedly fight and fight well. And if by chance the expedition escaped and succeeded in effecting a landing, James had, under his hand, an effective fighting force of men in perfect condition, well-trained and disciplined. The mass of the English people could be relied upon to remain quiet and to continue their daily avocations. The odds against William

[1] Evelyn's *Diary*, 14th, Oct., 1688.

were exceeding heavy. The only further items in the final reckoning were the Prince of Orange's own ruthless ability, and the unknown factors which might turn the scale, James's behaviour and the loyalty of his men.

PART V

FAILURE

CHAPTER XI

WILLIAM OF ORANGE

'Heaven's favourite, for whom the skies do fight,
And all the winds conspire to guide thee right.'

Claudian.

ON October 19th, 1688, the wind blew from the north-east, and William of Orange set sail for England. He embarked 'during the silence of the night; so that no sounds were to be heard, except those which arose from the unfurling of sails, the hauling of ropes, and the voices of the commanders.'[1] The expedition comprised sixty-five ships of war, an equal number of vessels bearing supplies and the best artillery the States could offer, and five hundred transports, carrying some sixteen thousand men. The latter were a motley collection of Dutch veterans, French Huguenots and German mercenaries, with six British regiments, mostly composed of political refugees. In the van of the fleet sailed Admiral Herbert, a man of proud and sullen humour, whose jealousy had been kindled in England by James's preference for Dartmouth, and whose conscience, quiescent in matters of ordinary morality, had manifested itself when he was asked to change his religion. Burnet, although he did not like him, admitted that his behaviour had gained him such a reputation in England that William must perforce suffer and cajole him. 'The managing him,' he added, with feeling, 'was in a great measure put on me; and it was no easy thing.' The other men of consequence upon whose open adherence the success of the venture depended, waited in

[1] I have based this account on the excellent chapter in Dalrymple's *Memoirs*, vol. II, 189 *seq.*

England; should they fail, William's army would be inadequate to face the trained forces of the Crown. But all except twelve vessels of the Dutch fleet had been called into service, so that should it be impossible to avoid the English navy, there would be no necessity to refuse battle.

The fleet weighed anchor at Helvoetsluys. During the night the wind changed to the north-west and blew with gale force. By daylight the ships were scattered, forced to take refuge where and how they could. 'The Prince re-entered Helvoet with only four ships of war, and sixty transports, but with a mind calm and unruffled, which reflected more splendour upon him than all the pomp, which two days before had attended him.' The only casualties were a large number of horses who had died for want of air; one transport, which happened to have more than her full complement of men, was driven on to the shore of England and was captured, thereby giving an erroneous impression of the size of William's army, which he was careful not to dispel. Nor did he contradict the rumours of disaster, willing that the English government should believe that the expedition had been laid aside till the ensuing spring. In fact, a week's work sufficed to collect the scattered ships and restore order among the transports. On November 1st, he set sail for the second time before a strong easterly breeze, which had been named the Protestant wind by those who saw the finger of Heaven in the variable ways of Nature.

For twelve hours, the Prince steered northwards to encourage the belief that he meant to land in Yorkshire and to trick James into dispatching a part of his army thither. But on the morning of November 3rd, William's fleet appeared at the mouth of the Channel, a point it had attained under the shelter of a sea-mist, while in the mouth of the Thames the English Navy struggled in vain, though not perhaps with the united heart with which it would have struggled in 1665, to raise anchor and sail out to intercept the Dutch. The wind, which drove the enemy so easily on their way, effectively bottled the English fleet in the river mouth. James assured Dartmouth later that he was fully satisfied. 'You did all that you could, and . . . I am sure all knowing seamen must be of the same mind.' George Legge, Lord Dartmouth, whose father had accompanied Charles I on his last bid for freedom that ended at Carisbrooke, would not obliterate the memory of years of friendship and service because now his master's actions made him wretched. But though he could not consider disloyalty and could not doubt that British seamen would fight, with him as with them a feeling of relief at the waywardness of winds and weather must have had an enervating effect upon endeavour.

The wind still blew, clearing away the mist, and revealing the Dutch fleet stretched in a long line between Calais and Dover. Both shores were thronged with people, the volubility of the Gallic spectators matched by the conflicting emotions of those who watched from England, partisans of King and Prince united only in foreboding at the prospect of civil war. From ten in the morning till five in the evening, through the cold and brief November day they watched the vessels pass; and saw them congregate in mass and dispose themselves in fresh formation as William held a council of war, partly to ascertain if any had intelligence of the English fleet, mainly to impress the watchers and 'to conquer first the imagination of those he was invading.' The expedition swept down the Channel. The Prince hoped to land on November 4th, which was his birthday and the anniversary of his marriage; even in him the drama evoked an unaccustomed strain of sentiment. But this was impossible, and his English companions assured him that no better date could be found than November 5th, the day of Gunpowder Treason. It was hoped to reach Torbay early that morning. But for a moment his fortunes wavered; his pilot misreckoned and when day came, both Torbay and Dartmouth lay to the east. They dare not tack for fear of the English, who had achieved the open sea in face of the wind and were pursuing them down the Channel. They must make Plymouth, where they had reason to expect an unfriendly reception.

At this crisis, Providence – or chance – came to their aid in a manner so remarkable that even William's phlegm yielded to a brief essay in cheerfulness. 'He took me heartily by the hand,' wrote Burnet, 'and asked me if I would not now believe predestination.' The wind veered suddenly to the south and as night fell wafted them gently into Torbay, while the weather, in keeping with the wind, became unseasonably mild and enabled the soldiers, who were quickly disembarked, to encamp in the open without serious consequence. And then the south wind, freshening to a gale, blew up the Channel and kept the English fleet powerless and inactive, somewhere off Portland Bill. William and his men gave thanks to God on the shores of Devon for their safe landing and Providence's assistance. In the new chapel of Whitehall, the priests exposed the Host and the King made his earnest devotions, and through the length and breadth of England anxious men and women prayed for peace.

The Prince marched immediately from Torbay to Exeter. Two hundred English gentlemen led the van, each with a negro-attendant, a piece of exoticism, not likely to be appreciated by the Devon men who watched them with slow suspicious glances. They had hailed a deliverer once, less than four years ago; they had not forgotten what came afterwards. And he was their own beloved Duke; this was a foreign army. Behind the English came some Swedish horsemen and the French, under the Count of Nassau; about the Prince were his Dutch guards, and in the rear were the Brandenburghers and the Swiss veterans under Schomberg, the famous soldier of fortune. It was six hundred years since foreign troops had marched on English soil; William arriving at Exeter, found the gracious city mindful of its loyal traditions. The bishop betook himself to James in London, rather than receive his unwelcome guests. When Burnet preached in the Cathedral, the clergy refused to attend. Nor were the dissenters more forthcoming. Ferguson, the attendant spirit of revolt, asked for the keys of the chapel. They were denied him. 'I will take the kingdom of heaven by violence,' he cried, and broke open the door with a hammer. Men of the West Country are courteous by nature, and they looked coldly on this breach of good manners.

For ten critical days, William stayed in Exeter. He had no intention of trying to conquer England with a foreign army. He knew he would not succeed, and his sense of justice was too strong for him to attempt it. The English gentry had invited him and he had come. If they wanted him, they must take the next step by joining him openly. If not, he would go home to Holland. So he waited. It was the most difficult thing he had to do, during the whole course of the Revolution. A few adherents drifted in, but their coming merely stressed the dilatory behaviour of the majority. Once the Prince faltered in his pose of unconcern; he exclaimed in a voice that had a peevish ring, that he would depart immediately and let the English and their King settle their differences at their leisure among themselves. But after a week, the appearance of things began to change; the gentlemen of Devonshire and Somerset came to pay their respects: Sir Edward Seymour, the proud Tory, who to the Prince's courteous words, 'I believe, Sir Edward, you are of the Duke of Somerset's family,' gave the answer, 'No, Sir; the Duke is of mine.' Whigs came as well as Tories, the brother of Lord Russell and former friends of Monmouth's. William greeted them with the remark, that he had expected to see them sooner.

At Whitehall the King was bewildered, though not as yet distracted. There were three alternatives before him, flight, resistance or compromise. He was hemmed in by a multitude of counsellors, anxious courtiers and frightened Romanists, soldiers who wished to fight and bishops who urged a treaty. In the latter course alone lay safety, for many Tories, hating the idea of Revolution, would have rallied to the defence of their lawful sovereign, had they been given a reasonable pretext. As a statesman, James should have taken it; though it may be questioned whether an immediate desertion of his Catholic friends would have argued him a better man. He himself, with his loathing of disloyalty, was not prepared to countenance such a course; he barred the way to compromise, by refusing to summon a free Parliament until William of Orange should leave the country and by including two Catholics upon the commission, to which he entrusted the government when he went down to join his army. For, of the other alternatives, it was natural that he should choose resistance. Cowardice was as hateful to him as disloyalty. Moreover he had a picked army of trained men: here was an opportunity to test the machine created so zestfully in the previous years. But the hours spent in his oratory had softened James's nature; the commandments of Christ were frequently on his lips. However faulty his methods, he was at bottom sincere in his religion. The idea of going out to fight his son-in-law, and of throwing away in civil strife the men, whom he had loved to imagine warring against the infidels, grieved his heart and paralysed his nerve. He had decided to resist but he could not bring himself to offer battle.

The third alternative of flight was whispered in his ear by the crafty Barillon; Louis would give him refuge, Louis would help him to strike at William from without, with Louis at least his son would be safe. In an agony of fear for his wife and child, James listened only too readily to these insidious counsels. Not yet for himself, but for them, he accepted Louis's aid, and trusting the baby Prince to the care of Lord Dover, who had shown himself more than a fair-weather friend, he sent him down to Portsmouth, with instructions to Lord Dartmouth to smuggle him across to France.

For the prospect was deplorable. Bad news had reached Whitehall. The advance-guard of the royal army was already at Salisbury. On November 16th, eleven days after William's landing, three regiments rode out from the King's camp behind Lord Cornbury, the Earl of Clarendon's son. Their supposed objective was the town of Dorchester. Gradually it dawned upon the troops that they were on their way to Exeter. Then, certain of their number turned back whence they had come, but Cornbury rode on and deserted to William of Orange.

The news came to London, before the stragglers had returned to Salisbury, and a complete loss of three regiments was reported. Nor did it matter much what the men had done. Feversham was anxious about the loyalty of his officers, and Cornbury's defection underlined his doubts. James was going into dinner, when the couriers arrived. 'His concern was too great to think of anything but how to remedy the comfortless situation of his affairs, so calling for a piece of bread and glass of wine, went immediately to consult what measures were fittest to be taken; at which time the Lords Sunderland, Churchill and Godolphin . . . were seen unawares going hand and hand along the Gallery in the greatest transport of joy imaginable.'[1] Lord Clarendon was inconsolable. 'Oh, God! that my son should be a rebel,' was his bitter cry. That afternoon he sought audience with the King. James was at his best, letting no reproach fall upon his unhappy relative, and quieting his confusion with the assurance that he pitied him with all his heart. On this occasion, he could understand and sympathise with one who came to him for pardon. He too had a child, who had dismayed him by disloyalty.

The next day, previous to his departure to Salisbury with the main body of his army, James summoned the general officers into his presence. He assured them that

[1] Clarke. *James II*, p. 218. Evelyn records Sunderland's flight on Dec. 9th – the D.N.B. places it in November.

he was resolved 'to quiet his people's minds' by securing their religion, laws and liberties. 'If you desire anything more, I am ready to grant it. But if after all this, any of you is not satisfied, let him declare himself. I am willing to grant passes to all such as have a mind to go over to the Prince of Orange, and spare them the shame of deserting their loyal sovereign.' It was the honest speech of a soldier, to whom treachery was a heinous sin; some might doubt whether he could or would have quieted the minds of his people, had William been forced to quit the kingdom, but those who doubted should have left James then and declared themselves openly. No counsel for the defence, however brilliant or vituperative, can excuse what followed. The officers showed no signs of wavering in their obedience. They cheered their King, declaring that they were ready to spill the last drop of their blood in his service. The cheers were led by Colonel Churchill.

Although he had played in turn with every possibility, showing a vaccilation of spirit more in keeping with his father's nature than his own, James reached Salisbury with the full intention of fighting. His army had been reinforced by three thousand Scots, under Douglas and Claverhouse, upon whom the King had conferred the title of Marquis of Dundee. It would have been easy to check the enemy, who had advanced to Axminster, and possible by promptitude and vigour, to defeat him. For though the loyalty of the officers might be doubtful, the men of the ranks, inured to the habit of obedience and proud of their soldiering, had no intention of letting Dutchmen and Brandenburghers walk through England without a challenge. Feversham, the commander-in-chief, the butt of more subtle men, was as loyal to his King in his emergency as he had been through the years to his own Protestant faith. He suggested to James that he should deplace the suspected officers and put the most trusted sergeants in command. One of the Scots pleaded for permission to attack, and Dundee, in a passion of loyalty, staked his own head upon the success of the venture. The King, nerved by the men about him, felt the pull of his military training and arranged to visit the outposts at Warminster, preparatory to an advance.

And then his nose began to bleed. For three days the violent hemorrhage continued, disenabling him and paralysing his initiative. The physical collapse was accompanied by a nervous breakdown. Absolutely nothing was done. He refused to let the Scots 'throw away the lives of so many brave men' in an action which could not be decisive. At a council of war on the evening of November 24th, it was decided to retreat on London. In vain Dundee urged the King to fight, or to go to William in person to demand the reason for his presence in England. The King was a sick man, unnerved by the reports of insurrection in the north and west, and cowed by the unbelievable news that an officer of the navy had deserted to the Dutch. On the morning of the 25th, he received a shock more close at hand. A letter was brought to him from Colonel Churchill. With apologies and acknowledgments of past indebtedness Churchill informed him that he had left the camp. In company with Colonel Kirke and the Duke of Grafton, Charles II's natural son, he had joined the Prince of Orange. Like many other Tories, they had been in an honest dilemma and had chosen to betray their sovereign rather than their church. But Churchill's position of trust in the King's army, the close association of years of friendship and his effusive professions of loyalty, which continued to the eve of his last-minute desertion, make it impossible to excuse an action that belied the fundamental decency of human relationships. The Jacobites used to say that when Churchill reached the enemy camp, the mercenary Schomberg looked him up and down, declaring with curious scorn 'that he was the first Lieutenant-Generall he had ever heard of that had deserted from his Colours'.

James and his army retired to Andover. There, word

was brought him that young Ormonde and George of Denmark had left the camp. Prince George was a dull man whose chief conversational gambit was the query 'Est-il possible?' The loss of a good trooper had been of greater consequence, but to the King his going was another proof of the treachery that was on every hand, a disloyalty that took no heed of any tie of family or of friendship. 'So "Est-il possible?" has gone too,' he commented. These desertions unmanned him, more than any danger. There was only one thing left to do, to preserve the lives of the remnant, who still knew how to be loyal. And so the retreat continued, while the common soldiers wept.

In London, the morale of the court had broken. Father Petre had wisely retired to the Continent; and some time before the month was out, Sunderland had fled disguised in woman's dress. He had played for high stakes and lost. That summer he had declared himself a Catholic, carried away by the force of the enthusiasms he had engendered. As soon as he realised the imminence of disaster, he had made a panic retreat, at first in political concessions now in actual flight. He could lie low in Holland, revert unostentatiously to Protestantism and emerge when the time served, to argue or ingratiate, to intrigue and to triumph. Untrammelled by ties of love and loyalty, life for him was a great game of chance, in which the thrill of the gamble outweighed the loss or gain. He was not concerned with those he had left behind, to whom he had brought tragedy. The Queen, bereft of husband and son, maintained the pretence of certain victory, but wrote from her heart to her uncle the cardinal. 'In charity, remember me in your prayers, and ask God to give me strength to suffer what seems insufferable to human nature, but which Divine Grace can make bearable.' Her discomfort was increased by the crowds who thronged the palace in search of news, imagining the facts they could not ascertain and disseminating idle rumours through the town. One morning, when the word ran round that the Princess Anne was missing from her chamber, the city was in an uproar. Her attendants in a panic cried that 'the Papists had murdered her in the night,' and it was fortunate for the Queen that the truth was soon discovered. Accompanied by Bishop Compton, who had once been her spiritual adviser and had no reluctance in becoming her temporal guide, fastening pistols to his holster and accoutred more like soldier than like priest, she had ridden north to Nottingham, to raise rebellion and eventually to join her husband.

This was the news which greeted James on his return to London on Monday, the 26th. If there lingered in him any power to retrieve his cause, his daughter's action destroyed it. He burst into tears, with the cry 'God help me. My own children have deserted me.' Two weeks lay ahead of him, full of confused action and belated parleying. But during those days he was seriously ill, in body as well as mind; much of his time was spent in his oratory, and the only constructive thought which emerged from his mental chaos was the determination not to risk the lives of the loyal few in a fruitless battle. A consciousness of his own sins pressed in upon him, and the Revolution appeared as a just retribution for his sexual indulgences in the past. He could not withstand the righteous anger of God. He put neither his heart nor his will into his public acts; each day he longed more acutely, for the quiet that only France could give.

Three weeks too late to be effective, he adopted in form, though not in sincerity, the alternative of compromise. On Tuesday, November 27th, he summoned a council of Peers. He met the Earl of Bedford that morning and asked his aid in conciliating the lords. Bedford, who believed that James's ruthlessness had prevented King Charles from sparing Russell in 1683, looked sadly in his sovereign's face. 'I once had a son,' he answered, 'who could have served your Majesty upon this occasion.' The Peers were not inclined to half-measures. Taking their lead from Clarendon's pedagogic utterances, they adjured James to dismiss the Catholics from office and to send a deputation to treat with William. On Wednesday, writs were issued summoning a Parliament and Nottingham, Halifax and Godolphin set out to confer with the Prince. London settled down again to quiet living, still confident, in spite of the evidence, in the efficacy of conference and debate.

William was advancing steadily and playing for time, knowing that every day of unsettled rule would make the community more willing to accept his dictates. By one subterfuge after another he postponed seeing the delegates until ten days had passed. On Saturday, December 8th, they eventually met at Hungerford. William, the least emotional of men, was surprised into sentiment when a formal dispatch, written in diplomatic French, was handed to him from the King. Recollecting the friendly correspondence of years, he commented that this was the first letter he had ever received from James, written in a strange language by another's pen. But he continued the task on hand, which was to instruct the nobility about him to frame an answer to the King's envoys, he himself retiring from the room that no charge should lay against him of interfering in England's private concern! But when he saw the finished articles and thought his friends had acted foolishly in demanding the recall of the writs for Parliament, he did not scruple to insist on the deletion of the clause concerned. The terms offered to James included the demands that all Catholics should be disarmed and removed from office, that the custody of the Tower and Tilbury should be in the hands of the City of London, and that if James remained at Whitehall, William and his guards should also reside in the capital during the forthcoming Parliament. They were the terms of a victor, but when news of them reached James on the following day (Sunday, 9th December) he expressed neither disappointment nor approval. Forced into the negotiation by the Tories whose reproaches had exacerbated his sorrow, he regarded them as little more than a cover, until his plans were made for leaving the country. By the end of the first week after his return from Salisbury he had planned for the Queen to go to France, on the day that the Prince was to sail from Portsmouth. She herself was torn between fear and love; anxiety for her child struggling with the proud recollection that she had never yet left her husband in emergency. At first she refused to go, and only complied when she realised that his assurances that he would follow were sincere. For she found her anchor in this darkest hour, as in the years to come, in implicit obedience and devotion to the man, who had lost everything except her love.

On December 3rd, he had received the final blow in a letter from Dartmouth, refusing with gentle firmness to commit the technical treason of removing the Prince from the country. The letter made it clear that James must not rely on the loyalty of the fleet. To the King, this defection was almost more bitter than his children's treachery. He had loved the ships and their crews and 'gloryed in nothing more than that he had shar'd with them in the hardships and dangers of defending the Dominion of the seas. . . .' He knew them for honest sturdy men; if they had no use for him, nothing remained but refuge in a foreign land.

The Count Lauzun, soldier-adventurer and the somewhat flamboyant champion of ladies in distress, had come post-haste from Paris and placed himself at the Queen's service. It was arranged that she should flee with the Prince of Wales as soon as Lord Dover could bring him safely back from Portsmouth. It was no easy task. Dover and his companions left the town at five in the morning. A company of the King's guards were to act as escort, but they missed each other, and Dover followed a countryman's directions, and came safely by Petersfield to Kingston and Whitehall, narrowly escaping an enemy ambush. The King's guards, returning to the Palace by another route were mobbed in Southwark and forced to disperse, each man looking to his own safety. The Prince was brought to London on December 8th, the very day that the envoys met William at Hungerford. In the early hours of the following night, the Queen fled from Whitehall. As she bade her husband farewell, she threw herself into his arms and begged to stay with him. But he urged the child's safety and promised to follow immediately. She controlled herself and turned to put on the rough dress that had been provided for her. She had come to England fifteen years before with the great ambitions, the proud certainties of youth; she went, humbly, a woman who had known sorrow.

The arrangements for flight had been made by an Italian wardrobe-keeper, Francesca Riva, who had a boat waiting at the horse ferry[1], furnished with provisions and a gun to give colour to the pretence of a shooting expedition on the river. He and Lauzun, who alone were to accompany the refugees, secreted some jewels about their persons to the irritation of the King and Queen, who could think of nothing but the child's safety. Mary Beatrice with the baby and two nurses, went out to the waiting coach. It was two o'clock in the morning. They drove through Westminster, Riva sitting by the coachman to see he went aright. It was extremely dark, and as they groped their way into the small dinghy, Riva was smitten with realisation of the folly of their venture. One cry from the baby and all was lost. But the skill of the nurse and God's merciful providence prevailed; the six months' old infant slept on, unconscious alike of wind and rain and his mother's breaking heart. They crossed the river with difficulty in the teeth of the storm, and were met by a Page of the Back-stairs who reported a coach and six in readiness at an adjacent inn. As she waited for its coming, Mary of Modena leant in the rain against the wall of Lambeth Church, the tears streaming down her cheeks as she gazed at the pin-points of light across the river, the last she would ever see of the Palace of Whitehall. The coach came up,

[1] Where Lambeth Bridge now stands. Hence Horseferry Road.

and at the same moment an interested spectator made his way up to the Queen. A sudden jolt from the watching Riva landed both him and the curious stranger in the muddy road, where the latter was overwhelmed by such profuse apologies from the Italian, that he rose quickly in acute embarrassment and looked no further at the interesting young woman. The refugees drove eastward to Gravesend, where by previous arrangement a boat awaited them, to take them to a yacht. Lauzun engaged the captain of the yacht in talk upon politics, while the Queen came upon board, and gave him two hundred guineas to land 'his Catholic friends in France'. The captain took the guineas and consented. He told the Count, when France was reached, that he had recognised the Queen, but was only too happy to do her service.

On Tuesday, the 11th of December, Mary Beatrice and her son landed in France. On the same morning James made his first attempt to follow. Sunday had been a terrible day. The solitude of Whitehall without her encouraged him to thoughts of his own capture and to reflections on his father's saying, that 'small was the distance between the prisons of princes and their graves.' He thought a great deal of his father at this time; there was always at the back of his mind the probability of a like ending for himself. And death was horrible. Nobody must die. It had become an obsession. He wrote to Feversham, disbanding the troops from whom he had hoped so much; 'there remains nothing more for me to do but to thank you. . . .'

It seemed to his staunchest friends that he belied his soldierly training and his reputation for courage. Ailesbury, his devoted servant, urged him to a final stand. If they marched north, he declared, they would find new adherents and could face the enemy with fresh courage. Years later, Ailesbury told the Earl of Danby of his advice. 'Was the Devil in you, and what did you mean by it?' Danby asked.

'To knock you on the head in the first place if you had resisted.'

'Your most humble servant and good friend is much obliged to you.'

'What course would you have taken?' asked Ailesbury, and Danby replied without hesitation, 'What course? To submit ourselves and to crave his pardon.'

These very words prove that had James followed Ailesbury's advice, Tory support would have enabled him to resist William. Civil war would have resulted. This the King was determined to avoid. He could have fought William when he regarded him merely as a foreign invader; he refused, when he realised that half the English kingdom was behind him, in goodwill if not in actual fact. To condemn James's flight is easy, but since compromise was only possible if he were willing to betray his fellow Catholics and his belief in the Divine Right of Kings, and resistance would have plunged his country into bloodshed, it is fairer to criticise his insincere negotiations and the precipitancy of his departure without any provision for a regency, than the actual surrender to tragic circumstance.

James left the Palace soon after midnight on December 10th. His companion was the Catholic officer, Sir Edward Hales, who had figured in the famous law case of more prosperous days. They took hackney coach to the horse ferry as the Queen had done, and rowed across to Vauxhall. As they went James cast into the river the Great Seal of England, his formal act of abdication. It was in part the angry gesture of an unbalanced man, in part a spiteful attempt to increase the difficulties of his opponents at the expense of his people's security. A passing barge rescued the seal a few days later – an anti-climax, typical of the English story. Making eastward, the fugitives crossed the Medway about seven on the Tuesday morning, and reached the Kentish port of Feversham about ten. A Custom-house brig was waiting for them by arrangement, but the master knew nothing of the rank of his passengers. A fresh breeze was blowing, and the ship needed more ballast before she set out to sea. This occasioned some delay. The day passed, while the fugitives chafed in idleness. Hales sent out a servant with a letter, and his livery drew attention to the boat. A constant stream of fugitives had passed through Feversham in the previous weeks and 'a priest codding' had become a profitable pursuit. Some fishermen determined to board and search the yacht, and their hope of finding suspect passengers was fulfilled when they discovered the King, whose lantern-jaws convinced them that he was a priest. James was in his cabin with his two gentlemen, when the captain, who rejoiced in the satisfactory name of Amis Sat, came to examine him. Hales, drawing him aside, clapped fifty guineas in his hand and said he should have a hundred more, if he could get them away. The rogue's reply was to anchor the ship off Feversham, to go ashore ostensibly to see what he could do, and to advise the refugees to entrust their jewels to his keeping lest the fishermen, left on guard, should plunder them. He went and did not return till next morning, with word that they must appear before the Mayor. Meanwhile, the fishermen had treated their captives with scant courtesy, rifled their persons and only just failed to find a bodkin of the Queen's and the coronation ring, which James had secreted in his pants. Some diamond buckles they did find, but thinking them only glass, returned them to the King.

In the morning they were taken ashore and as they passed through the crowds, James saw that in spite of his black periwig, he had been recognised. As the rumour spread, some were incensed against him, others wept and pleaded for pardon, while the fishermen vowed that no hair of his head should be hurt but gave him no chance to escape. He was housed in an inn, where the seamen kept guard and never had James Stuart known such a bitter moment as when their self-appointed leader demanded his sword from him. He never forgave them. The authorities were in a dilemma and James wrote to his Council at Whitehall and waited to be rescued. It was at once absurd and pitiful.

At Whitehall, some hours had passed before the King's flight had been discovered. On Tuesday morning the usual crowds had assembled for the levee at the Palace. When the doors of the King's bedchamber were thrown open, the Duke of Northumberland, the gentleman-in-waiting, emerged alone. Then having kept his uncle's secret till the last, he went down to the regiment of guards which he commanded and rode out to join his brother, Grafton, with the Prince of Orange. The news spread like wildfire, and consternation prevailed. There was no settled government, and there was nothing to prevent panic except the citizen's fundamental respect for the law. It is one of the truly great things about the Revolution that in this emergency, a sense of law and order prevailed over mob-violence and fear of the uncertain future. There was inevitably some street-riotings, and Catholic chapels were pillaged and destroyed. On Thursday (the 13th) a strange incomprehensible rumour swept the town, caused no doubt by the fact that Feversham had disbanded his army. Most of the men had gone quietly home, bitterly disappointed. But it was said in London that Irish troops were rioting through the country, cutting the throats of all they met, burning the farmsteads and advancing upon the capital. People thronged the city in terrified excitement; the militia was called out, and, as the winter darkness fell, every house was lit. They were massacring the Protestants in the very next street – the rumour passed from mouth to mouth; 'some added circumstances to what they had heard and when these were related back to themselves, or when they had often told them, they believed them to be true'. The story appeared at the same moment in different parts of England, very much in the same way as that of the Russian troops appeared in 1914. But as the hours passed and nobody was actually killed, the myth of the Irish soldiers dwindled into the limbo of inexplicable legends; the passion for getting things done triumphed over the love of gossip; folk went back to their jobs; the authorities kept order in the city and such peers as were in town joined them at the Guildhall and formed themselves into a provisional government. They passed resolutions censuring the King's flight, and applied to the Prince for protection. Men still went up and down the streets singing 'Lillibulero', the Irish marching song, but the majority went to bed early and kept their shutters closed.

The nearest approach to tragedy occurred at Wapping. Jeffreys, the Chancellor, had decided to flee. To his credit be it recorded that until the King went he stood firm. Least of all men, could he hope for mercy when the Whigs triumphed. He cut off his eyebrows and disguised himself as a seaman, but missing the tide in London, came down to Wapping in the hope of obtaining a ship. He was in terror of his life, and taking refuge in an ale-house from the passers-by, whose every glance seemed to threaten danger, he hired some ruffians to keep guard without. Their foul language and filthy tales collected the very crowd Jeffreys hoped to avoid. He sat on within not daring to emerge, and the story went that as he raised his head to drink, a clerk looking through the window saw the Chancellor's face. Once he had been a witness in a court over which Jeffreys had presided; he had been bullied, until he turned sick with the thought of it; at sight of the face in the inn he felt again the sensation of nausea, and only then did he recognise, beneath the disguise, the features of the most hated man of England. Recognised Jeffreys was by one means or another, and apprehended by the constables who found him, according to another report, lying between two blankets in an upper room of the hostelry. As they took him to the house of a magistrate near by, the yelling mob pelted him with mud and stones, and the officers had much ado to prevent him being torn to pieces. With the help of a company of the trained bands, they took him by coach to the Lord Mayor of London, who was startled at dinner by the apparition of a wretched man, mumbling for mercy at his feet. When he recognised the Chancellor of England, the Lord Mayor swooned with the shock. Eventually Jeffreys reached the welcome quiet of the Tower, in such a state of exhaustion, and so belaboured by the crowds, that his body already worn out in luxurious living could not recover its equilibrium, and not long afterwards he died. It was a wretched and perhaps a fitting end.

On December 13th, as the provisional government sat in council, news came that a messenger was without. He bore a letter from the King, stating briefly that he was detained at Feversham. The Lords heard without comment. There was silence, broken at long last by Ailesbury. They must ask his Majesty to return. The Lords admitted their duty, reluctantly. James, out of England, was an insoluble problem solved; the officious seamen had done a bad day's work in intercepting him. But there was no alternative. Ailesbury was deputed to ride at once and inform the King that representatives of his Household were coming down to escort him to London. Ailesbury slept that night at Dartford, and early on Friday morning he rode out through Rochester and Sittingbourne calming the townsfolk, who were still exercised by the Irish myth. At Rochester they were cutting down the bridge in belief that Dartford was on fire; 'a man in a red coat' had told them so; no one had seen him since. At Sittingbourne, the women stood at their doors keeping their children by them and crying quietly to themselves. Ailesbury as he galloped past, covering the eight and thirty miles in the course of the morning, shouted the good news that all was well. There was no massacre; nothing was happening in London. The people of Rochester and Sittingbourne, with ready faith, went home to their dinners, and Ailesbury wearily pushed on. He reached Feversham at one o'clock. He found James, his shoulders twitching beneath the same dirty shirt in which he had been captured, unshaven and wearing his hat. Ailesbury was struck by his likeness to his father as the latter had appeared before the Court of Justice. James was in a bad humour, he gave his friend a cold welcome, asking him for news with the sneer, 'You were all kings when I left London.' Ailesbury, hungry and aching from his long journey, did not mince his words. 'But for our care and vigilance the city of London might have been in ashes,' he replied, upbraiding James for not leaving a Regency. The two men looked at each other and realised the deep affection, of which the angry words were but the froth. The King's dinner was brought in and Ailesbury served him with ceremony, offering the food upon his knee and thus soothing James's outraged kingship. Afterwards, too weary to eat himself, he retired.

Feversham and a contingent of the guards arrived shortly afterwards, and the Keeper of the Wardrobe with some welcome new linen. Next morning the return journey began. At Sittingbourne a company of guards, lined the route and asked the King's permission to do him honour as he passed. Tears of joy ran down the men's faces as they gave the royal salute. That night they slept at Rochester and on Sunday, December 16th, they returned to Whitehall, with the exception of Feversham, whom James had sent to the Prince of Orange at Windsor, with an invitation to come to London to negotiate. But William considered that James by his flight had forfeited his right to parley. He detained Lord Feversham as a prisoner, and ordered the Dutch Guards to march on London, while he himself advanced to Sion House. In fact he felt, not without justification, that he had wasted six weeks in England and that it was time that something conclusive happened.

The King rode to Whitehall through the city. The people, whose levity in matters political never ceased to astonish and dismay the foreigner, gave James a great reception. Their enthusiasm was largely due to their desire to have a king of some sort, since a king was synonymous with settled government, while it was increased by their good-natured affection for royalty in distress, combined with their liking for an orgy of sentiment. James was comforted by it but did not allow himself to believe that it had any real significance. The emptiness of Whitehall held more meaning than all the huzzas of the crowd. He was pitifully anxious for Ailesbury not to leave him, and when the latter had to slip home to change his clothes and reassure his wife, the King asked anxiously, 'But you will be here to wait at supper.'

Monday was a melancholy day. It was a fine morning and James expressed a wish to walk in the Park. Two loyal Scots were with him, Dundee and Balcarres. After all, James was a Stuart, and at the end it was his own countrymen who stood by him. He had no hope in England, but it was still possible that he might come into his own again, by way of Scotland. They spoke of it that morning. Balcarres vowed that twenty thousand men would be at the King's service, if he spoke the word. But James's heart was full of mistrust; he could do nothing till he had sorted out friend from foe. He looked at them curiously. Why were they with him, when all the world was at Sion House with William? They answered that they could not fail to be faithful to so good a master. Incredulously, he asked if they still cared for him, and they gave him their hands upon it. One day, he promised they should hear from him again.

But the walk ended. There was nothing else to do. Meanwhile, the Dutch Guards, who had been ordered to take up their position at Whitehall, advanced through Kensington to Chelsea. The short December day was coming to an end as they halted at the riverside village, for rest and refreshment. It was dark when they set out again, and rumour had gone before them and enlarged their numbers, so that the exhausted citizens believed that a whole army, not a mere detachment, was to march on them at midnight. At Whitehall the officer in command was Lord Craven, an old man of seventy, who had been the trusted friend of Elizabeth of Bohemia. Unconcerned with political subtleties, he knew that a soldier's duty was to die at his post. He drew up his men and prepared to fight, while the Dutch, disturbed in their turn by report, marched through St. James's Park at eleven o'clock at night, with drums beating, matches lit, and in order of battle. But James, realising the danger, sent down orders to Craven to make no resistance. There was almost a mutiny in the English ranks; with angry murmurs and resentful backward glances, the men retired. But Craven like Claverhouse, his second-in-command, had but one rule to guide him as a soldier. It was to obey. Sorrowfully, they sheathed their swords, and by midnight the Dutch stood on guard before Whitehall.

At one o'clock that night, commissioners arrived from William to speak with the King. Lord Halifax was the uncomfortable spokesman.[1] The Prince had decided that James should not be allowed to stay longer in London; Halifax, Shrewsbury and Delamere had been chosen to deliver the message. They had been delayed on the road, but dare not wait till the morning to see the King, as William planned to reach Whitehall on the Tuesday afternoon. At three in the morning, James was awakened from his sleep and received them in his bedchamber. Halifax, with an assumption of indifference, informed the King that he must retire at once to Ham, the remote river home of the Earl of Lauderdale. Shrewsbury, a soldier and a gentleman, echoed the words with greater warmth of feeling. James complied, but in place of Ham, suggested Rochester. He spoke calmly but his heart was in turmoil. For Ham, buried in the luscious shades of the Thames valley, meant imprisonment; in time without a doubt, mock-trial and execution. Rochester meant the sea below his window, and with good fortune, escape and freedom. William, when he heard the King's request, perceived its significance

[1] Halifax had returned to the Prince after finding that James had fled on Dec. 9th.

and readily assented. He did not believe in unnecessary martyrdoms. All he wanted was to have James out of the way.

On Tuesday, December 18th, the King set out from Whitehall for the second time. A few Scottish lords accompanied him; Dutch guards rowed before and aft the barge. To their commander, whom he had known in happier days, James was polite as one soldier to another. He told his companions to offer him refreshment, and heard Arran mutter that he would rather throw him into the Thames. 'My Lord, you are a good subject but a very bad Christian,' James reproved him. 'He is a man of honour and does his duty.'

As they passed the Tower, he commented on the instability of life; from 'above twelve million of subjects, he had only five friends to attend him'. But the die was cast; he need no longer struggle against circumstance nor inveigle himself in tortuous paths of policy. He was calmer than he had been for many days.

They had missed the tide at Whitehall so did not reach Gravesend till seven in the evening, and there they stayed the night. Next day they went overland to Rochester; James, of his own choice, went on horseback, riding for the last time on English soil. Ailesbury went in the royal coach and as it jolted over the bad roads, he dozed, wearied by uncertain days and excess of emotion. And as he slept, he was roused repeatedly by the coachman's angry curses: 'God damn Father Petre!' 'Dixey, what harm hath he done you?' remonstrated Ailesbury. 'Damn him. But for him, we had not been here,' quoth Dixey, the King's faithful servant for many long years. He had to curse somebody, in case he wept.

They came to Rochester, and as they went into the castle, they noticed a strong display of guards, at one entrance only. It was a broad hint from William, not to be disregarded. Yet the King hesitated. At Rochester, he was allowed to communicate with London. Friends came down to see him, and a letter arrived from the bishops, urging him not to leave England. But they could not promise him security, and the news of William's triumphal entry into the capital and of the convocation of the Lords and Commons seemed to underline his own impossible position. He tried to excuse his flight to Ailesbury, in whose blunt Scottish face he sensed disapproval. 'I shall certainly be sent to the Tower,' he argued, 'and no king ever went out of that place but to his grave.' So, years before he had cried to his brother, 'Remember Edward II, remember Richard II, remember our own father.' The ghosts of murdered kings were uneasy bedfellows. He recollected his promise to the Queen, distraught that he had not followed her, and his thoughts turned continuously to France. A coincidence evoked recollections of his first exile, in retrospect a not unhappy time. Each morning, mass was said in the castle and the soldiers on guard attended. One of them was an elderly infantry officer, of whom James inquired his religion. The old soldier replied that his sword was his religion; he would fight for them who paid him well. The honest answer pleased the King, and looking more closely at the man, he recognised him with the happy Stuart gift for remembering faces. 'I am sure I have seen you formerly,' he said, and so he had. They found that they had fought together at the Dunes.

On Saturday, December 22nd, the Duke of Berwick came down from London. He was only eighteen, but he had already experienced war and in him, with a father's imagination, James saw his own youth repeated. For him there was no question of betrayal; he was to be his father's steady comrade in the forthcoming years. Berwick brought word that a vessel was in readiness, and about midnight, the King embarked. This time there was no mistake, though the voyage was far from easy. The fugitives rowed out from the unguarded postern-gate in a small shallop, that was to take them to a fishing smack, lying off Sheerness. But a hard head-wind was blowing and they were forced to take refuge on a fireship, which was fortunately commanded by an officer of proved loyalty, who knew how to manage his men. They rested there till daylight, and were then able to transfer to the fishing vessel. The gale was blowing hard, and throughout that day they made little progress and were forced to anchor under the lee of the Essex shore. During the night the storm slackened; they were under way before sunrise and passed safely through the Downs. The wind was blowing from the east and a thin snow was falling upon an empty sea. Late at night the weather cleared and they saw above them the high land of France. They ran along the coast till they reached Ambleteuse.

For the King, it had been a strange and rough passage. The loss of three kingdoms became for the time being nothing more than an aching background to his immediate hardships. He sat with Berwick, cooped up in a narrow cabin, fearful of pursuit, frozen to the marrow, and hungry. Gradually all his sufferings and his wrongs were concentrated in the fact of hunger. The captain seized an ancient frying-pan and stuffed a hole in it with an old tarred rag. He fried his King some bacon, and offered him a drink of beer in a rusty mug. As James felt the cold touch of the metal on his lips and the coarse smell of the frying bacon assailed his nostrils, the chimeras of the immediate past faded into the winter darkness, and he laid hold again upon life and sanity.

At three o'clock next morning they reached France and safety. It was Christmas Day.

CHAPTER XII

'. . . AND PEACE AT THE LAST'

'On the heights of Killiecrankie,
Yester-morn our army lay:
Slowly rose the mist in columns
From the river's broken way;
Hoarsely roared the swollen torrent,
And the Pass was wrapt in gloom,
When the clansmen rose together
From their lair amidst the broom.

'But he raised his hand for silence –
"Soldiers! I have sworn a vow:
Ere the evening star shall glisten
On Schehallion's lofty brow,
Either we shall rest in triumph,
Or another of the Graemes
Shall have died in battle harness
For his Country and King James."

' "Strike! and when the fight is over,
If you look in vain for me,
Where the dead are lying thickest,
Search for him that was Dundee!" '

Aytoun's '*The Burial March of Dundee.*'

A SCHOOLGIRL listened to King James's story. 'He should have died!' she exclaimed, with youth's sublime indifference to Death. She was right. If James had fallen in 1688, fighting at the head of the men whose lodestar was duty and to whom treachery was but an idle tale, his end would have been in harmony with a life from which the best had been evoked by action and high endeavour. Men would have remembered, then, the sacrifice of his youth and the dream of religious freedom that sanctified his age. They would have forgotten or excused the rigidity of mind, the self-centredness which is the negation of charm, and the paucity of imagination, that alone can induce sympathy and understanding. They would have recalled his unsettled childhood, burdening his spirit with a fear of revolt and a hatred of the bourgeoisie; they would have pleaded that his politics, however erroneous, were founded upon a consistent philosophy, and his downfall would have become a martyrdom for a great idea.

But he did not die – nor did he by a full and free retirement achieve a yet more difficult and glorious end, in the thorough manifestation of the other-wordliness years of devotion had gradually inculcated. The riddle of his behaviour in 1688 is only satisfactorily explained, if one credits him with a distaste for fighting with one-time friends which grew into a determination not to give the country, for whom he had planned prosperity, the parting curse of civil war. But James's religion, though it coloured his whole life, never quite made a new man of him. The King of England was at constant friction with the servant of Christ; the man of pleasure with the son of the Church. It may have been this inability to achieve poise, as much as the actual physical effect of his immoralities, which weakened his resistance to the shocks of the Revolution, and made him at the crisis of his life, a sick man in body and spirit, who wasted days in indecision and fled because he must, rather than because he would. And so when his physical vigour had returned, his old cravings for power and kingship returned also. From the tone of his last paper it would appear, that James had hoped by his retirement to give his people a chance to come to their senses. He could not believe that William would establish a settled government or manage those Lords and Commons, who had been a thorn in the flesh of every Stuart. When the spring of 1689 proclaimed to the world that the Revolution was an accomplished fact, James would perhaps have been more than human if he had not accepted Louis's offers of French aid, the loyal support of the Scottish clansmen, and the devoted if unruly service of the Catholic Irish. In 1689 and 1690 at the battles of Killiecrankie and the Boyne, the Revolutionary settlement stood the challenge of the sword. Only when Louis had made peace with William at Ryswick in 1697 did James turn aside from the lures of worldly power. Such a surrender, it may be, had no value. But in his last years, God gave him the gift of peace.

William and Mary became King and Queen of England, not without much heart-searching and a large number of speeches. William entered London on the day of James's departure, and a mob of jubilant citizens, waving oranges upon the end of sticks, assured him of the capital's support. The Tory Peers were not too pleased with his quiet assumption of authority; but James's flight took the wind out of their sails and they had perforce to accept the inevitable. A Convention Parliament was summoned by William's authority to meet on January 22nd. Both common sense and the fundamental tenet of political theory, that whatever the circumstances the work of government must be carried on, made his position unassailable. His chance of securing the throne was further increased by the comparative unanimity of his supporters. They formed two-thirds of the new House of Commons and though numerically less potent in the Lords, the leadership of Halifax strengthened their position. They considered that James had forfeited the Crown by his behaviour, and that William was the best man to succeed him. But the Tories were divided. A few remained staunchly Jacobite. Others were for a Regency, believing that no circumstance could justify the deposition of a King; many, under the guidance of Lord Danby, declared that James had abdicated and that Mary of Orange should be Queen. They soothed their consciences by questioning the Prince of Wales's birth, or disallowed his claim because of the religion into which he had been baptised.

In both parties many, who agreed as to final action,

differed over procedure. Few of the members who flocked up to town on January 22nd, had sat in James's single ill-starred Parliament, so either they were new to Westminster or had not been there for nearly eight years. In their country homes, they had few opportunities of correlating their opinions with those of their fellow Whigs and Tories. Now each of them aired his own views with vigour, displaying some amazing discrepancies. Academic theories about the social contract were bandied about with hot-headed arguments that James should be formally impeached. Not only in the House but in the streets the Englishman's genius for political debate indulged itself to the full, 'even women became politicians and filled all places, where they came, with noise and altercation'.

Only William of Orange remained calm amid 'the universal ferment', courteous yet aloof, neither stooping to flatter nor permitting himself to interfere with the efforts of an honest but muddle-headed people to work out their own salvation.

On the 28th of January, the Commons passed the motion 'that King James the Second having endeavoured to subvert the constitution of the Kingdom, by breaking the original contract between King and people, and having, by the advice of Jesuits and other wicked persons, violated the fundamental laws, and withdrawn himself out of the kingdom, has abdicated the government, and that the throne is thereby vacant'. On the same day the Tories raised the question in the Lords: 'Whether a Regency . . . would be the best and safest way to preserve the Protestant religion, and the laws of this kingdom'. In debate, the laurels went to Rochester, emerging from a self-imposed obscurity to fight for the principle of hereditary right, but through the defection of Danby and his friends, too deeply alienated from James to consider this solution, the Tories lost their motion by two votes only, and by the voices of fifty-one peers as opposed to forty-nine, England declared against a regency, and struck the death blow at the Stuart philosophy of kingship by divine right.

Next day (January 29th) the Lords considered the Commons vote that the throne was vacant. Determined to begin at the beginning, they embarked upon a philosophical discussion as to whether or not there was an original contract. William with his passion for getting things gone, must have writhed in anger when he heard; but only a few hours and a great deal of breath was wasted and the existence of a contract was carried by seven votes. The Lords then proceeded to the essential point of the vacancy of the throne. To this, the Tories could not agree, since it conflicted with their whole theory of hereditary kingship. The Danby contingent having returned to the Tory ranks, it was resolved in the negative by fourteen votes, and an impasse was reached, Lords and Commons having arrived at diametrically opposed conclusions.

There were five days of dangerous stalemate, while the tempers of the anxious citizens rose to fever heat and angry petitions were presented at Westminster, urging Parliament to crown both the Prince and Princess of Orange and to act speedily for the security of religion and property.

William decided that something must be done. Mary's loyalty helped him at the critical moment. She had replied to a letter of Danby's, suggesting her sole sovereignty, with a rebuke that he should attempt 'to divide her interest from her husband's'. She had sent the correspondence to William. The latter summoned a few of the leading peers before him, and told them plainly that he would neither accept the office of Regent, nor would he exercise power in England, in a position inferior to his wife or any other woman. They must make up their own minds; it was their own affair: for himself, he was ready to go back to Holland. After that, there was little further point in political disquisitions. If William went back to Holland, there would be civil war, and a complete disintegration of trade and the routine of life. The Lords revoked their amendment, agreed by twenty votes that the throne was vacant, and carried without a division the proposal that William and Mary should be declared King and Queen. The Commons invested the executive powers of the Crown in William, making him in effect sole ruler. On February 13th, the Prince and Princess of Orange were formally proclaimed in London William III and Mary II of England.

On the previous day, Mary had reached England, from The Hague. It was Shrove-Tuesday and a day of carnival. Mary came to Whitehall through a haze of bells and bonfires. Genuinely happy to be with her husband again, relieved beyond measure that matters were settled at last, and quietly thankful that she had been able to ease William's path, she turned her thoughts resolutely from the memory of her father. She was at once excited and uneasy, resolved above everything not to displease her husband by any display of regret for a past that could not be recalled. It was in a mood of feverish gaiety that she came to London. A Scot would have called her fey and understood: her English subjects looked askance at a behaviour, that seemed to lack good form. 'She came into Whitehall laughing and jolly as to a wedding, so as to seem quite transported,' wrote Evelyn. 'She rose early next morning, and in her undress as it was reported . . . before her women were up, went about from room to room to see the convenience of Whitehall, lay in the same bed and apartment where the late Queen lay, and within a night or two sat down to play at Basset, as the Queen her predecessor used to do. She smiled upon and talked to everybody. . . .' It was in part a habit that had grown upon her, in an attempt to counteract the silence and stiffness of her husband. In Holland it had made her popular. Now, at this crisis she over-acted, as she often admitted to herself in later years, when she sat in lonely retrospect over her embroidery frame, in the new grandeur of Hampton Court or the more homely rooms of Kensington. At the time, she had been possessed by two ideas, not to disappoint her husband, and not to think. But the early morning visit, so maliciously reported, may not have been what it seemed. Perhaps it was nothing more than an hour's escape from the necessity of pretence, to wander among the ghosts of a happy childhood.

At least she did not shirk her new responsibilities. By her husband's side, she sat in the great Banqueting Hall of the Palace, and heard the Speaker of the House of Lords offer them the joint crown and read the Declaration of Right. The latter had been a hasty measure, which dealt in a somewhat perfunctory way with the Crown's dispensing power and the need of frequent Parliaments. As the basis of a constitutional sovereignty it was faulty, but it suited the genius of a people, whose idea of justice is based on case-made law and who have always preferred experience to theory. The absence of too many rigid rules left the way open for development and readjustment. The real revolution lay not in the declaration, but in the motions which the Lords had done well to scrutinise and debate so fully. The transfer of the crown ended once for all the sovereign's claim to absolute power, and the fact that the transfer had been effected peaceably, by Parliamentary resolutions, marked the triumph of representative government. James's political beliefs were shattered. But his religious ideals were maintained, if somewhat grudgingly, in the Toleration Act of 1689, which gave to Protestant dissenters the liberty of conscience they had earned so well. Political and social equality they were not given, nor was the legal position of the Catholics improved for over a hundred years.

. . . .

On his first arrival at St. Germain, James's predominant mood seemed to be one of indifference. King Louis treated him with excessive courtesy and genuine goodwill, but the French as a whole, fighters to their finger-tips, were out of conceit with him, impatient of his preoccupation with his religious devotions and unable to understand the calmness with which he spoke of his deposition. They made slighting comparisons between his behaviour now and when he was Duke of York; their opinion was summed up by the lady who exclaimed, 'Our King does well to treat the King of England kindly, for he will never be anything but poor man's sauce.' So different was he not only from the fighting Duke but from the proud King of 1685, that men used to say it were safer to belong to William's party, since the latter pardoned so reluctantly while James was always ready to forgive. He wished also to be understood and he wasted his energy on recurrent declarations, reiterating excuses for his flight, righteously indignant at the denial of his son's true birth, and stressing his ideal of religious liberty. But in spite of much that was reasonable in his words, he failed to grasp that the loss of mutual confidence between himself and his subjects had undermined the foundations of his rule and proved, beyond denial, that no theory of kingship could work in the absence of sincerity and trust.

Yet two months after his arrival in Paris, James set out for Ireland. The support and stimulus of Louis, and his wife's eager temper, urged him to strike again for his son's inheritance. In February 1689, he sailed from Brest, accompanied by twenty-two French ships and financed by French gold, though he still refused the offer of French troops. 'I will recover my own dominions with my own subjects, or perish in the attempt.' Louis had furnished him with costly accoutrements and the gift of his own sword. In parting he assured his cousin 'that for his honour and glory he trusted he might never see him in France again'. But Mary of Modena sobbed and swooned, and the onlookers marvelled at the intensity of her love for the old man, who had failed her.

James landed at Kinsale on March 12th, 1689, and was received in Cork and Dublin as hero and as King. Tyrconnel had remained loyal to his old friend and master after some vaccillation which, for his own peace of mind, James regarded as a pose to deceive William. Dick Talbot's hobby since he became omnipotent in Ireland had been the collection of regiments of giants. Thirty thousand well-trained men and eight thousand horse were at the King's service: the country was on fire with joy at his coming; only Ulster, dour and Protestant and hostile to all things Stuart, had proclaimed William King. In the autumn, Tyrconnel had attempted to quarter men in Londonderry; had he succeeded, Ulster too would undoubtedly have been subdued. There had been much debate among the citizens of Derry, as to whether to resist, and those whose opinion counted for most had no wish to attempt the impossible. 'But when the troops came within an hundred yards of the walls, a handful of youths rushed forth from their companions, pulled up the draw-bridge, shut the gates and drew the bars.' Arms were hastily distributed and a defence was organised. Londonderry's refusal to receive Tyrconnel's men inspired the other northern towns to a like defiance, and the action of the nine young men saved Ulster for William, and in the event preserved the Revolution.

While James was enjoying unwonted popularity in Ireland, a convention in Edinburgh had offered the Crown of Scotland to William of Orange. Dundee, in whom loyalty burnt like a flame, and Colin Lindsay, Earl of Balcarres, whose love for the Stuarts had the quiet fixity of a delicate and cultured mind, had refused to submit. Claverhouse rode out of Edinburgh, clambering up the impregnable slopes of the castle and urging revolt in vain upon the Duke of Gordon, who met him at a postern gate. As he rode on, some asked him whither he fared. 'Wherever the spirit of Montrose shall direct me,' Dundee answered. Raising the clans, who came gladly to the call of 'dark John of the Battles', he begged James to cross from Dublin and put himself at the head of his own people in Scotland, 'where hosts of shepherds would start up warriors, at the first wave of his banner upon their mountains.' Others urged him to cross to England with his Irish army to overwhelm the new King, while affairs were still unsettled, and if he failed 'to fall in the heart of his kingdom, in the eyes of his native subjects, pitied and respected even by those who conquered him.'

But the Irish themselves, headed by Tyrconnel, and the French officers, who surrounded James, had no desire for his restoration in England or Scotland. The Irish hated their Saxon conquerors and saw in the Revolution an opportunity to obtain the separation from England for which they yearned. Their eagerness to welcome James was occasioned not merely by his religion, but also by the very fact that he was no longer King across the sea. To France the prospect of Ireland as a separate unit, under French protection, had much to recommend it, and it was with considerable asperity, that at the end of March D'Avaux, the French Ambassador, was forced to accompany the King on a harassing and exhausting march towards Ulster, where James intended to summon Londonderry and on its submission to cross to Scotland and join Dundee. Unhappily for the Stuart cause, the King was affected by the disapprobation of those about him, and went half-heartedly, only too ready for an excuse to return to Dublin. Londonderry gave him excuses, and to spare!

The governor of the town was a Jacobite at heart and had informed James that immediate surrender would greet his coming. But, inspired by a certain Captain Murray, a soldier of tried worth, the townsfolk determined to stand firm. Lundy the governor was kept a prisoner in his house and the command of the town was given to a Major Baker. Murray was made Captain of the Horse, and an elderly clergyman, George Walker by name, who had come into the town from a neighbouring parish, took charge of the supplies and the control of the civil population. Lundy was wisely allowed to escape, disguised as a porter with a load upon his back. Next morning, when

James advanced within a hundred yards of the city gate, a shout of 'No surrender' rose from the assembled citizens, and a shot from the walls killed the officer walking by his side. James retired. The siege of Londonderry had begun, and the King's army of some 20,000 troops prepared to subdue a town manned by 7,000 untrained men and hampered with the additional burden of close on three times that number of unarmed inhabitants.

The Siege of Londonderry, gave to tradesfolk and dissenters the chance to show that courage and devotion was no monopoly of Highland cavaliers. The story is in the true succession of the Iliad, telling of man's indomitable pluck in the face of overwhelming odds. After the first assaults upon the city, James retired to Dublin. It was expected that a few energetic assaults would soon break the defence. But Murray did not wait to be attacked, and harassed the enemy in frequent sallies. When May came, two French banners, captured from the enemy, hung in the cathedral from whose roof the cannon thundered, while within the Anglican liturgy was read each morning to sustain and cherish the devout, while every afternoon the dissenters came together to seek God, and strengthen their souls with simpler prayers.

A final assault failed and the besiegers resorted to blockade. The shortage of supplies made eventual success more than likely. Among the besieged, meal was doled out in minute quantities and horseflesh was already a luxury. As May gave way to June, the heat of summer strengthened the grip of pestilence upon the starving town. Hope deferred sickened their hearts. Relief arrived from England, under Kirke that man of ill-omen, but upon the sight of the boom which the enemy had constructed across the Lough, to cut off the town from the sea, Kirke and the ships retired and waited inactive six miles away.

Only a good supply of salted hides kept Londonderry from starvation. Fifteen officers died in one day from the pestilence and Major Baker eventually succumbed. But there was no weakening of spirit, though men tottered at their posts and every day their numbers lessened till the women filled the gaps. When their ammunition failed, they used bricks for cannon ball, covered in lead. Towards the end of June a fiery Lithuanian, von Rosen by name, with the genius for brutality that at times characterises the races of northern Europe, came to take command of the besieging army. Accustomed to elaborate continental sieges, he fumed at the disgrace of being defied by a paltry Irish town. Sweeping up the remnants of Protestant families, still to be found outside the city – old men, ailing women and children, wretched in a cruel world – he drove them all under the walls of Derry declaring that their relatives within should watch them starve at leisure. The besieged replied, by erecting a gallows on the wall and bidding their enemy send their priests to confess the prisoners, about to die. But the gesture having failed, von Rosen let his victims go and the gallows were removed. Word of the atrocities came to James in Dublin; and he at once repudiated the action, angrily recalling von Rosen whom he termed a 'barbarous Muscovite'. The town was now desperate: the very rats, who fed on the unburied corpses, were chased and eaten. Legend asserted that the only fat man in the town kept close in his house, dismayed by the cannibalistic glances of his wretched fellow-citizens. They still said 'No surrender', with the bitter whisper after, 'First the horses and hides; and then the prisoners and then each other.' A few days more must have seen the end of it. Then relief came. On the night of July 31st, as darkness fell, two brigs bearing supplies, protected from the fire of the enemy by an accompanying warship, crashed into the boom. It broke, but one of the brigs ran upon a sand-bank, and the besieged, peering eagerly through the twilight, heard the enemy's triumphant shout and knew despair that made their very faces lose the hue of life. But the tide rose and gently bore the ship of salvation on her way. She rode into harbour, and within a brief hour, cheeses, butter, bacon, beef – unbelievable plenty – were landed in the town. The enemy fired their guns, powerless through the night, and the clanging bells of the cathedral answered in joyous defiance. On the morning of August 1st, the aching eyes of the remnant still left in Londonderry looked out to see an abandoned camp, and knew their ordeal over. The amazing fortitude of man had triumphed.

While Walker urged his comrades to incredulous heights of courage against the armies of the Stuart, in Scotland Dundee had struck nobly for King James. On March 30th he had been proclaimed a traitor in the Edinburgh Convention. He rode into the Highlands, and prepared to face the army which William had dispatched into Scotland under a skilled and prudent soldier, General Hugh Mackay. The clans, whom Dundee rallied round him, were inspired less by love of James than by devotion to himself and hatred of the Campbell. But while Macdonalds and Camerons joined him readily enough, others equally powerful, the Macphersons and Macleods, remained aloof, regarding Mackay with greater coldness than Claverhouse but unprepared to fight for either. Except for the Grants, Mackay at Inverness had few recruits. Compared with this intensely personal attitude, the political claims of William or James counted for little, only the King's own presence might have stirred the country as a whole with a reminder that he was a Stuart and a Scot. And James did not come. Dundee spent the weeks in winning the affection and confidence of the clansmen. He worked harmoniously with Locheil the Cameron chief and submitted to his judgment that he must make the best of the Highlanders as they were, and not attempt to train them to the type of disciplined warfare, to which he himself was accustomed. Towards the end of July, he marched on Blair, and on Saturday, the 27th, Mackay advanced from Dunkeld to its relief, through the Pass of Killiecrankie. Dundee called a council of war; he was expecting recruits, and some urged that it would be more prudent to avoid an engagement until their arrival. But Locheil advocated immediate battle, as soon as Mackay's men were through the pass. Dundee was delighted that the old chief's wisdom matched the temper of his own daring. He had no fear of defeat, for, in his own words, 'there is no proportion betwixt loyalty and treason; nor should be any betwixt the valour of good subjects and traitors.' It was agreed that they should fight. Locheil, on behalf of them all, begged leave to command that day. Let Dundee give his orders but let him, Locheil, execute them; on Dundee's life rested the fate of Scotland and King James; it should not be risked in battle. But the impetuous spirit of Claverhouse could bear no such restriction. Next time, let it be as Locheil suggested. Having shown the Highlanders his metal, he would be content to hearken to wisdom. But, he concluded, 'Give me one Shear-Darg (harvest day's work) for the King, my master, that I may show the brave clans that I can hazard my life in that service as freely as the meanest of them.'

At ten in the morning, Mackay reached the mouth of the Pass. Toilsomely, his doubting army climbed the narrow defile, with eyes expectant for the attack that at any moment might swoop down upon them, with minds oppressed by the wild grandeur of the scene. The barren hills and the ceaseless roar of the torrent seemed to mock at the odysseys of pigmy men. In the weary day's march through the unfriendly pass, full of healing to those who belonged to it, accursed to those who came hither to destroy, half the battle was won as the men's spirits wavered beneath its spell. Towards sunset, they emerged on the level ground at its head. Dundee's army awaited on the hills to their right, ready to sweep down upon the enemy. In vain Mackay endeavoured to re-order his ranks, so as to meet the attack. As darkness fell, each general made a final speech to his troops. Mackay, as he indicated the river below and the narrow pass behind them, urged the men to fight as they could not flee; Dundee reminded his captains that they gave battle in the best of causes, for their King, their religion and their country. The Highlanders' shout rent the sharp northern air, as they threw aside their plaids and their shoes, and prepared to charge. 'Courage, the day is our own,' cried old Locheil, as he heard the enemy's feeble reply, the whimper of unnerved men. The enemy fired as the clansmen descended the hill. But before they could fix their bayonets, the latter were upon them, claymores in hand and death upon every side. Mackay's regiments broke and fled, hurtling to destruction in the river below, leaping bush and boulder down the dark mouth of Killiecrankie. But one, ere he ran, fired a musket shot at a figure that advanced, urging on his men, riding the black horse that was too well-known for safety. Dundee fell and died. The battle had been won, but the victory was an empty mockery. For the clansmen without a leader, there was no purpose in the struggle and the campaign frittered its way into oblivion. The news of Killiecrankie came to London, and his advisers urged William to send an army into Scotland. 'It is needless,' he said, 'the war ended with Dundee's life.' And James had lost the most faithful servant he had ever known; one to whom crooked dealing was anathema, and cowardice a negation of manhood, who had reduced life to the simple rule of obedience to God and to those set in authority over him.

But no romance of Cavalier devotion nor Derry's epic struggle for love of the Protestant faith can disguise the fact that James, once a soldier of repute, no longer participated in great affairs. In Dublin, he met his Irish Parliament, and under his ægis, an Act of religious toleration was passed. But he could not stem the tide of petty persecution with which the triumphant Catholics wreaked vengeance on the hated Protestants. By approving the repeal of the Act of Settlement, he alienated his friends in England who were dismayed at the separatist policy that was being countenanced at Dublin. Yet it should be recorded that James was actuated by his sense of justice rather than his own interests in allowing the repeal, and though he failed to accomplish much in the wilderness of Irish politics cleverer men than he had failed before and since. He wasted two years in Ireland, unhappy amid a multiplicity of counsellors, Irish nationalists, suspicious Jacobites and disgruntled French. The latter wrote home grumbling of dullness of life in Dublin and mocking at the King's flirtations with two ugly women. The only event that boded good to James's cause in 1689 was the success of the French fleet in a skirmish with the English off Bantry Bay. The French at Dublin magnified it into a naval victory. 'It is not worth calling a battle,' cried Dover, insolently, while James, when he was told that the English fleet had fled, replied tersely, 'It is the first time then.' He vowed that only their reluctance to fight against their rightful King had occasioned their defeat, an opinion creditable to his sentiments as an Englishman but not conducive to harmony in his relations with his French allies.

An army from England under the veteran Schomberg landed in Ireland in August, 1689, but sickness ravaged his troops, and he avoided an engagement. James retired to winter-quarters, well satisfied with the campaign, talking of a spring invasion of England and only perturbed by his incredible shortage of money. Rashly he had tampered with credit and embarked on a fatal system of inflation. According to report in England, he had 'coined a new sort of money, made of copper, about the bigness of half a guinea' to which the value of sixpence was arbitrarily attached. Mary Beatrice was urged to persuade Louis to send over old cannon and other supplies of brass. She did her utmost for James both in regard to money and in maintaining a secret correspondence with the malcontents in England. But she wrote to Tyrconnel pleading with him to safeguard the King's person and dissuade him from any rash action. 'I dare not lett myself go upon this subject. I am too full of it. I know you love the King. I am sure you are my friend, and therefore I need say the lesse to you.' Mary Beatrice had forgotten that worse things might befall her husband, whom she herself had urged to defend his rights, than to die fighting in an honourable cause.

In the spring of 1690 William III arrived in Ireland, to lead his army in a decisive campaign. He came to Ulster, and the bells pealed forth their welcome. 'This is a country worth fighting for,' he cried. In June, James marched out of Dublin with an army of some twenty-six thousand men. The horse were in good condition and led by able officers, and a reinforcement of French troops under Lauzun might be trusted to give a good account of themselves. But the Irish foot were ill-disciplined and unused to the ordeal of fire. No attempt had been made to instil into them on the march or in the camp, the qualities of control and obedience, which alone could ensure firmness in the field. William's army was even more varied than his opponents. Dutch guards, English regiments, Danish and German mercenaries, unconquerable Ulstermen and French Huguenots, to whom James and his Papist friends were little better than the agents of the Devil, marched behind a Prince, who, freed from the enervating atmosphere of politics, regained new energy of body and elasticity of mind, as he rejoiced in the hardships and dangers of the campaign. On the last day of June the two armies faced each other north of Dublin, on either side of the river Boyne. The Jacobites wore white emblems in honour of the Bourbons; William's men fastened boughs to their caps, bright with the summer green of Irish trees. William and his staff went out to view the enemy's line, and across the river he was recognised, and shots were fired. A bullet scraped his shoulder and he fell forward in his saddle. For a moment, a thousand hearts knew exultation or dismay. But William raised himself. 'There is no harm done, but the bullet came near enough.' The wound was dressed and he continued in the saddle; he was too accustomed to ill-health to be put out by a little pain.

At dawn on July 1st, day of tragic memories for the Irish race, the English advanced. The pass-word was 'Westminster', the soldier's tribute to the faculty of reason which had made him King. William had detached a force and sent it some miles up the river, to cross by the nearest bridge and turn James's left flank. The Irish who held the bridge did not make a stand, and Lauzun, fearing that James would be surrounded, detached his troops from the other flank and marched behind the royal army towards the bridge. This left James's right wing dangerously weak and here the main force of the enemy attacked, plunging across various inadequate fords, with a disregard of personal danger and an assurance of success that demoralised the Irish foot, who turned to flee. The horse stood firm, and in the brief but bitter struggle that ensued, Schomberg fell, and Walker the hero of Londonderry, who had just been made bishop of that city by his grateful sovereign. But William's appreciation had been dulled by Walker's insistence upon following the army; it was not a layman's business to fight, let alone an ecclesiastic's.

William made the crossing, with aching wounded shoulder and the tide running swiftly against him. He, who was never affable in court or council, had won the hearts of the Ulstermen by choosing them as his guards, with a soldier's words, 'I have heard much of you.' But James left the field and rode for Dublin, while the remnant of Irish horse, their leader captive and themselves decimated, yielded at length to inescapable defeat. On them, the whole brunt of battle had fallen; elsewhere the bloodshed had not been excessive and William did not press the pursuit. He was too exhausted, and Schomberg his second-in-command had gone. He feared, too, that he might capture James. Between them a living ghost hovered, the spirit of

Queen Mary, wife and daughter. Her distress that her father and husband should meet at last upon the field of battle had moved William to unusual feeling. The fear of meeting his nephew in combat may also have influenced James. This fighting against his nearest relatives, was unnatural: the horror of it persisted, weakening his will, making the situation utterly impossible.

Yet whatever the excuses, the fact remains that James did badly. The reputation, sullied in 1688, was not retrieved. He rode for Dublin, urged his friends not to raze the town, and set out at once by speedy and secret stages to France. There he endeavoured to persuade Louis to engineer an invasion of England, while William was absent in Ireland. Two days before the Boyne, the French had beaten the English in the Channel off Beachy Head. There had been a week of panic in London before it was allayed by news of the Boyne. In one sense, James was right. William's absence left England far from impregnable. Now if ever was the time to attack. The first glamour of the Revolution had worn thin. Clarendon, the leader of the Tories, and many lesser men were in close touch with St. Germain; even the Whig Shrewsbury, that youthful Admirable Crichton, had dipped his fingers in intrigue and murdered his peace of mind. Invasion from without and revolt within – the plan was feasible. But Louis, as courteous as ever, firmly ignored James's suggestions for another military venture. The invasion of England had to go by the board.

Yet it was conceived and attempted by Louis himself in 1692, after Jacobite intermediaries had sounded no lesser men than the brilliant Churchill and the indispensable Godolphin. Both these appeared to be genuinely contrite about past treacheries. Godolphin in particular required a special pardon from the Queen. But there was not complete trust on either side. James and William were both disillusioned on the subject of loyalty. What James failed to realise was that Louis's support, which at first glance appeared the mainstay of his cause, was in reality its curse. Revolt and invasion were mutually incompatible. The moment a French fleet dominated the Channel, intrigue gave place to a narrow but deep-rooted patriotism. James himself was not free of it. The scheme of 1692 foundered because the French fleet was engaged by the British off the coast of Brest and after five days' hard fighting was beaten and destroyed. From the cliffs, whither he had come ready to embark, James watched the engagement. As he saw the seamen swarming up the high sides of the French boats, he cried, 'None but my brave English could do so brave an action.' Beachy Head was avenged; the navy he had fostered was worthy of his love. He saw his last hopes of kingship vanish with the foundering fleet and was conscious not of despair but of exhilaration.

There was inevitable reaction. 'Heaven fights against me,' he sighed as he retired to his own tent, and with a new humility he thought not of himself, but of Louis. 'My evil star has influenced the arms of Your Majesty, ever victorious, but when fighting for me. I entreat you therefore,' he wrote, 'to interest yourself no more for a prince so unfortunate but permit me to withdraw, with my family to some corner of the world, where I may cease to be an interruption to Your Majesty's wonted course of prosperity and glory.' There was only one more serious attempt to regain the throne when Berwick in 1696 went to England to organise rebellion, while James waited at Calais to the amusement of the sceptical Parisians who offered a mock reward to any who would bring him back to St. Germain. As all sensible men recognised the inevitability of William's rule, the level of morality in the conspirators had been lowered, and in London Berwick found himself in the midst of uncongenial talk of assassination. He came back to France at once; he was too much of a soldier to like underhand methods and too honest a man to remain where he could not approve. The plot was hatched but discovered, and eight people were executed. Nothing else resulted from this last endeavour. James's own complicity is doubtful, and there is no proof that he ever consented to an assassination scheme.

The current opinion of the exiles is reflected in the letters of Charlotte Elizabeth, Orleans's second wife and the granddaughter of Elizabeth of Bohemia. Madame, caustic, witty and at bottom extremely good-natured, bore hardly with the stupidity of her second cousin King James, 'a child of seven would not make such silly mistakes as he does.' 'The more one sees of this King the more favourably one feels towards the Prince of Orange. . . . I would rather have [his] intelligence than the other's handsome face.' 'It is often wise of him to keep his tongue between his teeth,' is another scathing comment upon James, but in October, 1690, after a few months' longer acquaintanceship, she admits, 'Now that I have come to know more of this good King, I like him better. He is the best fellow in the world, and I pity him with all my soul, for he sometimes sighs fit to break your heart. He took me aside once and put me through a veritable catechism to find out whether his daughter, the Princess of Orange, had really taken his misfortunes so much to heart that she would not dance when the Electress of Brandenburg visited the Hague. . . .' As the years passed, people forgave his mediocre brains, his growing stutter and his simple talk (and they were hard things for Frenchmen to forgive) as his gentleness and piety won him the affection of his little court, and the people among whom he lived. It was a strange contrast to the reputation he had borne in youth.

The Queen had been bitterly disappointed by the failures of 1690. At first her irritability extended to her husband. Madame related a conversation, as the Stuart exiles rode with the Duke and Duchess of Orleans. Monsieur, a connoisseur of furniture, asked James, 'And has Your Majesty, who had such great wealth, not built and furnished some beautiful home?' 'Money!' exclaimed the Queen, 'he never had any. I never knew him to have a halfpenny.' To which the King replied, 'I had lots but I never bought gems or furniture with it. Nor did I build palaces. I spent it all on making great ships and cannons and guns.' 'Yes,' said the Queen, 'and a lot of good they did you. Why, they have all been used against you!'

That money worried Madame. She always wanted to ask James, 'Why he did not use the thirty thousand pistols which he had in his chamber in England in doing good and attaching the hearts of his subjects to himself, so that they would remain faithful to him. . . .' Shrewd as she was, she had apparently not realised that the heart of the tragedy lay in that very fact that James had endeavoured to do good according to his lights. He had been in turn arrogant and unwise, regardless of his subjects' wishes even to the point of insanity, but he had never been merely selfish or lazy. He had always a goal, greater than himself.

Mary Beatrice's ill-humour had been due not only to the frustrated ambitions of a Princess of the proud House of D'Este. In James's absence she had suffered again the heart-burnings of a jealous woman. Even yet she could not be sure that James's besetting sin was entirely overthrown. 'I am sure she wishes that her husband may never see any ladies more beautiful than I am,' wrote the not too charitable Madame. 'Then her mind will be at rest and she won't be troubled with jealousy, and dear King James won't have his ears boxed.' But a succession of quiet days in 1691 darkened though they were by William's subjugation of Ireland and Scotland, restored Mary Beatrice's nerve, while the careful organisation of the little court at St. Germain gave a semblance of normality to their daily lives.

On June 26th, 1692, the Queen bore her last child. The calumnies of 1688 were silenced. 'See what heaven has sent us to be our comforter in the land of exile,' wrote the King, and to him his little daughter remained the 'child of consolation'. In August, Louise Marie was christened, and Louis XIV and Madame were her sponsors.

She grew and prospered, a healthy and happy child of gentle ways and trim figure and very beautiful eyes. She was only known to lose her temper once, when she was scarce out of babyhood and heard that the Duke of Burgundy, King Louis's handsome grandson, was to marry someone else. At St. Germain she lived among a crowd of youngsters, the children of the men and women who had chosen voluntary exile rather than submit to William, the usurper. Their ring-leader was the Prince of Wales, who was said by some to resemble his mother, by others to have something in him of his uncle Charles II. He had an innate sense of dignity and a royal bearing, which to the careful observer seemed of itself to dispose of the slander of a suppositious birth. His nickname was 'little Blackbird'. There was a touch of Stuart obstinacy in him, underneath the surface. If one attempted to drive him, his easy chatter ceased and he withdrew into himself; but by his affections it was easy to lead him. Madame forgot to be critical in his presence . . . 'It is impossible to see him without falling in love with him. . . . I think that in time he will become a great King, because although he is only nine years old, I am sure that already he would rule better than his father did.' Thus, England expelled the Stuarts, and in 1714 chose a mediocrity to rule, at the very time a Stuart had grown to manhood who combined his father's moral and religious sense with his uncle's ability to charm. Perhaps it was as well for the development of democratic institutions, but it was tragic for him who was to be called James III, that his life should have so sparing a fruition. At least in the end, he died with a quiet conscience, knowing that not even for the sake of the three crowns had he betrayed the faith his father taught him. But by then his nickname had changed to 'Mr. Melancholy'.

James loved the children, his own and the others. There was one naughty child, who used to be confined as punishment in a passage of the Palace. There was a window in the passage that looked into the King's closet. The young miscreant used to tap upon the glass, and the child's mother would invariably find her daughter happily ensconced at the King's feet or upon his knee. For James was satisfied increasingly by simple things. He was grateful for King Louis's friendship and especially for the respect he showed to Mary of Modena. But he refused to take more from him than an adequate pension. His court was not unhappy in spite of its sobriety. Berwick, his son, whose close likeness to his half-sister Mary cut his father to the heart, was an ornament to any circle, a man of honour and of reputation. Men of letters, poets and painters frequented St. Germain, Anthony Hamilton the wit, and Tyrconnel's beautiful widow, whose sister was John Churchill's wife: existence was full of such sudden reminders of the tragic past.

After William had subdued Scotland, a body of Scottish gentlemen repaired to Saint Germain. They were the pick of Dundee's officers, who asked James's leave to place their swords at Louis's service. He received them at his levee and gave his consent. A few days later, as he set out to hunt, he passed a body of men, in the dress of French soldiers, lined up to salute him. Upon inquiry he found they were the Scots in borrowed garb. He could not go on with the hunt; his heart was too full. He reviewed them, later, and wrote his name in each man's pocket-book. He bade them think of him as their father and friend, and in the end left them in tears. The Prince of Wales emptied out his slender purse and told them that all that he possessed was theirs. These were the men who had been loyal, and to this pass their loyalty had brought them. They saw service on the Spanish frontier and on the Rhine, were cheated by their French officers, bore hardships and poverty and disease and death, until after six years' absence, four only returned to Scotland to tell the tale of a brave though barren Odyssey.

James turned from the unhappy contemplation of the tragedies of the Jacobite cause, to the consolation of hard exercise, the joy of the hunt had never failed him, to the children and to his prayers. In 1694, the death of his daughter Mary of England, unrepentant and unforgiven, and of Mary Beatrice's brother, the young Duke of Modena, afflicted them both grievously. Louis's personal kindness did not falter but at the treaty of Ryswick in 1697 he abandoned them politically and acknowledged William III. Then James achieved serenity. As the stormy century drew to a close he wished intensely for speedy death. The longing was not the expression of despair, but a growing confidence in an eternity of joy, after the purging of his sins.

His religious meditations written at St. Germain have been preserved.[1] They are sufficient justification for stressing the religious rather than the political side of the years of exile, the aspirations towards sainthood, rather than the feeble efforts to regain an earthly throne. Written at first clearly and vigorously, they throw much light on his conversion to Catholicism and contain some common-sense advice on educating the young of which the warning to keep novels out of the hands of young women and to avoid laziness at all costs are characteristic. But with the passing of years the notes grow indeterminate, the sentences incomplete, the confusion of thought deplorable. There is no sequence; only the outpourings of a man, sadly conscious of sin. He had apprehended the truth at last that no theories, no bribes, neither the tyranny of a Jeffreys nor the amiable philosophy of a Penn could convert a people; only a saintly life might have achieved the impossible and he, who had hoped to bring back England to the fold had never even succeeded in governing himself. His vices had begun gradually, and before he knew his danger he was enslaved to sex. He had presumed too much on his own strength, instead of relying on the Grace of God. 'I abhor and detest myself for having lived so many years in almost a perpetual course of sin.' He even wondered if he had

[1] *Papers of Devotion of James II*, Ed. G. Davies. (Roxburgh Club.)

the right to pray for forgiveness in the hope of shortening his time in purgatory: surely instead he should spend his last days in intercession, praying for charities and the souls of the faithful departed. We are told elsewhere that he made himself a spiked iron scourge, which he wore next to his skin. He was shy of his self-abasement, and much embarrassed when one day by accident his wife came upon the instrument of penance. She only adored him the more, speaking of him always as the 'dear good King'.

It was in reaction from his own youth that he urged upon Berwick and the young Prince of Wales, care in the choice of friends, suspicion of playhouses and abstinence from the tables, writing of the card-players with something of his old spirit, 'no slave in the Galleys, no labouring man, but has more quiet and rest than they, very often they do not give themselves to eate, drinke or sleepe, are enraged when they lose, and when they win are vexed it is not more'.

James's own day at St. Germain when it approximated to the ideal he set before him, had the touch of red tape about it which showed the lingering bureaucrat. He rose at 7 or 7.30, after not more than eight hours sleep. He knelt by his bed for his first morning prayers as soon as he had thrown something over his shoulders, and immediately he was dressed retired to his oratory for half an hour's ordered devotion. Then came the first public Mass, to be followed by the business of the day, succeeded in turn by a short walk or other exercise and a quiet time spent in reading or writing. A second Mass brought the morning to a close. After dinner, James would habitually spend some time in conversation with his friends or with visitors from England or elsewhere; he then retired for his afternoon rest, generally with some good book to bear him company. Evening prayers were said at three o'clock, to be followed by any social occasion, or further exercise. On every third Wednesday in the month, there was a special fast and suitable prayers for the re-establishment of the

Catholic religion in the three kingdoms of England, Scotland and Ireland.

This was the technique of James's religion. The spirit behind it was one of resignation. 'Nothing does amuse and astonish me so much as to see so many witty and ingenuous men of most proffessions, so industrious and diligent in pursuing their worldly and temporal advantage and so negligent and remiss in what concerns their eternal good, when every day we see that all we grasp at is but vanity and vexation of spirit and that nothing but the love of God can fill and satisfy the heart of man.'

King James died, to his own joy and relief, in September, 1701. He was not granted an easy death. In the spring of the year, on March 4th, he had fainted while in Chapel, but had soon recovered. A week later a partial paralysis gave warning of the end, and he was sent to take the waters at Bourbon, but though he recovered the use of his limbs, his lungs appeared to be affected and he frequently spat blood. He came back to St. Germain in June, so as to be at home for the children's birthdays. He had little hope of recovery, and not even the Queen's bewailing could render him desirous of life. He longed only for freedom from the corruptible body and the perils of the world. As he stood in Chapel on the first Friday of September, as the same anthem was being sung as six months before, again he fainted, rallied next day, but relapsed on Sunday, vomiting blood and calling for the Sacrament, in immediate expectation of the end. But for two weeks, Death delayed its coming, while in the crowded room of the Palace, James lay with eyes closed, lest the bustle around him should detract his thoughts from holy things. The King of France visited him frequently; those, who had ruined their lives to serve him, crowded round their lord, who in the fortitude of his death was justifying their faith and loyalty. From his lips they heard the words of pardon for his enemies. By the side of his couch, Mary Beatrice shrunk upon the ground; he stirred himself to comfort her, but took little notice of anybody else except when the kneeling priests repeated prayers. Then by the movement of his lips they saw that he was alive and understood. Occasionally the children were brought into the room, but the sight of the Prince of Wales still had power to shake the calm of the dying man. The thought that the child had lost his inheritance alone troubled a mind in tune with Death.

On the 13th of September, King Louis came for a third time to visit his cousin, and this time he came with a great resolve. There had been high debate in council as to whether, upon King James's death, Louis should acknowledge the Prince of Wales's claim. Such an avowal would be contrary to the Treaty of Ryswick. That it would be injudicious and even dangerous, that it would stir the dormant hostility of William, that it would be more prudent to take the opportunity of making a break with ill-starred Jacobitism every statesman knew, none better than the King himself. But there were others who influenced Louis. There was Madame de Maintenon whose chief counsellor was her conscience, who believed in the Prince's right and was Mary of Modena's friend. And in council the young blood of the House of Bourbon spoke out, and the princes refused to abandon their kinsman. Louis was fired with the idea of a great sacrifice. He came to St. Germain, and calling for the Queen and Prince, told them of his determination to uphold the latter's claim against William, and to acknowledge him as James's son and heir. He went into James, who lay so still that at first he thought him dead. But he rallied when they told him that the King of France was there. 'Where is he?' he asked. 'Sir, I am here and am come to see how you do.' James began to pour out words of gratitude for his kindness, and then Louis told him of his great decision. 'I will take your family under my protection and will treat your son as Prince of Wales.' The words fell as healing balm on the wounds that had been made by the slanders of his enemies, and in the chamber, heavy with the nearness of death, an amazing scene was enacted. Those who heard Louis's declaration burst into cries of joy, wept in their emotion, seized the French King's feet, kissed the hem of his garments. The news spread without and the cheers of the people, excited to enthusiasm by the generous action, brought a breath of the outside world into the darkened room. Louis himself felt the tears upon his cheek and turned aside, while vainly above the babel, the dying king tried to express his thanks. Louis rode away, happier than he was ever to be again. The road to Blenheim and to Ramillies, to the stormy sunset of his glorious reign, had opened before him with his acknowledgment of James's son. By a single act of magnanimity he had rendered futile years of toil, watered with the lives of men. For what he had done meant war, and in due course defeat. But the act of acknowledgment in the death-chamber of St. Germain, if it robbed the King of France of success at the end, gave a lustre to his life it had hitherto lacked, and showed that in him as in other men lurked the divine spark that could give without counting the cost.

James lingered for three more days and died on Friday, September 17th, 1701. It made little difference to the world. Most unfortunate of men, he achieved neither understanding in his lifetime nor justice after his death. Yet little loved though he had been, a man who had counted as his friends Turenne and Pepys, the Coventrys and Bishop Ken, William Penn the Quaker and Graham of Claverhouse, must have had in him something worth the loving. Their friendship and his wife's devotion plead for him at the bar of history. There the verdict must go against him because he was a Stuart, callous in his choice of means, and prostituting his judgment to the ill-balanced advice of ill-chosen counsellors, because his political creed was arbitrary and unprogressive, because of the cruelty of 1685 and the cowardice of 1688. Yet something may be said on his behalf. England swept on her way, through much that was selfish and unworthy to a future indubitably great, best and greatest when she upheld those reasoned ideals which had made the Revolution glorious. Liberty under the law and ordered progress that respects the life and opinions of every individual are challenged to-day as never before since the seventeenth century died. England defended them then and must defend them still. But the corollary of such ideals in political life was reasonable freedom in matters of religion. Toleration, the chief constructive idea of the years after 1660 grew at length into real humanitarianism and made possible the adventures in social service which were the true glory of a later age. James deserves the honour due to a pioneer. Nor did he err in principle in his endeavour to give to his fellow-Catholics the right to serve their King. It was the harmony, in which men of different faiths had fought side by side under Turenne, that had first fired his young imagination. Toleration is a milk and water virtue when accompanied by indifference; James aimed at combining it with deep religious convictions and zeal for the service of the Church and State. Not till his last days did he achieve the supreme virtue of charity. But he had worked hard and well at ships and soldiering, and round the council-table; he had given up his work and risked all for the sake of his faith; he had been loyal to his friends, and suffered the supreme tragedy of knowing his friends disloyal. Often harsh, often stupid, lacking, like every Stuart save one, the excellent gift of true imagination, he yet remained a King who preferred to lose his crown than to betray his religion, and living in an age that flouted authority, never hesitated to look beyond present gain in an endeavour to obey the dictates of his God. Remembering these things and recalling in judgment, not only his inglorious triumphs but the failures that were laudable, let those who came to censure remain to pity and forgive.

NOTE ON SOURCES

[*Reference is made to the main sources, only*]

The journals and memoranda kept assiduously by James II from the age of sixteen were bequeathed by him to the Scotch College in Paris. At the time of the French Revolution, the papers were sent to the house of a Frenchman in St. Omer, who was assisting to smuggle them out of France for their greater security. He was arrested on suspicion and his wife, fearing that he might be compromised by the possession of English manuscripts, embossed with the Royal Arms, buried them in her garden and subsequently burnt them.

Fortunately voluminous extractions had already been made from the papers in order to compile a life of James II, shortly after his death. These survivals were brought to England during the Napoleonic wars, and form the basis of the *Life of James the Second* published by the Rev. J. S. Clarke, librarian to the Prince-Regent. In his preface he acknowledges the 'able assistance' of Mr. Walter Scott, which came 'like the cheering radiance of an autumnal evening after days of anxiety and labour'. Extracts from James's original manuscripts are also included in Macpherson's *Original Papers*; and his account of his campaigns form a volume of Ramsay's *The History of Henri de la Tour d'Auvergne, Viscount de Turenne*.

The political side of the first exile is illustrated by the letters of Hyde, Nicholas etc., in the *Clarendon State Papers* and the *Correspondence of John Evelyn* (Ed: Bray). Clarendon's *Life and Continuation of his history of the Grand Rebellion* carry on the story to 1667. The best contemporary history of the whole period is G. Burnet's *History of my own Time*, but in addition to having a strong Whig bias, it is less valuable for James II's reign than the earlier period, as Burnet was out of England.

Contemporary comment on personages and affairs is provided by the reports and news-letters in the *Venetian* and the *Domestic State Papers.* The former are only calendared up to 1661; the latter up to 1683. Pepys's *Diary* illuminates the first years of Charles II's reign and comments freely on the Duke of York and Admiralty matters. Bryant's *Samuel Pepys* is a modern essay on the man and his work, and Tedder's *The Navy of the Restoration* is a competent monograph on the subject.

The more scandalous side of Restoration life is depicted by Hamilton in his *Memoires de la vie du Comte de Grammont* and Andrew Marvell's *Political Poems* should be consulted if only to illustrate the disgusting insinuations of which 17th century pamphleteers were capable. Marvell's *Letters* are a more restrained exposition of the point of view of the Country Party. John Evelyn's *Diary* contains many useful references to public affairs, but his interests were not in politics. After 1675, *The Memoirs of Sir John Reresby* give the point of view of a moderate Tory; the unreliable but vivid *Memoirs of Thomas, Earl of Ailesbury* are most valuable for the account of Charles II's death, and the events of 1688.

In an age which gloried in self-expression, there are numerous collections of letters, of which the most useful are Henry Sidney's *Diary and Correspondence*; the *Saville Correspondence*; the *Diary and Correspondence of Henry Hyde, Earl of Clarendon,* and the *Ellis Correspondence* (the comments of a shrewd observer during the reign of James II). *Reliquiae Baxterianae* (Baxter's narrative of his life and times) is important in religious history.

Numerous letters are scattered among the *Reports of the Historic Manuscript Commission* of which the most valuable are the naval letters and George Legge's correspondence in the *Dartmouth MSS.*; the letters of Coventry and other statesmen in the *Ormonde MSS.* and the Scottish papers in the *Buccleugh and Queensberry MSS. at Drumlanrig.*

Narcissus Luttrell's *Brief Historical Relation of State Affairs* provides a formal diary of events after 1678. Dalrymple's *Memoirs* contain invaluable correspondence between James Duke of York and William of Orange, Barillon and Louis XIV, Anne of Denmark and Mary of Orange, etc. The latter's *Memoirs* (Ed: Doebner) are illuminating, and the *Letters of Madame* (Charlotte Elizabeth, Duchess of Orleans) include interesting comments on the Jacobite exiles.

Among secondary authorities containing much original material are Christie's *Life of Shaftesbury* and Foxcroft's *Life of Halifax.* Martin Haile's *Mary of Modena* includes numerous letters from foreign observers in England, and correspondence from the Papal Nuncio is attached to Mackintosh's *History of the Revolution.* Similarly, important Barillon correspondence is included in Fox's *History of the early part of the reign of James II,* a fragment mainly of interest as the work of the great Whig statesman. Miss Blundell's *Cavalier* illustrates from contemporary documents the life of the Catholics of the day. A Layman's *Life of Thomas Kern* is of value for the story of the seven Bishops.

Ralph's *History of England during the reigns of King William, etc.,* has an introductory sketch of the period, 1660–88. The histories of Macaulay and Ranke remain masterpieces, the one for its brilliance, the other for its erudition. Outstanding books on the period recently published are Bryant's *King Charles II* and Ogg's *England in the reign of Charles II.* Churchill's *Marlborough* is a timely vindication of a great man, but occasionally it has the character of special pleading. Pollock's *The Popish Plot* is invaluable; Parry's *Bloody Assize* also deals with a special incident. *The Old Chevalier* by A. and H. Taylor is a life of the Prince of Wales. Belloc's *James II* is a slight but brilliant study, written from the Catholic point of view.

NOTE ON SOURCES

The *Papers of Devotion of James II* published by the Roxburgh Club and edited by Godfrey Davies from James's original MSS. remain the best key to the King's strange and thwarted personality.

INDEX

INDEX

INDEX

INDEX

INDEX

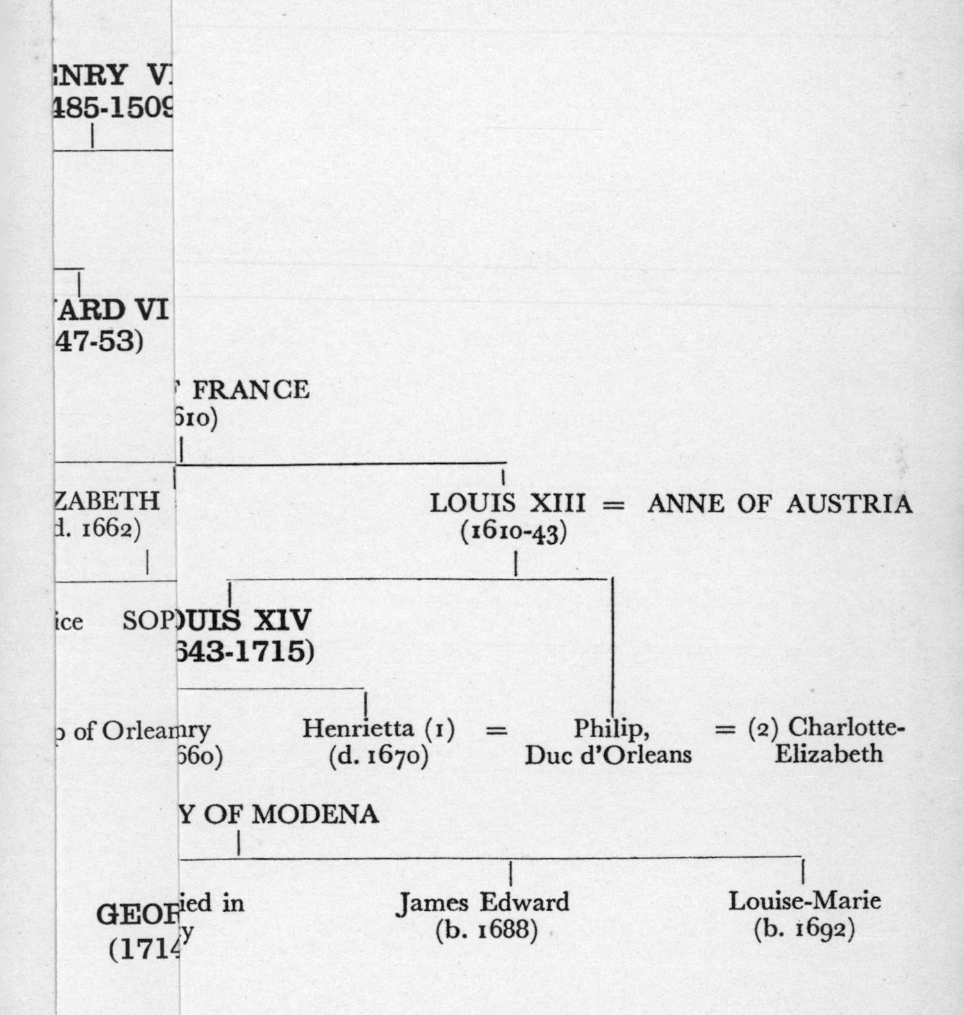

ENRY VI
485-1509
ARD VI
47-53)
FRANCE
610)
ZABETH
d. 1662)
ice SOP
LOUIS XIV
643-1715)
LOUIS XIII = ANNE OF AUSTRIA
(1610-43)
of Orleans
nry
660)
Henrietta (1) =
(d. 1670)
Philip,
Duc d'Orleans
= (2) Charlotte-
Elizabeth
Y OF MODENA
ied in
y
GEOR
(1714
James Edward
(b. 1688)
Louise-Marie
(b. 1692)